Terraform Associate Certification

Study Guide with Practice Questions & Labs

Second Edition

www.ipspecialist.net

Document Control

Proposal Name   :   HashiCorp Certified Terraform Associate
Document Edition   :   Second Edition
Document Release Date :   15th June 2022

Copyright © 2022 IPSpecialist LTD.
Registered in England and Wales
Company Registration No: 10883539
Registration Office at: Office 32, 19-21 Crawford Street, London W1H 1PJ, United Kingdom
www.ipspecialist.net

All rights reserved. No part of this book may be reproduced or transmitted in any form or by any means, electronic or mechanical, including photocopying, recording, or by any information storage and retrieval system, without the written permission from IPSpecialist LTD, except for the inclusion of brief quotations in a review.

Feedback:

If you have any comments regarding the quality of this book, or otherwise alter it to better suit your needs, you can contact us through email at info@ipspecialist.net
Please make sure to include the book's title and ISBN in your message.

About IPSpecialist

IPSPECIALIST LTD. IS COMMITTED TO EXCELLENCE AND DEDICATED TO YOUR SUCCESS.

Our philosophy is to treat our customers like family. We want you to succeed, and we are willing to do everything possible to help you make it happen. We have the proof to back up our claims. We strive to accelerate billions of careers with great courses, accessibility, and affordability. We believe that continuous learning and knowledge evolution are the most important things to keep re-skilling and up-skilling the world.

Planning and creating a specific goal is where IPSpecialist helps. We can create a career track that suits your visions as well as develop the competencies you need to become a professional Network Engineer. Based on the career track you choose, we can also assist you with executing and evaluating your proficiency level, as they are customized to fit your specific goals.

We help you STAND OUT from the crowd through our detailed IP training content packages.

Course Features:

- Self-Paced Learning
    - Learn at your own pace and in your own time
- Covers Complete Exam Blueprint
    - Prep-up for the exam with confidence
- Case Study Based Learning
    - Relate the content with real-life scenarios
- Subscriptions that Suits You
    - Get more and pay less with IPS subscriptions
- Career Advisory Services
    - Let the industry experts plan your career journey
- Virtual Labs to test your skills
    - With IPS vRacks, you can evaluate your exam preparations
- Practice Questions
    - Practice questions to measure your preparation standards
- On Request Digital Certification
    - On request digital certification from IPSpecialist LTD.

About the Authors:

This book has been compiled with the help of multiple professional engineers who specialize in different fields, e.g., Networking, Security, Cloud, Big Data, IoT, etc. Each engineer develops content in his/her own specialized field, which is then compiled to form a comprehensive certification guide.

About the Technical Reviewers:

Nouman Ahmed Khan

AWS-Architect, CCDE, CCIEX5 (R&S, SP, Security, DC, Wireless), CISSP, CISA, CISM, Nouman Ahmed Khan is a Solution Architect working with a major telecommunication provider in Qatar. He works with enterprises, mega-projects, and service providers to help them select the best-fit technology solutions. He also works as a consultant to understand customer business processes and helps select an appropriate technology strategy to support business goals. He has more than fourteen years of experience working in Pakistan/Middle-East & the UK. He holds a Bachelor of Engineering Degree from NED University, Pakistan, and an M.Sc. in Computer Networks from the UK.

Abubakar Saeed

Abubakar Saeed has more than twenty-five years of experience managing, consulting, designing, and implementing large-scale technology projects, extensive experience heading ISP operations, solutions integration, heading Product Development, Pre-sales, and Solution Design. Emphasizing adhering to Project timelines and delivering as per customer expectations, he always leads the project in the right direction with his innovative ideas and excellent management skills.

Dr. Fahad Abdali

Dr. Fahad Abdali is a seasoned leader with extensive experience managing and growing software development teams in high-growth start-ups. He is a business entrepreneur with more than 18 years of experience in management and marketing. He holds a Bachelor's Degree from NED University of Engineering and Technology and a Doctor of Philosophy (Ph.D.) from the University of Karachi.

Mehwish Jawed

Mehwish Jawed is working as a Senior Research Analyst. She holds a Master's and Bachelors of Engineering degree in Telecommunication Engineering from NED University of Engineering and Technology. She also worked under the supervision of HEC Approved supervisor. She has more than three published papers, including both conference and journal papers. She has a great knowledge of TWDM Passive Optical Network (PON). She also worked as a Project Engineer, Robotic Trainer in a private institute and has research skills in the field of communication networks. She has both technical knowledge and industry-sounding information, which she utilizes effectively when needed. She also has expertise in cloud platforms, such as AWS, GCP, Oracle, and Microsoft Azure.

Hareem Khan

Hareem Khan is currently working as a Technical Content Developer, having command over networking and security. She has completed training in CCNA and Cybersecurity. She holds a BE in Telecommunications Engineering from the NED University of Engineering and Technology. She has strong knowledge of all the basics of IP and Security Networks and Routing and Switching Protocols.

Free Resources:

For Free Resources: Please visit our website and register to access your desired Resources Or contact us at: helpdesk@ipspecialist.net

Career Report: This report is a step-by-step guide for a novice who wants to develop his/her career in the field of computer networks. It answers the following queries:

- What are the current scenarios and future prospects?
- Is this industry moving towards saturation, or are new opportunities knocking at the door?
- What will the monetary benefits be?
- Why get certified?
- How to plan, and when will I complete the certifications if I start today?
- Is there any career track that I can follow to accomplish the specialization level?

Furthermore, this guide provides a comprehensive career path towards being a specialist in networking and highlights the tracks needed to obtain certification.

IPS Personalized Technical Support for Customers: Good customer service means helping customers efficiently, in a friendly manner. It is essential to be able to handle issues for customers and do your best to ensure they are satisfied. Providing good service is one of the most important things that can set our business apart from the others of its kind.

Excellent customer service will result in attracting more customers and attain maximum customer retention.

IPS offers personalized TECH support to its customers to provide better value for money. If you have any queries related to technology and labs, you can simply ask our technical team for assistance via Live Chat or Email.

Our Products

Study Guides
IPSpecialist Study Guides are the ideal guides to developing the hands-on skills necessary to pass the exam. Our Study Guides cover the official exam blueprint and explain the technology with real-life case study-based labs. The content covered in each Study Guide consists of individually focused technology topics presented in an easy-to-follow, goal-oriented, step-by-step approach. Every scenario features detailed breakdowns and thorough verifications to help you completely understand the task and associated technology.

We extensively used mind maps in our Study Guides to visually explain the technology. Our Study Guides have become a widely used tool to learn and remember information effectively.

vRacks
Our highly scalable and innovative virtualized lab platforms let you practice the IPSpecialist Study Guide at your own time and your own place as per your convenience.

Exam Cram
Our Exam Crams notes are a concise bundling of condensed notes of the complete exam blueprint. It is an ideal and handy document to help you remember the most important technology concepts related to the certification exam.

Practice Questions
IP Specialists' Practice Questions are dedicatedly designed from a certification exam perspective. The collection of these questions from our Study Guides is prepared keeping the exam blueprint in mind, covering not only important but necessary topics as well. It is an ideal document to practice and revise your certification.

Content at a glance

Chapter 01: Introduction...19

Chapter 02: Getting Started with Terraform......................................35

Chapter 03: Understanding Infrastructure As Code 55

Chapter 04: IaC with Terraform 69

Chapter 05: Terraform Fundamentals 83

Chapter 06: Terraform CLI...113

Chapter 07: Terraform Modules.. 167

Chapter 08: Built-in Functions and Dynamic Blocks....................211

Chapter 09: Terraform State 237

Chapter 10: Terraform Cloud and Enterprise................................ 261

Answers 275

Acronyms 301

References.. 303

About Our Products 307

Table of Contents

Chapter 01: Introduction 19
Introduction 19
What is DevOps? 19
    How Does DevOps Work? 20
What is Infrastructure as Code? 21
    What Does IaC Come To Solve? 21
What is Terraform? 22
    How Does Terraform Work? 22
    Why use Terraform? 24
    Use Cases of Terraform 25
    Terraform versus Alternatives 27
Terraform Associate Exam 30
    Introduction 30
    Exam Objectives 30
    Exam Questions 31
Mind Map 32
Practice Questions 32

Chapter 02: Getting Started with Terraform 35
Introduction 35
Getting Started 35
    Install Terraform 35
    Launch AWS EC2 instance using Terraform 40
Mind Map 53
Practice Questions 54

Chapter 03: Understanding Infrastructure As Code 55
Introduction 55

Infrastructure as Code (IaC) 55

IaC solves real-time problems 55

Why is IaC important for DevOps? 56

IaC techniques 57

Manage any Infrastructure 58

Standardize your deployment workflow 58

Track your Infrastructure 59

Collaborate 59

Benefits of IaC 60

Key Challenges for IaC 60

Cloud Agonistic IaC with Terraform 61

Providers 61

Mind Map 65

Practice Questions 65

Chapter 04: IaC with Terraform 69

Introduction 69

What is the Terraform Workflow? 69

terraform init 70

Terraform Key Concepts: Plan, Apply and Destroy 70

terraform plan 70

terraform apply 70

terraform destroy 71

Resources Addressing in Terraform: Understanding Terraform Code 71

CDK for Terraform 73

How does CDK for Terraform work? 74

When to use CDK for Terraform? 75

Demo 4-01: Create Terraform Infrastructure with Docker 75

Mind Map 79

Practice Questions 79

Chapter 05: Terraform Fundamentals 83

Introduction 83

Installing Terraform and Terraform Providers 83

    Method 1 84

    Method 2 85

    Terraform Providers 85

Terraform State: The Concept 86

Terraform Variables and Outputs 88

    Variable Validation 88

Terraform Provisioners: When to Use Them 89

    Best Practices 90

Lab 5-01: Installing Terraform and Working with Terraform Providers 91

    Introduction 91

    Problem 91

    Solution 92

Lab 5-02: Using Terraform Provisioners to Set up an Apache Web Server on AWS 101

    Introduction 101

    Problem 101

    Solution 101

Mind Map 108

Practice Questions 109

Chapter 06: Terraform CLI 113

Introduction 113

Terraform CLI 113

    Initializing Working Directories 113

    Remote Terraform Execution 114

Demo 6-01: Initialize Terraform Configuration 115

Terraform fmt, taint, and import Commands 124

    fmt Command 124

    taint Command 125

    untaint Command 126

    Import Command 126

    Terraform Block 127

Terraform Workspaces 128

    Terraform Workspaces Subcommand 128

    Terraform Dot Workspace 129

Debugging Terraform 129

Lab 6-01: Terraform CLI Commands 129

    Introduction 129

    Problem 129

    Solution 130

Lab 6-02: Using Terraform CLI Commands (workspace and state) to Manipulate a Terraform Deployment 140

    Introduction 140

    Problem 141

    Solution 141

Lab 6-03: Build Infrastructure – Terraform Azure Example 154

    Introduction 154

    Problem 156

    Solution 156

Mind Map 163

Practice Questions 163

Chapter 07: Terraform Modules 167

Introduction 167

Accessing and Using Terraform Module 167

    Accessing Terraform Modules 167

    Using Terraform Modules 168

Interacting with Terraform Module Inputs and Outputs 169

    Terraform Module Outputs 169

Lab 7-01: Building and Testing a Basic Terraform Module 170

    Introduction 170

    Problem 170

    Solution 170

Terraform Workflow 177

    Workflow steps 178

Lab 7-02: Deploying a VM in AWS Using the Terraform Workflow 179

    Introduction 179

    Problem 179

    Solution 179

Lab 7-03: Automate Infrastructure Deployment with Terraform and Azure Pipeline ... 187

    Introduction 187

    Problem 187

    Solution 187

Mind Map 206

Practice Questions 207

Chapter 08: Built-in Functions and Dynamic Blocks 211

Introduction 211

Terraform Built-in Functions 211

    General Syntax 211

Functions 211

    Some Useful Functions 212

    Function Testing 212

Type Constraints 214

1. Primitive: 214
2. Complex types: 215
any constraint 216
Dynamic Block - The Complex Variable Example 217
Dynamic Blocks in Terraform 219
Lab 8-01: Using Terraform Dynamic Blocks and Built-in Functions to Deploy to AWS 221
Introduction 221
Problem 221
Solution 222
Mind Map 233
Practice Questions 234

Chapter 09: Terraform State 237

Introduction 237
Terraform State Command 237
- Scenarios 237
Demo 9-01: Terraform command 238
Local and Remote State Storage 241
Local State Storage 241
Remote State Storage 242
Output Values 243
Demo 9-02: Persisting Terraform State in AWS S3 244
Lab 9-01: Exploring Terraform State Functionality 248
Introduction 248
Problem 248
Solution 248
Mind Map 257
Practice Questions 257

Chapter 10: Terraform Cloud and Enterprise 261

Introduction 261

Terraform Cloud and Terraform Enterprise 261

Benefits of Sentinel - Embedded Policy as Code Framework 261

    Introduction 261

    Benefits 262

    Use Cases 262

    Sentinel Sample Code for Terraform 262

Best Practice: Terraform Vault Provider for Injecting Secrets Securely 263

HashiCorp Vault 263

Why Do We Need Vault? 263

Vault workflow is used to inject secrets into Terraform during a deployment, on the fly. 264

-    Scenario: 264

    Benefits of Vault Provider to Inject Secrets into Terraform 265

Terraform Registry 266

Benefits of Terraform Registry 266

-    You can collaborate with other contributors to make changes to providers and modules 266

-    You can publish and share your modules 266

-    Can be directly referenced in your Terraform code 266

Terraform Cloud Workspaces 266

Difference between Terraform OSS and Terraform Cloud Workspaces 267

Features and Benefits of Terraform Cloud 268

Mind Map 269

Practice Questions 269

Answers 275

Chapter 01: Introduction 275

Chapter 02: Getting Started With Terraform 276

Chapter 03: Understanding Infrastructure As Code 277

Chapter 04: IaC with Terraform 280

Chapter 05: Terraform Fundamentals 283

Chapter 06: Terraform CLI 285

Chapter 07: Terraform Modules 287

Chapter 08: Built-in Functions and Dynamic Blocks 290

Chapter 09: Terraform State 292

Chapter 10: Terraform Cloud and Enterprise 296

Acronyms 301
References 303
About Our Products 307

About this Certifications

HashiCorp has launched a new certification program called Terraform Associate. It is for folks who have some Terraform experience but are not quite ready to take the full-fledged "HashiCorp Certified Engineer" exam. The certification's purpose is to assist applicants in improving their grasp of Terraform and its key ideas so that they may become more successful Terraform users. HashiCorp's suite of tools, which includes Packer, Serf, Consul, and Vault, is a leader in the DevOps sector. As a technical certification, the Terraform Associate exam is an excellent opportunity for applicants to demonstrate their knowledge of HashiCorp's most popular product.

Pre-requisites

- Terminal skills are fundamental.
- Basic knowledge of on-premises and cloud architecture is required.

Objectives

The HashiCorp Terraform Associate Exam is a certification exam that assesses and validates an individual's expertise. HCPAE is another name for it. HashiCorp is in charge of organizing and managing the exam. The exam is designed to evaluate candidates' understanding of a certain set of skills or technology. The candidate's ability to start, provide, manage, govern, and maintain infrastructure on public cloud platforms is assessed in this test. Terraform Associate Dumps includes all of the practice questions and answers from the HashiCorp Terraform Associate exam. This certification is intended to assess a candidate's professional abilities and knowledge of the HashiCorp Terraform software, which allows him or her to build up, deploy, and manage cloud-native applications in a variety of contexts.

HashiCorp Certified: Terraform Associate

Exam Questions	Case study, short answer, repeated answer, MCQs
Number of Questions	50-60
Time to Complete	60 minutes
Exam Fee	70.50 USD

How to become HashiCorp Certified Terraform Associate

You must pass the HashiCorp Terraform Associate Certification to become a HashiCorp Terraform Associate. The exam is a one-shot test with a two-year certification period. It is made up of only one question. The Associate test is the first step on your path to professional certification. It is intended to be a simplified version of the professional exam, with just enough content to give you a sense of how a true professional-level Terraform project may look. The Assistant test is also intended to be the first step in a more extensive process. We know that most users would not take the complete professional certification right away; instead, they will start using Terraform on their own projects and work their way up as they get more experience.

Recommended Knowledge

- Understand infrastructure as code (IaC) concepts
- Understand Terraform's purpose (vs. other IaC)
- Understand Terraform basics
- Use the Terraform CLI (outside of core workflow)
- Interact with Terraform modules
- Navigate Terraform workflow
- Implement and maintain state
- Read, generate, and modify the configuration
- Understand Terraform Cloud and Enterprise capabilities

The following general domains and their weights on the exam are included in this exam curriculum:

	Domain
Domain 1	Infrastructure as Code (IaC)
Domain 2	Terraform Basics
Domain 3	CLI, modules, and workflow
Domain 4	Configurations
Domain 5	Terraform Cloud and Enterprise capabilities

Chapter 01: Introduction

Introduction

Infrastructure-as-Code (IaC) is a method that has gained popularity among public cloud providers such as AWS, Google, and Microsoft. In a nutshell, it entails managing a set of resources (computing, networks, storage, and so on) in the same way developers manage application code.

In this lesson, we will take a quick tour of Terraform, one of the most popular tools used by DevOps teams to automate infrastructure chores. The fundamental appeal of Terraform is that we specify what our infrastructure should look like, and the program determines which activities must be made to "materialize" that infrastructure.

What is DevOps?

The phrase DevOps is a mix of the development and operations of the term, and it refers to a collaborative or shared approach to the work performed by an organization's application development and IT operations teams.

DevOps, in its broadest sense, is a mindset that promotes greater communication and collaboration among these teams – and others – inside a business. In its most limited sense, DevOps refers to the use of iterative software development, automation, and programmable infrastructure deployment and maintenance. Building trust and cooperation between developers and system administrators and aligning technology projects to business goals are examples of culture shifts. DevOps can transform the software delivery chain, services, job roles, IT tools, and best practices.

While DevOps is not a technology, DevOps environments use common approaches. These are some examples:

- Continuous Integration and Continuous Delivery or Deployment (CI/CD) tools that focus on task automation
- Systems and tools that support DevOps; examples of such systems and tools are real-time monitoring, incident management, configuration management, and collaboration platforms
- Use DevOps methodologies to implement Cloud computing, microservices, and containers

Chapter 01: Introduction

Adopting DevOps culture methods and tools allows teams to respond to customer requests better, boost confidence in the applications they produce, and achieve business goals more quickly.

How Does DevOps Work?

DevOps is an approach for improving work across the software development lifecycle. A DevOps process can be represented as an infinite loop, with the sequence:

- Plan
- Code
- Build
- Test
- Release
- Deploy
- Operate
- Monitor
- Via feedback – plan, which resets the loop

DevOps ideally means that an IT team creates software that perfectly satisfies user requirements, installs quickly, and operates optimally on the first try. To achieve this purpose, organizations employ a combination of culture and technology.

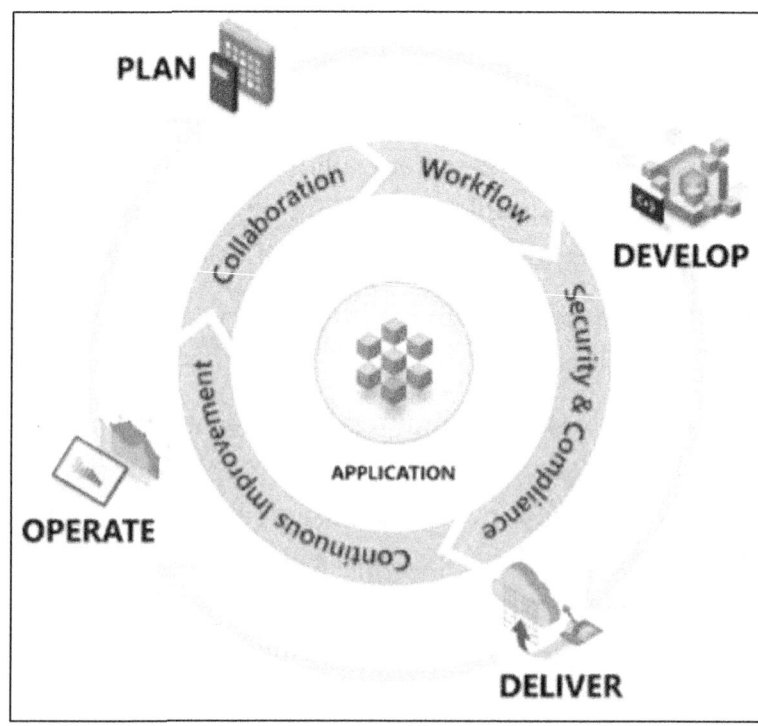

Figure 1- 01: DevOps Life Cycle

Chapter 01: Introduction

To ensure that software meets expectations, developers and stakeholders communicate about the project, and developers work on incremental updates that are released independently.

IT teams utilize CI/CD pipelines and other automation to move code from one development and deployment stage to another to eliminate waiting times. Teams may instantly review modifications and enforce regulations to ensure that releases match requirements.

DevOps practitioners employ containers or other approaches to ensure that software behaves consistently from development through testing and production. They roll out modifications one at a time to ensure that they can track down problems. Teams use configuration management to provide consistent deployment and hosting environments.

What is Infrastructure as Code?

Infrastructure as Code (IaC) manages the server, storage, and networking infrastructure in datacenters. Every configuration change in traditional datacenter infrastructure management requires manual intervention by operators and system administrators. With IaC, infrastructure configuration information is stored in standardized files that software can read and monitor the infrastructure's state. Because it removes human configuration processes, IaC can boost productivity and dependability.

All actions can be automated when using IaC for cloud infrastructure management. IaC enables system components to be configured and provisioned using Terraform and Kubernetes, saving time, money, and effort. IaC enables operations ranging from database backups to new feature releases to be completed faster, better, and at lower cost.

Infrastructure as a service Code and automation are two concepts that are closely linked yet mean quite different things. The goal of infrastructure as code is to keep the configuration or state of the datacenter infrastructure consistent. Automation is mainly concerned with automatically putting the state into and preserving it in the infrastructure.

What Does IaC Come To Solve?

An Infrastructure as Code method modernizes the laborious, time-consuming process of managing IT infrastructure. You must recruit experts for each stage of the process without IaC, from network engineers to hardware maintenance technicians. Furthermore, datacenters would need to be built, which would raise expenses tremendously. Because of their limitations, manual configurations may struggle with speed and access spikes. It

forces businesses to put up backup servers or even datacenters to prevent the application from being unavailable for an extended period.

Enterprises can use Infrastructure as Code to do unit testing, functional testing, and integration testing to drastically reduce the number of product lifecycle errors. Furthermore, it allows for errors to be detected early in the process, removing the chance of costly reworks late in the process. The requirement for written documentation is also nearly gone. Because the code itself documents the machine's status, infrastructure documentation is always up to date.

As all environments are produced and configured automatically, Infrastructure as Code provides continuity. It eliminates the possibility of human error, dramatically accelerating and simplifying software development and infrastructure operations.

What is Terraform?

Terraform by HashiCorp is an IaC solution that allows you to specify cloud and on-premises resources in human-readable configuration files that you can version reuse, and share. Terraform can manage low-level components such as computing, storage, and networking resources and high-level components such as DNS records and SaaS services. After that, you may utilize a standardized procedure to provide and manage all of your infrastructures throughout their lifecycle.

Terraform is quietly revolutionizing DevOps by altering how infrastructure is handled and making DevOps initiatives faster and more efficient to execute. Although it has the same underlying premise as other DevOps technologies (i.e., infrastructure as code), this infrastructure builder is unique. It concentrates on the automation of the infrastructure itself. This means that Terraform can describe the complete cloud infrastructure.

How Does Terraform Work?

Terraform uses application programming interfaces to construct and manage resources on cloud platforms and other services (APIs). Terraform can now operate with nearly any platform or service with an API.

Chapter 01: Introduction

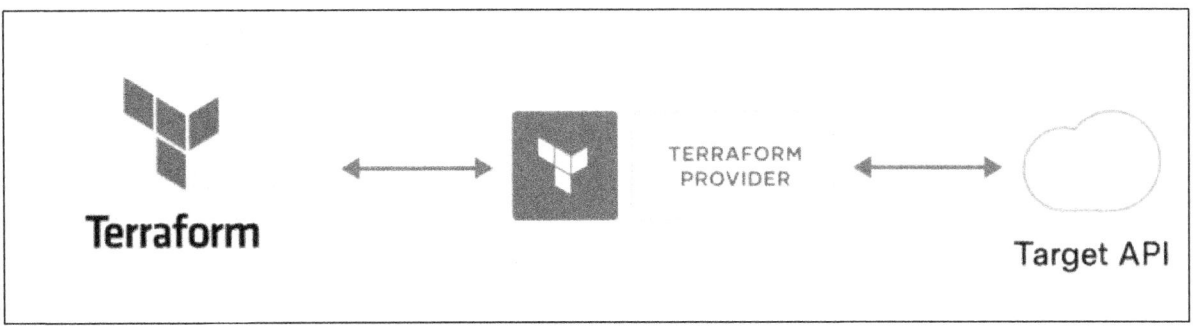

Figure 1-02: Terraform Workflow

HashiCorp and the Terraform community have already created over 1700 providers to handle thousands of various resources and services, and the number is growing. The Terraform Registry lists all publicly available providers, including Amazon Web Services (AWS), Azure, Google Cloud Platform (GCP), Kubernetes, Helm, GitHub, Splunk, DataDog, and many more.

The Terraform workflow is divided into three stages:

Write: You define resources that may span several cloud providers and services. You could, for example, establish a configuration to deploy an application on virtual machines in a Virtual Private Cloud (VPC) network using security groups and a load balancer.

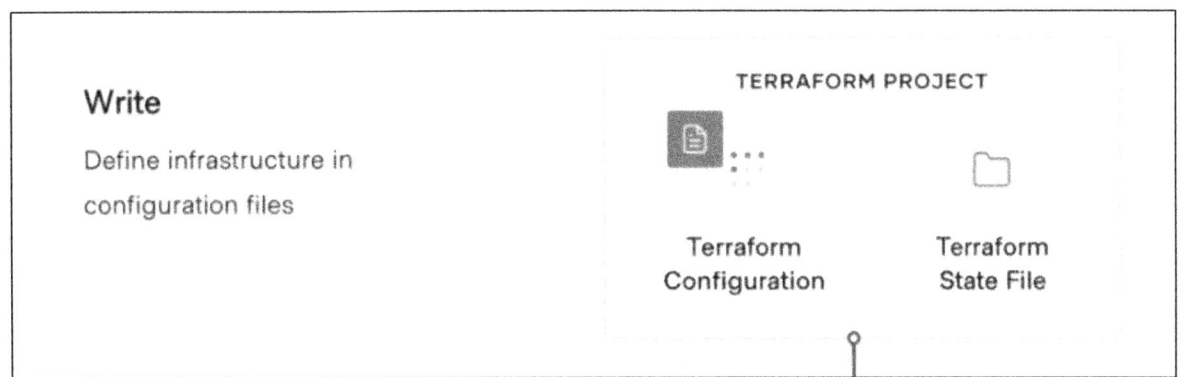

Figure 1-03: Write Stage

Plan: Based on the existing infrastructure and your setup, Terraform generates an execution plan that describes the infrastructure it will create, update, or delete.

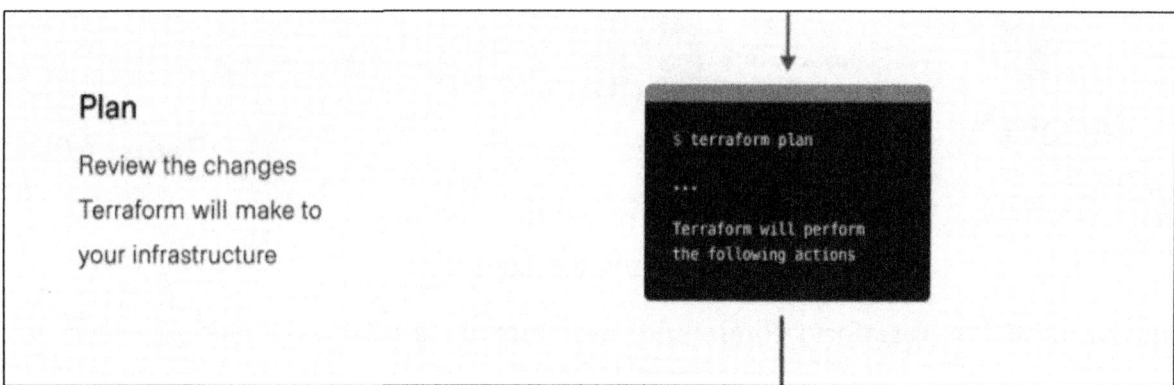

Figure 1-04: Plan Stage

Apply: Terraform executes the suggested actions correctly, taking into account any resource dependencies. For example, if you adjust the number of virtual machines in a VPC's settings, Terraform will recreate the VPC before scaling the virtual machines.

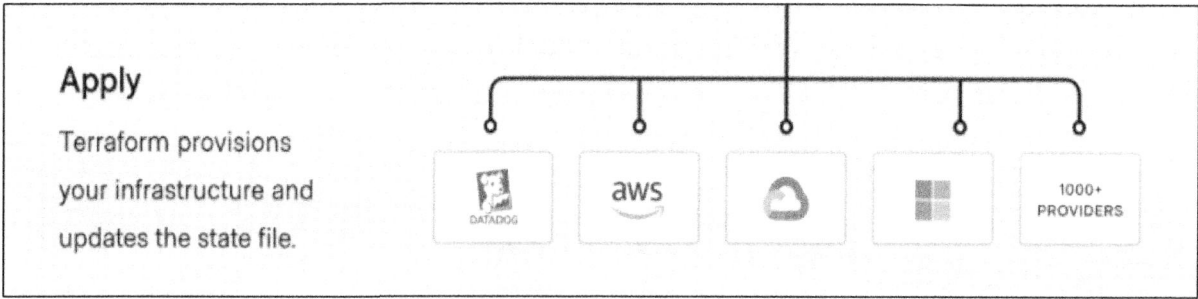

Figure 1-05: Apply Stage

Why use Terraform?

Unlike other related programs, Terraform is not platform-specific and works with all major cloud providers. There are a few more distinctions between equivalent technologies. One of these is Terraform's approach to failure. Terraform flags the questionable resource when provisioning fails and removes and re-provisions it in the following operation. The benefit of this technique for handling failed resources is that the system does not re-build successfully provisioned resources instead of focusing on contaminated ones.

When used as part of a multi-team DevOps approach, Terraform allows teams such as operations and security to collaborate with developers in parallel. Each step in the DevOps process has its tool, allowing teams to focus on their unique duties without interfering with other teams working on the project. It changes the DevOps process from a linear and time-consuming waterfall-style project to one where teams can operate in parallel.

Reasons to use Terraform

Manage any Infrastructure - In the Terraform Registry, you may find providers for many of the platforms and services you already use. You can also come up with your own ideas. Terraform takes an immutable approach to infrastructure, which makes updating and altering your services and infrastructure much easier.

Track your Infrastructure - Before altering your infrastructure, Terraform develops a plan and asks for your consent. It also keeps track of your real infrastructure in a state file that serves as your environment's source of truth. Terraform uses the state file to figure out what modifications need to be made to your infrastructure to match your setup.

Automate Changes – Terraform configuration files are declarative, which means they specify your infrastructure's final state. Terraform handles the underlying logic, so you don't have to provide step-by-step instructions to generate resources. Terraform produces or alters non-dependent resources while building a resource graph to detect resource dependencies. Terraform can now effectively provision resources.

Standardized configurations - Terraform configuration files are declarative, meaning they specify the ultimate state of your infrastructure. You do not have to offer step-by-step instructions to produce resources because Terraform handles the underlying logic. While building a resource graph to detect resource dependencies, Terraform creates or modifies non-dependent resources. Terraform can now provision resources efficiently.

Collaborate - You may commit your configuration to a Version Control System (VCS) and use Terraform Cloud to manage Terraform processes across teams because it's written in a file. Terraform Cloud enables safe access to shared state and secret data, role-based access controls, a private registry for sharing modules and providers, and more consistent, reliable environment.

Use Cases of Terraform

Terraform from HashiCorp is an infrastructure as code solution that allows you to create infrastructure resources in human-readable configuration files that you can reuse, distribute, and version. You can then utilize a consistent workflow to supply and manage your infrastructure in a safe and efficient manner throughout its lifecycle.

Multi-Cloud Deployments

Using several clouds to provision infrastructure improves fault tolerance and allows for a more smooth recovery from cloud provider failures. On the other hand, multi-cloud installations are more complicated because each provider has its own interfaces, tools, and workflows. Terraform allows you to manage numerous providers and cross-cloud dependencies with the same methodology. This makes large-scale, multi-cloud infrastructure management and orchestration easier.

Application Infrastructure Deployments, Scaling, and Monitoring Tools

Terraform can be used to quickly deploy, scale, and monitor infrastructure for multi-tier applications. N-tier application architecture separates concerns and allows you to scale application components independently. A pool of web servers with a database tier, as well as API servers, cache servers, and routing meshes, could make up an application. Terraform allows you to manage all of the resources in each tier at the same time, and it automatically handles tier dependencies. Terraform, for example, will deploy a database layer before the web servers that rely on it.

Self-Service Cluster

Your centralized operations team may receive several recurring infrastructure requests in a large organization. Terraform can be used to create a "self-serve" infrastructure paradigm that allows product teams to manage their own infrastructure. You may design and utilize Terraform modules to define your organization's rules for deploying and managing services, allowing teams to deploy services quickly and in accordance with your policies. Terraform Cloud can also work with ticketing systems like ServiceNow to create new infrastructure requests automatically.

Policy Compliance and Management

Terraform can assist you in enforcing standards regarding the types of resources that teams are allowed to provide and use. Ticket-based review processes can be a bottleneck in the development process. Instead, before Terraform performs infrastructure changes, you can utilize Sentinel, a policy-as-code framework, to enforce compliance and governance regulations automatically. Sentinel is a Terraform Cloud team and governance tier feature.

PaaS Service Setup

Platform as a Service (PaaS) companies like Heroku let you build web applications and add-ons like databases and email providers. Although Heroku may grow the number of dynos or workers on demand, most non-trivial apps require a large number of add-ons and other services. You may use Terraform to codify the Heroku application configuration, configure a DNSimple to set a CNAME, and set up Cloudflare as the app's Content Delivery Network (CDN). Without a web interface, Terraform can do all of this rapidly and consistently.

Software Define Networking

Terraform may work with Software Defined Networks (SDNs) to autonomously configure networks based on the applications' requirements. This allows you to go from a ticket-based to an automated approach, lowering deployment times.

For example, Consul-Terraform-Sync can produce Terraform configuration to expose suitable ports and alter network settings for any SDN that has an associated Terraform provider when a service registers with HashiCorp Consul. Without having to manually translate tickets from developers into the modifications you think their applications need, Network Infrastructure Automation (NIA) allows you to safely approve the changes that your applications require.

Kubernetes

Kubernetes is a containerized application workload scheduler that is open-source. Terraform allows you to both deploy and manage a Kubernetes cluster (e.g., pods, deployments, services, etc.). Through a Kubernetes Custom Resource Definition (CRD) and Terraform Cloud, you may also use the Kubernetes Operator for Terraform to manage cloud and on-prem infrastructure.

Parallel Environments

You might have staging or quality assurance environments where you test new applications before putting them into production. Maintaining an up-to-date environment for each stage of the development process becomes increasingly difficult as the production environment grows larger and more complicated. Terraform allows you to quickly provision and decommission infrastructure for development, testing, quality assurance, and production. It is more cost-effective to use Terraform to construct disposable environments as needed rather than maintaining each one indefinitely.

Terraform versus Alternatives

Terraform abstracts resources and providers in a flexible way. Everything from the actual hardware, virtual computers, and containers to email and DNS providers can be represented using this approach. Terraform's flexibility allows it to be used to tackle a wide range of challenges. This means that Terraform's capabilities overlap with those of a variety of other technologies. We compare Terraform to a few of these tools, but it's worth noting that Terraform doesn't have to be used in tandem with other systems. It can be used to manage a single application or a datacenter as a whole.

Terraform vs. Chef and Puppet

Configuration management software installs and manages applications on an existing PC. Terraform is not a configuration management tool, so existing tools can concentrate on what they do best: bootstrapping and initializing resources.

Terraform focuses on the datacenter and associated services at a higher level of abstraction, while allowing you to use configuration management tools on individual systems. It also intends to bring the same advantages of system configuration codification to infrastructure management.

If your compute instances employ traditional configuration management, Terraform can be used to configure bootstrapping software like cloud-init to activate your configuration management software on the first system boot.

Terraform vs. CloudFormation

The details of infrastructure can be formalized into a configuration file using tools like CloudFormation, Heat, and others. The configuration files allow the infrastructure to be established, modified, and removed on an as-needed basis. The issues they solve inspire Terraform.

Terraform is similar to Chef in that it uses configuration files to specify the infrastructure setup, but it goes one step further by being cloud-agnostic and allowing many providers and services to be merged and constructed. Terraform, for example, can orchestrate an AWS and OpenStack cluster at the same time, while also allowing third-party CDN and DNS providers like Cloudflare and DNSimple to be connected. Terraform can now represent and manage the whole infrastructure, including its supporting services, rather than just the subset contained within a single provider. Instead of requiring operators to utilize separate and non-interoperable tools for each platform and service, it provides a single universal syntax.

Custom Solutions

Most businesses begin by controlling infrastructure manually using simple scripts or web-based interfaces. As the infrastructure grows, any manual method to administration becomes both error-prone and time-consuming, therefore, many companies start using home-roll tooling to help automate the mechanical procedures.

Building and maintaining these technologies takes time and money. They are built to handle only the urgent needs as tools of necessity, representing the minimum practical characteristics required by an organization. As a result, they are frequently difficult to extend and maintain. Tooling becomes the limiting factor for how quickly the infrastructure can change because it must be updated in lockstep with any new features or infrastructure.

Terraform was created to address these issues. It has a simple, uniform syntax that allows practically any resource to be controlled without the need to learn new software. By capturing all essential resources, the dependencies between them can be automatically resolved, eliminating the need for operators to remember and reason about them. By removing the burden of tool development, operators may concentrate on their infrastructure rather than tools.

Terraform is also a free and open-source tool. In addition to HashiCorp, the Terraform community contributes to the development of new features, bug fixes, and documentation of new use cases. Terraform provides a standard that can be used to avoid reinventing the wheel between and within companies. Its open-source nature ensures that it will last a long time.

Terraform vs. Boto and Fog

Boto, Fog, and other libraries are used to enable native access to cloud providers and services via APIs. Some libraries specialize in certain clouds, while others try to bridge the gap between them all and hide the semantic differences. Application developers must construct their own tooling to build and manage their infrastructure because using a client library only provides low-level access to APIs.

Terraform is a high-level syntax for expressing how cloud resources and services should be built, provisioned, and merged. It is not meant to allow providers low-level programmatic access. Terraform is extremely adaptable, as it uses a plugin-based model to support providers and provisioners, allowing it to support nearly any service that exposes APIs.

Terraform Associate Exam

We will cover a couple of things on this topic. First, we will go over what to expect on the actual exam. Then we will learn about the primary goals that will assess, and finally, we will go through the types of questions you may expect on the exam.

Introduction

The Terraform Associate Exam will last one hour. It will consist of 50 to 60 questions, and you will be assessed on Terraform versions 12 and up. So, if you have worked with previous versions, be aware that there have been significant changes in the syntax and some logic since then. The exam will be proctored online. You must register on HashiCorp's official website. It will then take you to the exam portal, and you must ensure that your system meets the requirements for taking the exam. The certification is valid for two years from the date you pass the exam.

Exam Objectives

Objective 1: Understand Infrastructure as Code Concept

The first objective will assess your grasp of the Infrastructure as Code ideas. HashiCorp expects you to be able to explain what infrastructure as code, or IaC, is, as well as its merits and drawbacks.

Objective 2: Understand Terraform's Purpose (vs. Other IaC)

In the second objective, you must comprehend Infrastructure as Code from the standpoint of Terraform, what distinguishes it from other IaC tools, and demonstrate the benefits of some of Terraform's functionality and features.

Objective 3: Understand Terraform Basic

The third objective will test your grasp of Terraform's building blocks, its uses behind the hood, how it works to deploy infrastructure, and Terraform's numerous building blocks.

Objective 4: Use Terraform CLI (Outside of Core Workflow)

The fourth objective will take us deeper technically, as we will learn Terraform CLI commands and what circumstances to use those commands in a while adhering to best practices.

Objective 5: Interact with Terraform Modules

In the fifth objective, you will be tested on Terraform's modularization capabilities. For example, how can you make reusable code configurations not be required to rewrite code continually? Module inputs and outputs, as well as module versioning, will be tested. You will also need to understand variable scope when used within root or child modules, as well as the Terraform public module registry.

Objective 6: Navigate Terraform Workflow

The sixth objective will put your navigation and familiarity with the Terraform procedure to the test. All examples are local and remote backend storage for Terraform state files, state locking, the Terraform refresh, backend authentication, and managing sensitive data and state files.

Objective 7: Implement and Maintain State

The next objective will require you to understand how Terraform state is implemented and used. You should be familiar with the Terraform workflow, how Terraform configuration directories are populated, and how to use Terraform subcommands such as Terraform validate, plan, apply, and destroy.

Objective 8: Read, Generate, and Modify the Configuration

The eighth objective will put you to the test on Terraform's actual coding, and you will need to understand how to use variables and outputs in Terraform. You should also be familiar with built-in functions and dynamic blocks. Furthermore, you will need to understand the distinction between Terraform's resource and data blocks and when to use them. Finally, you must know how Terraform's resource addressing works and how you can reference distinct Terraform resources within the same Terraform code.

Objective 9: Understand Terraform Cloud and Enterprise Capabilities

The 9th objective will mostly test you on Terraform cloud and enterprise products, such as Sentinel, a HashiCorp policy enforcement framework that may be used in conjunction with Terraform. You will also need to understand the distinction between the capability of the workspace feature in Terraform's free offering and the identical feature in its corporate pricing. It would help to comprehend the major features of Terraform's managed cloud solution.

Exam Questions

We will now look at the types of questions you can expect on the exam.

First, we have the fundamental true and false question, in which you will be given a statement and must assess whether or not it is correct by selecting a true or false scenario. For example, suppose you are asked two options and must choose between true and false.

Following that are the standard multiple-choice questions, in which you will be given a situation, a statement, or a snippet of code and must select the single best answer from all

Chapter 01: Introduction

available possibilities. For example, you will be given a question, an excerpt of Terraform code, and asked to select the best potential answer. You may need to select more than one option when answering. So you have a question and five options, and you must select the correct two answers from the five offered.

Mind Map

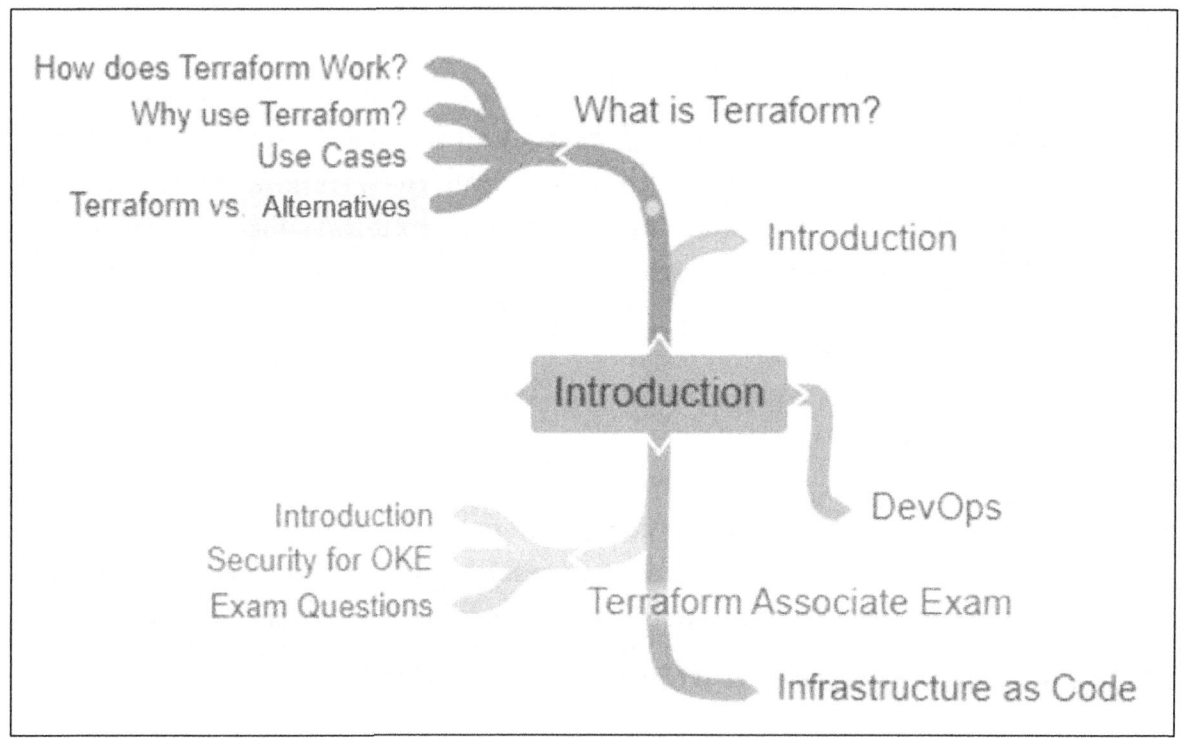

Figure 1-06: Mind Map

Practice Questions

1. IaC enables _____.
A. DevOps
B. Unit testing
C. Debugging
D. None of the above

2. The codification of deployment means that it can be tracked in _____.
A. Between the processes of testing
B. A website
C. Version control

Chapter 01: Introduction

D. None of the above

3. Which of the following is an example of IaC tools?
A. AWS Cloud Formation
B. Salt Stack
C. Terraform
D. All of the above

4. Terraform can be used to modify the configuration for _____.
A. Physical networks
B. Servers
C. SDNs
D. All of the above

5. In terraform, you cannot use two cloud providers for high availability. True or false?
A. True
B. False

6. Which of the following database providers is supported by Terraform?
A. MySQL
B. Influx DB
C. MongoDB
D. All of the above

7. Which of the following can be categorized as Terraform resources?
A. Compute Instance
B. VM
C. Virtual Network
D. All of the above

8. Which of the following statements is NOT true about Terraform?
A. Terraform is a set of tools
B. Terraform is free
C. Terraform is cloud agnostic
D. Terraform enables DevOps

9. Terraform is _____ tool.
A. Software Development

Chapter 01: Introduction

B. Orchestration
C. PAAS
D. None

10. Which of the following are the features of Terraform?
A. Remote Terraform execution
B. Workspaces for organizing infrastructure
C. Version control integration
D. All of the above

Chapter 02: Getting Started with Terraform

Introduction

HashiCorp's Terraform is a simple yet effective open-source infrastructure management tool. It allows you to manage your infrastructure safely and predictably by codifying APIs into declarative configuration files.

Within this chapter, you will be learned about the fundamentals of Terraform and integrated working with Cloud Service Providers. (CSPs).

Getting Started

Terraform is a fantastic suite of tools for automating infrastructure in both public and private cloud environments. This chapter will show you how to use Terraform to deploy infrastructure across various services in a consistent and repeatable manner.

Terraform must be installed before it can be used. Terraform is distributed as a binary package by HashiCorp. Terraform can also be installed using major package managers.

Install Terraform

Pre-requisites

There are various conditions that must be met before you begin the installation process:

- If you are installing on Windows, you will need a Windows PC.
- If you are installing on Linux, you will need a Linux system (virtual or local)
- A rudimentary understanding of the CLI

Installations

> 1. Go to Terraform's download page (https://www.terraform.io/downloads.html) to get started. Terraform downloads for various platforms should be listed. Go to the Windows area and get the appropriate version.

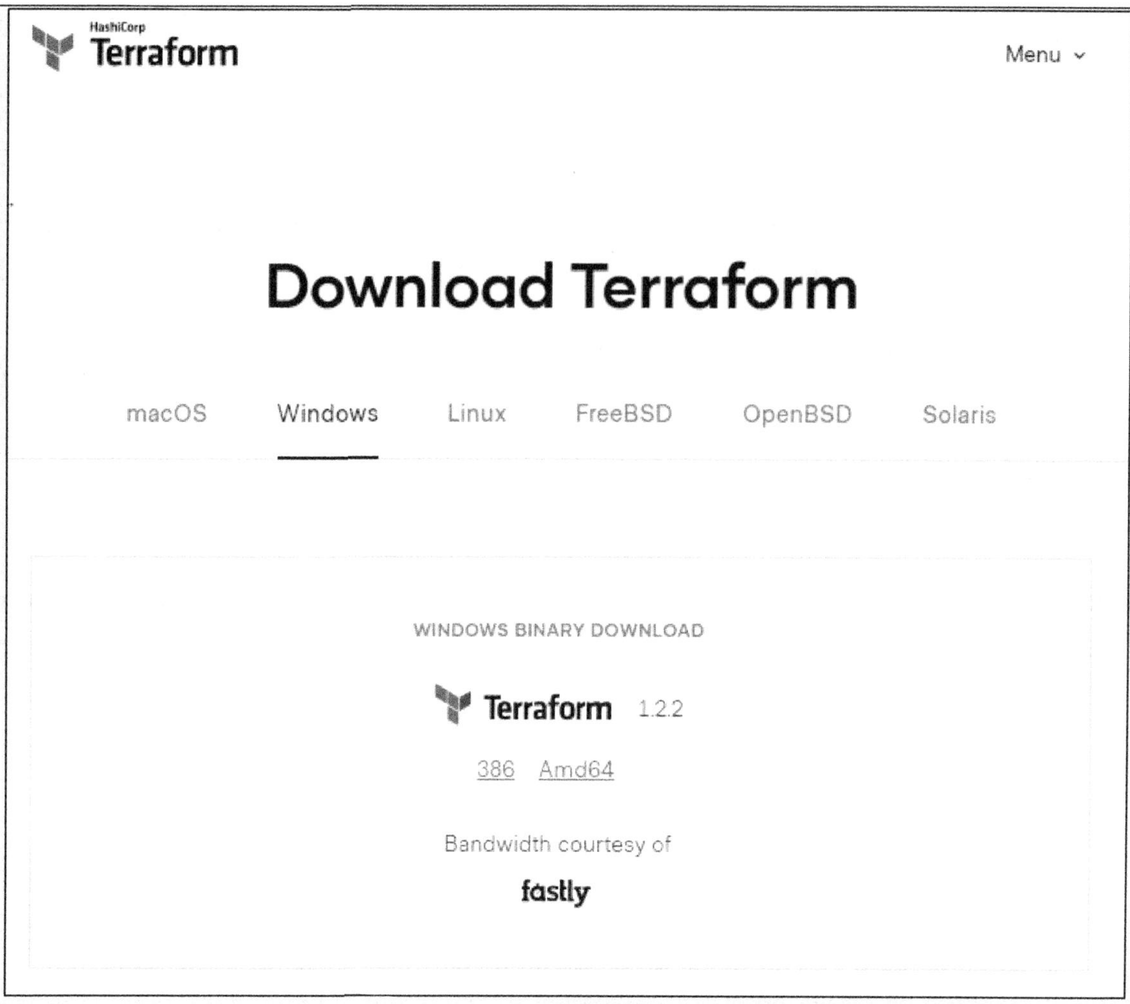

Chapter 02: Getting Started with Terraform

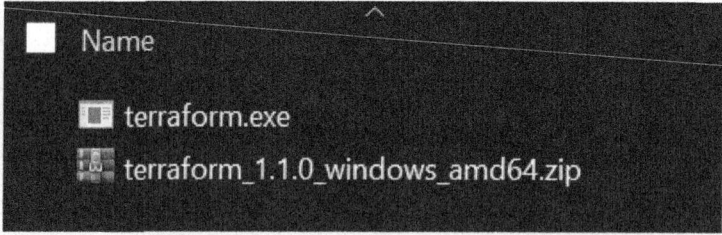

2. It will save a zip file to your computer. Make a folder named C:/terraform on the C disc. This folder contains a zip file that you can download. To get the .exe file, unzip the file.

3. Next, go to the Start menu and type Environment variables into the search box. Go to the Environment Variables page and change the settings.

Chapter 02: Getting Started with Terraform

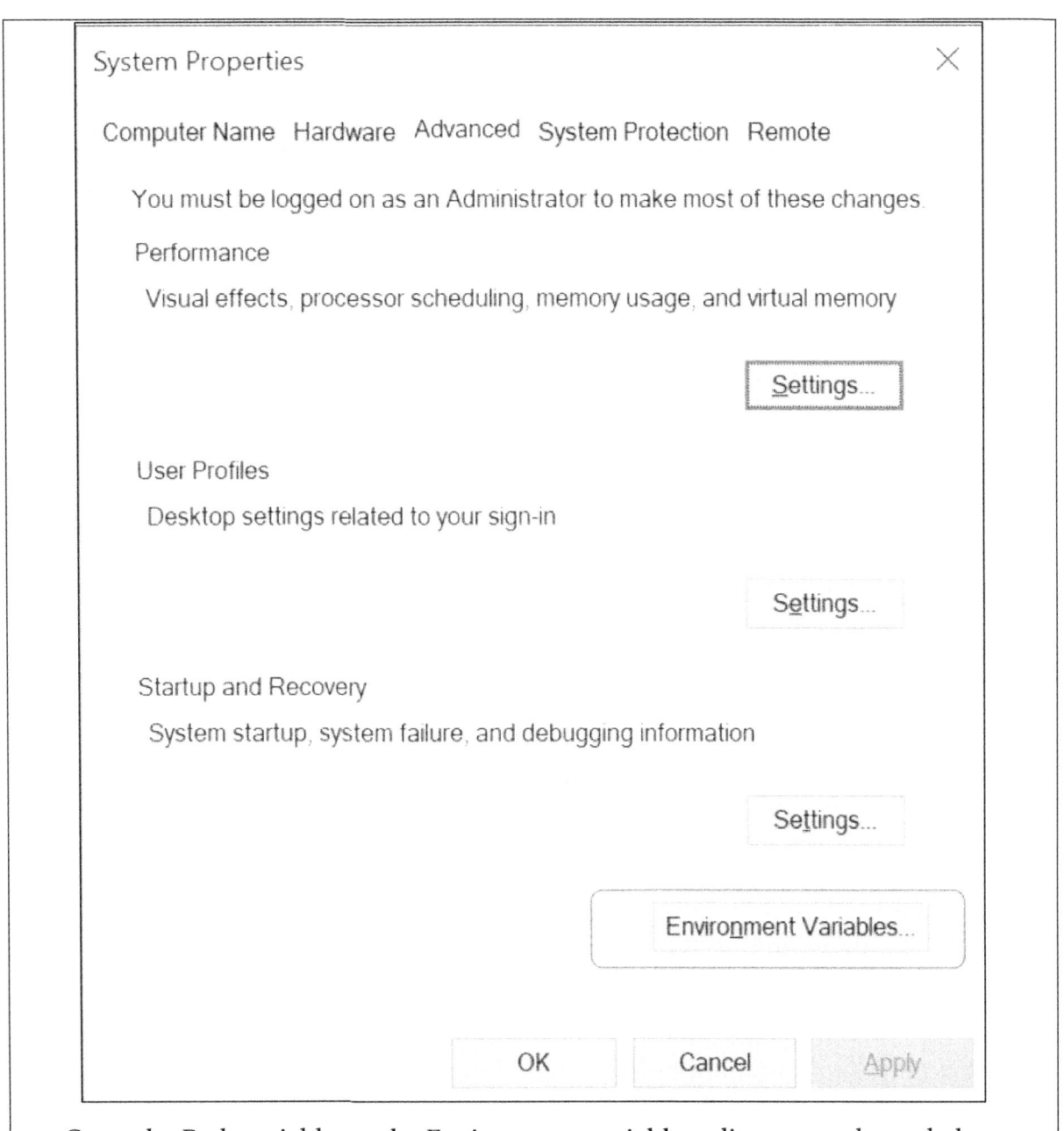

```
System Properties                                              ×

Computer Name  Hardware  Advanced  System Protection  Remote

  You must be logged on as an Administrator to make most of these changes.
  Performance
    Visual effects, processor scheduling, memory usage, and virtual memory

                                                    [ Settings... ]

  User Profiles
    Desktop settings related to your sign-in

                                                    [ Settings... ]

  Startup and Recovery
    System startup, system failure, and debugging information

                                                    [ Settings... ]

                                            [ Environment Variables... ]

                              [ OK ]      [ Cancel ]      [ Apply ]
```

4. Open the Path variable on the Environment variables edit page as shown below:

Chapter 02: Getting Started with Terraform

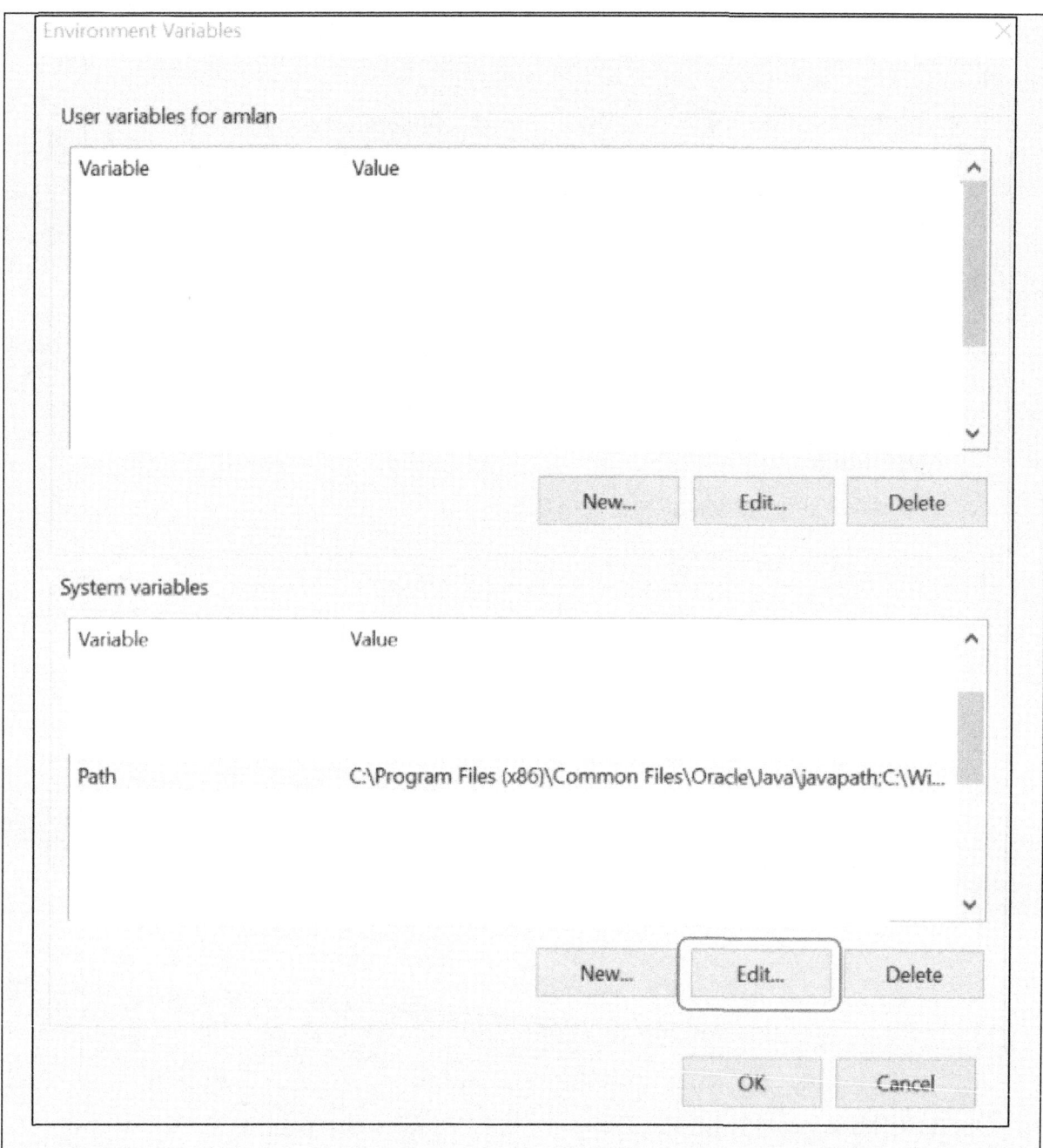

![Environment Variables dialog showing User variables for amlan and System variables with Path highlighted]

5. Click New on the Path pop-up to add the Terraform download folder. This is the folder (C:/terraform) where the zip file was downloaded and unzipped.

Chapter 02: Getting Started with Terraform

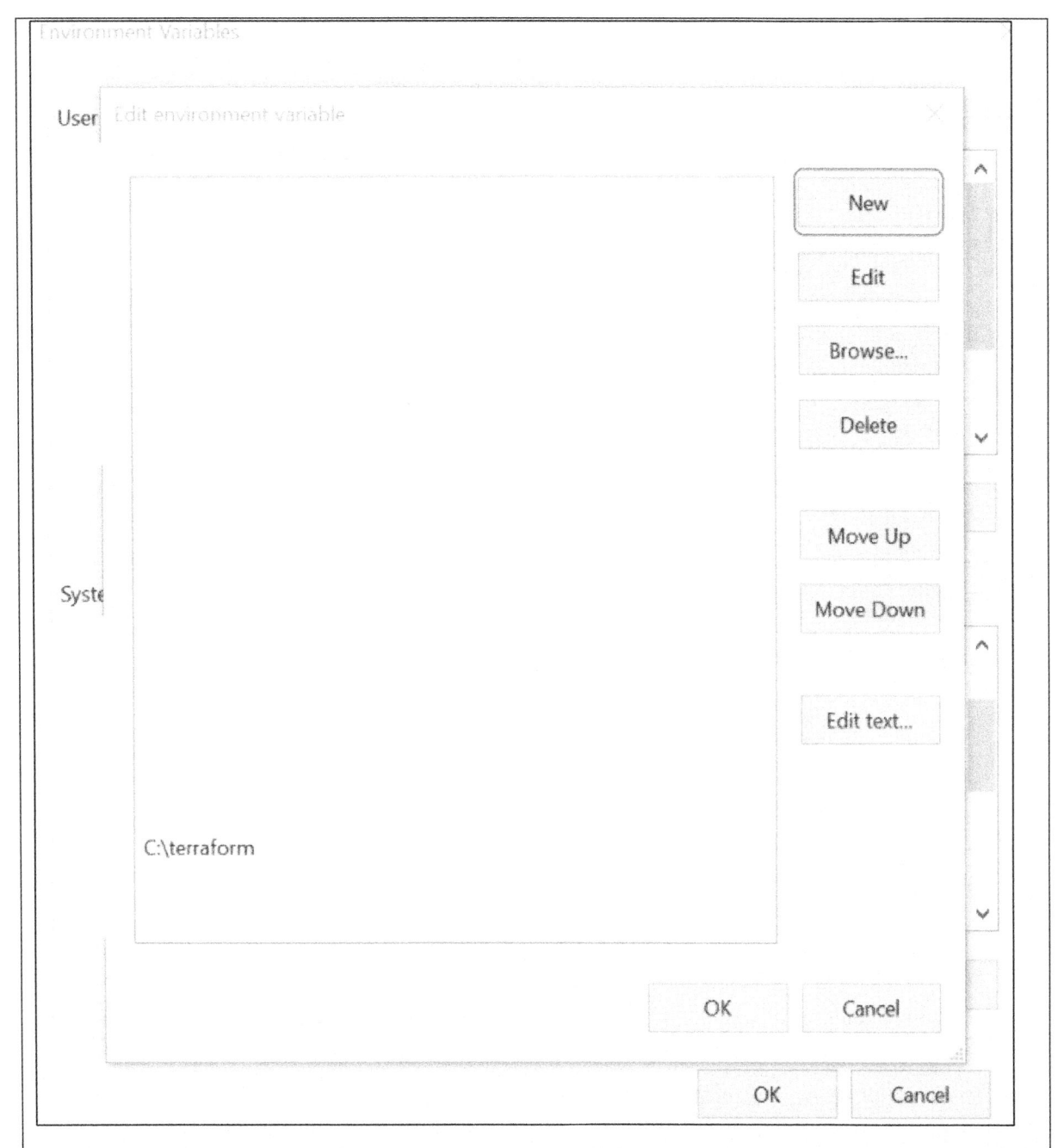

[Screenshot of Edit environment variable dialog showing C:\terraform entry with New, Edit, Browse, Delete, Move Up, Move Down, Edit text, OK, Cancel buttons]

6. To save the Path variable addition, click OK in the above dialogue. Restart your computer if necessary to effect the variable adjustments.
7. To ensure Terraform is installed successfully, open a command line and perform the following command:

```
C:\Users\amlan>terraform
Usage: terraform [global options] <subcommand> [args]

The available commands for execution are listed below.
The primary workflow commands are given first, followed by
less common or more advanced commands.

Main commands:
  init          Prepare your working directory for other commands
  validate      Check whether the configuration is valid
  plan          Show changes required by the current configuration
  apply         Create or update infrastructure
  destroy       Destroy previously-created infrastructure

All other commands:
  console       Try Terraform expressions at an interactive command prompt
  fmt           Reformat your configuration in the standard style
  force-unlock  Release a stuck lock on the current workspace
  get           Install or upgrade remote Terraform modules
  graph         Generate a Graphviz graph of the steps in an operation
```

8. Verify the installation using using version command.

```
C:\Users\amlan>terraform --version
Terraform v1.1.0
on windows_amd64
```

Launch AWS EC2 instance using Terraform

EC2 Instance

- Elastic Compute Cloud is how AWS describes it.
- It is a virtual world where you can "rent" your environment rather than buying it.
- These virtual machines are referred to as Instances by Amazon.
- Instances can be launched using pre-configured templates. Images are the names given to these templates. AMIs (Amazon Machine Pictures) are the images that Amazon offers (Amazon Machine Images).
- Allows you to add custom applications and services to your system.
- Infrastructure scaling, or scaling up or down, is simple depending on demand.
- AWS offers a variety of CPU, memory, storage, and other combinations from which you can choose the flavor that best suits your needs.
- There are no storage restrictions. Depending on the sort of instance you are working on, you can choose the storage.

- Instance Store Volumes are temporary storage volumes that are offered. When the instance is terminated, the data saved in this is erased.
- EBS (Elastic Block Store) volumes are persistent storage volumes that are available.
- Regions and Availability Zones are terms used to describe the multiple places where these instances can be put (AZ).
- You can disperse your Instances across many AZs (i.e., within a single Region) so that if one fails, AWS will immediately remap the address to a different AZ.
- It is possible to migrate instances from one AZ to another.
- You can optionally provide your own metadata to each resource in the form of tags to manage instances, pictures, and other EC2 resources.
- An AWS resource is given a label called a Tag. It has a key and an optional value, both of which you can define.
- On a per-Region basis, each AWS account comes with a set of default resource limits.
- Any increase in the limit must be requested through AWS.
- We use Key Pairs to interact with the instances we have built.

Terraform

- It is an open-source IaaC (Infrastructure as a Code) software platform that lets you design and creates resources using declarative configuration languages like JSON.
- You can package and reuse code in the form of modules with Terraform.
- It works with AWS, Azure, GCP, IBM Cloud, OCI, and other cloud infrastructure providers.

There are four main commands in Terraform:

- terraform init
- terraform plan
- terraform apply
- terraform destroy

Architectural Diagram

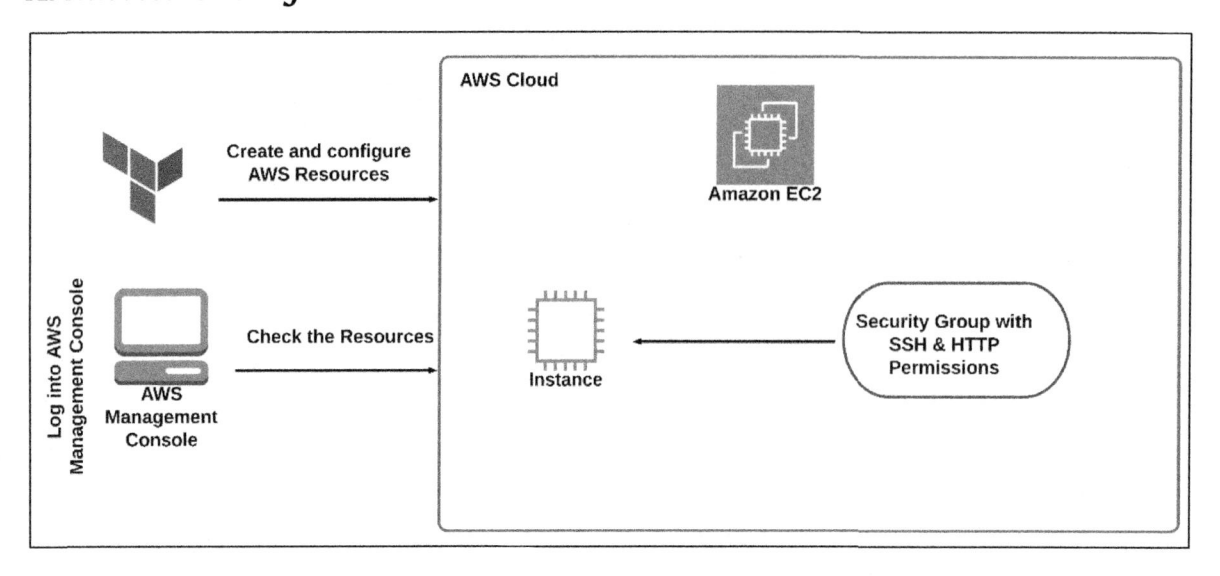

Figure 2-01: Architectural Diagram

Implementation Steps

- Create a new project in Visual Studio Code.
- Make a file called Variables.
- In the main.tf file, create EC2 and its components.
- Make a file called Output.
- Verify Terraform's installation by looking at the version number.
- Terraform setups should be used.
- Examine the HTML page.
- In the AWS Console, look at the resources.
- The lab is being validated.
- AWS Resources should be deleted.

Step 01: Log into the AWS Console.

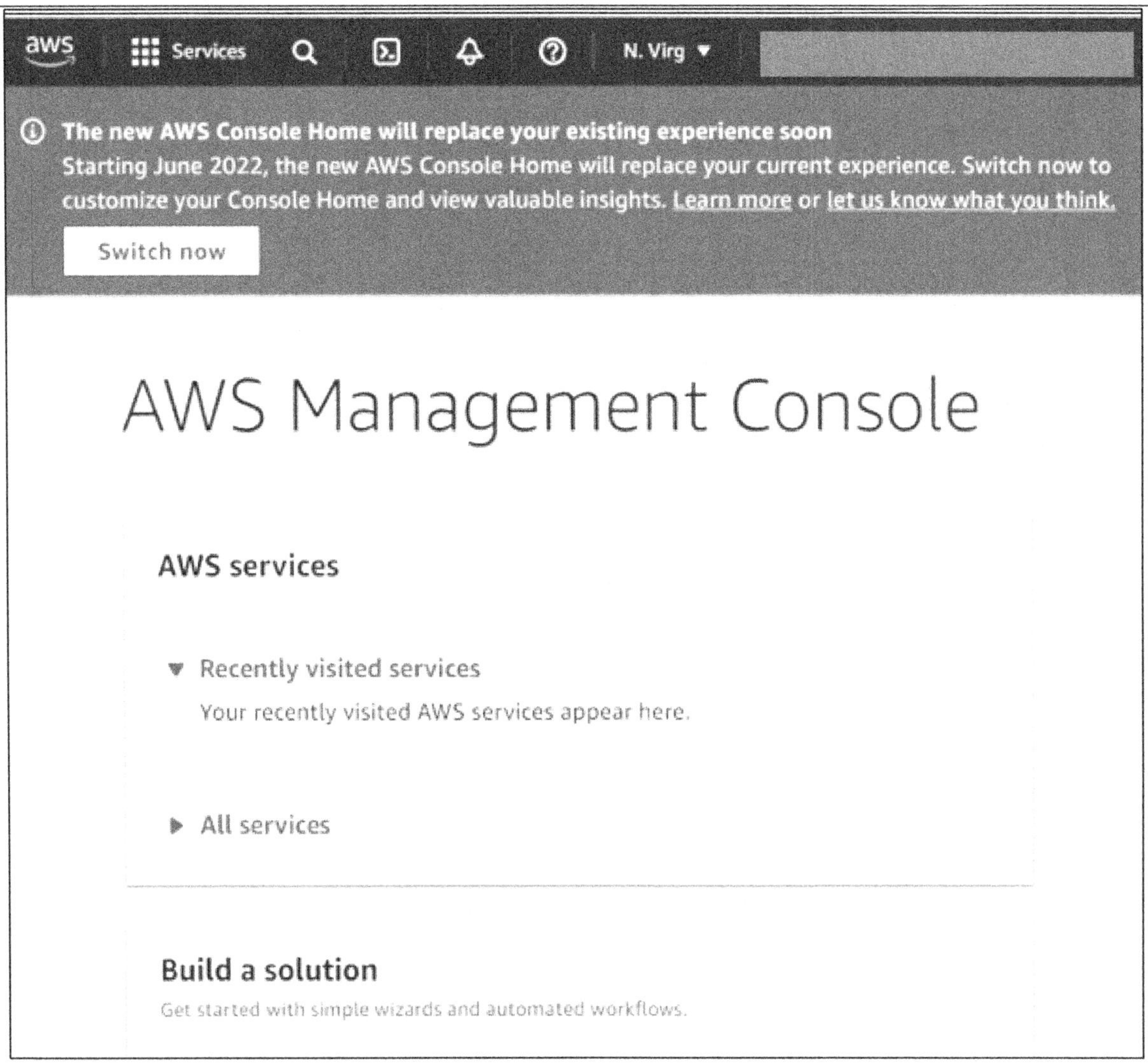
aws
Services
N. Virg
The new AWS Console Home will replace your existing experience soon
Starting June 2022, the new AWS Console Home will replace your current experience. Switch now to customize your Console Home and view valuable insights. Learn more or let us know what you think.
Switch now
AWS Management Console
AWS services
Recently visited services
Your recently visited AWS services appear here.
All services
Build a solution
Get started with simple wizards and automated workflows.

Step 02: Set up Visual Studio Code

1. Open the code in Visual Studio.
2. Open a new window if you already have Visual Studio Code installed and running.
3. A new file and release notes page will appear in a new window (only if you have installed or updated Visual Studio Code recently). Close the tab "Release Notes."
4. Select View from the Menu bar and Terminal from the drop-down menu.
5. The terminal window may take up to 2 minutes to open.
6. Let's go to the Desktop after the terminal is ready.

cd Desktop

7. Run the command below to create a new folder.

mkdir task_10001_ec2

8. Run the following command to change your current working directory to the newly created folder:

cd task_10001_ec2

9. Run the following command to find the current working directory's location:

pwd

10. Make a note of the location because you will need it in the next step.
11. Now, on the left sidebar, click the first icon, Explorer.
12. Open the folder **task_10001_ec2** by clicking the Open folder button and navigating to its location.

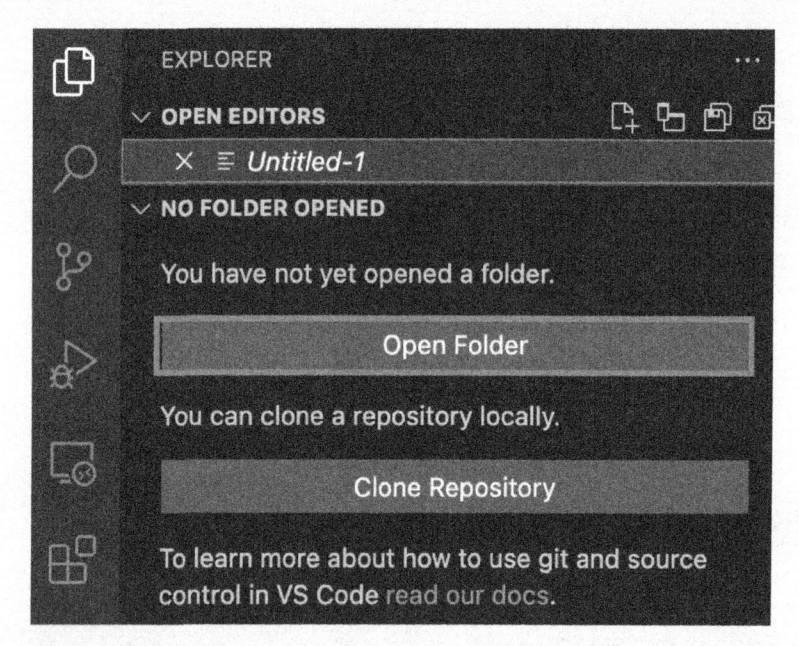

13. Allow Visual Studio Code to utilize the **task_10001_ec2** folder by clicking the Authorize button. This question will only be prompted after you have been using Visual Studio Code for a time and you are authorizing VSC to access a new folder.
14. It is now possible to use Visual Studio Code.

Step 03: Create a Variable File

1. This task requires you to build variable files in which you will declare all global variables along with a brief description and a default value.
2. To make a variable file, expand the folder **task_10001_ec2** and add the file by clicking the New File icon.
3. To save the file, type variables.tf in the filename field and hit Enter.

Note: Do not modify the new file's location; leave it as is, in the task 10001 ec2 folder.

4. In the variables.tf file, paste the contents below.

variable "access_key" {
   description = "Access key to AWS console"
}
variable "secret_key" {
   description = "Secret key to AWS console"
}
variable "region" {
   description = "Region of AWS VPC"
}

5. In the preceding material, you declare three variables: access key, secret key, and region, each with a brief description.
6. Save the file by hitting ctrl + S after pasting the preceding contents.
7. To add the file, expand the folder task 10001 ec2 and click the New File icon.
8. Save the file as terraform.tfvars by pressing Enter.
9. In the terraform.tfvars file, paste the following content.

region = "us-east-1"

access_key = "<YOUR AWS CONSOLE ACCESS ID>"

secret_key = "<YOUR AWS CONSOLE SECRET KEY>"

10. You are defining the dynamic values of variables stated previously in the code.
11. Copy the access key and secret key values from the lab page and replace them.
12. Save the file by hitting Ctrl + S after replacing the access key and secret key values.

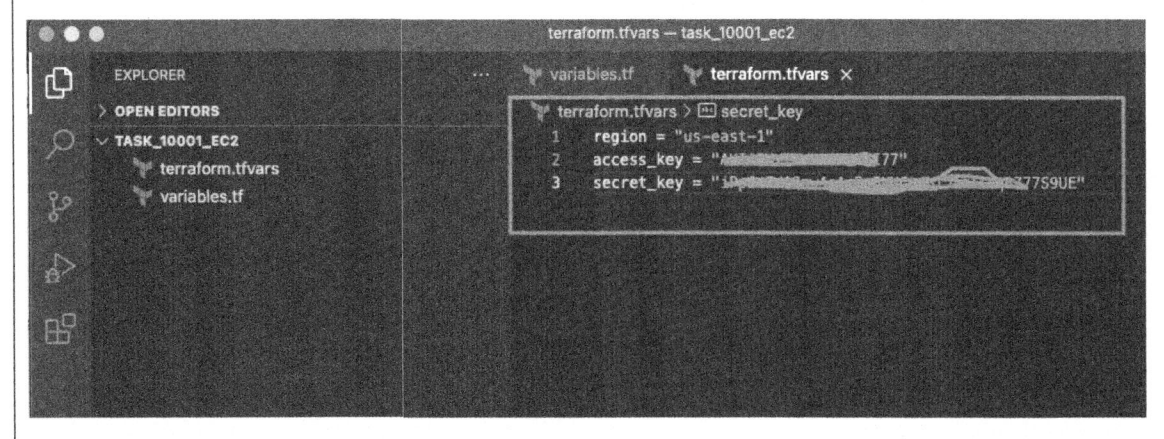

Step 04: Create EC2 Instance

1. In this task, you will construct a main.tf file in which you will enter the provider's and resources' information.
2. Expand the folder task 10001 ec2 and add the main.tf file by clicking on the New File icon.
3. To save the file, type main.tf and click Enter.
4. Copy and paste the content below into the main.tf file.

```
provider "aws" {
   region     = "${var.region}"
   access_key = "${var.access_key}"
   secret_key = "${var.secret_key}"
}
```

5. The provider is defined as aws in the code above.
6. Next, we will tell Terraform to construct an AWS EC2 Security Group and populate it with rules that allow traffic on particular ports. We are permitting the tcp port 80 in our scenario (HTTP).
7. We also want to ensure that the instance may connect outward on any port, so we've added an egress component below.
8. After the provider, paste the following content into the main.tf file.

```
resource "aws_security_group" "web-server" {
   name        = "web-server"
   description = "Allow incoming HTTP Connections"
   ingress {
      from_port   = 80
      to_port     = 80
      protocol    = "tcp"
      cidr_blocks = ["0.0.0.0/0"]
   }
   egress {
      from_port   = 0
      to_port     = 0
      protocol    = "-1"
      cidr_blocks = ["0.0.0.0/0"]
   }
```

}
9. Finally, after you have created a security group, add another set of code to the main.tf file to establish an EC2 instance.

```
resource "aws_instance" "web-server" {
  ami = "ami-02e136e904f3da870"
  instance_type = "t2.micro"
  key_name = "whizlabs-key"
  security_groups = ["${aws_security_group.web-server.name}"]

  user_data = <<-EOF
  #!/bin/bash
  sudo su
  yum update -y
  yum install httpd -y
  systemctl start httpd
  systemctl enable httpd
  echo "<html><h1> Welcome to Whizlabs. Happy Learning... </h1></html>" >> /var/www/html/index.html
  EOF

  tags = {
    Name = "web_instance"
  }
}
```

10. The Amazon Linux 2 AMI is defined in the code above. The above AMI ID refers to the us-east-1 region.
11. We have already mentioned which SSH key to use (which is already present in your AWS EC2 console). The security group ID is calculated automatically using a variable set during the creation process.
12. To install the Apache server, we added the user data.
13. Tags have been provided for the EC2 instance.
14. By using Ctrl + S, you can save the file.

Step 05: Create an Output File

1. In this task, you will create an output.tf file with the provider's and resources' information.
2. Expand the folder task 10001 ec2 and add the output.tf file by clicking on the New File icon.
3. To save the file, type output.tf and hit Enter.
4. Copy and paste the content below into the output.tf file.

output "web_instance_ip" {

  value = aws_instance.web-server.public_ip

}

5. The Public IP of the newly generated EC2 instance will be extracted and displayed in the code above once the instance has been created.

Step 06: Confirm the Installation of Terraform by checking the version

1. Open Terminal in Visual Studio Code by selecting View from the Menu bar and then Terminal.
2. If you are not in the newly created folder, run the command below to change your current working directory.

cd task_10001_ec2

3. To verify Terraform's installation, execute the command following to check the version:

terraform version

4. If you get the message "command not found: terraform," that means terraform is not installed on your computer.

Step 07: Apply Terraform Configurations

1. Run the following command to start Terraform.

terraform init

Note that terraform init will check for all plugin requirements and, if necessary, download them; this information will be used to build a deployment strategy.

Chapter 02: Getting Started with Terraform

```
PROBLEMS    OUTPUT    DEBUG CONSOLE    TERMINAL

        -Air task_10001_ec2 % terraform init
Initializing the backend...

Initializing provider plugins...
- Finding latest version of hashicorp/aws...
- Installing hashicorp/aws v3.63.0...
- Installed hashicorp/aws v3.63.0 (signed by HashiCorp)

Terraform has created a lock file .terraform.lock.hcl to record the provider
selections it made above. Include this file in your version control repository
so that Terraform can guarantee to make the same selections by default when
you run "terraform init" in the future.

Terraform has been successfully initialized!

You may now begin working with Terraform. Try running "terraform plan" to see
any changes that are required for your infrastructure. All Terraform commands
should now work.
```

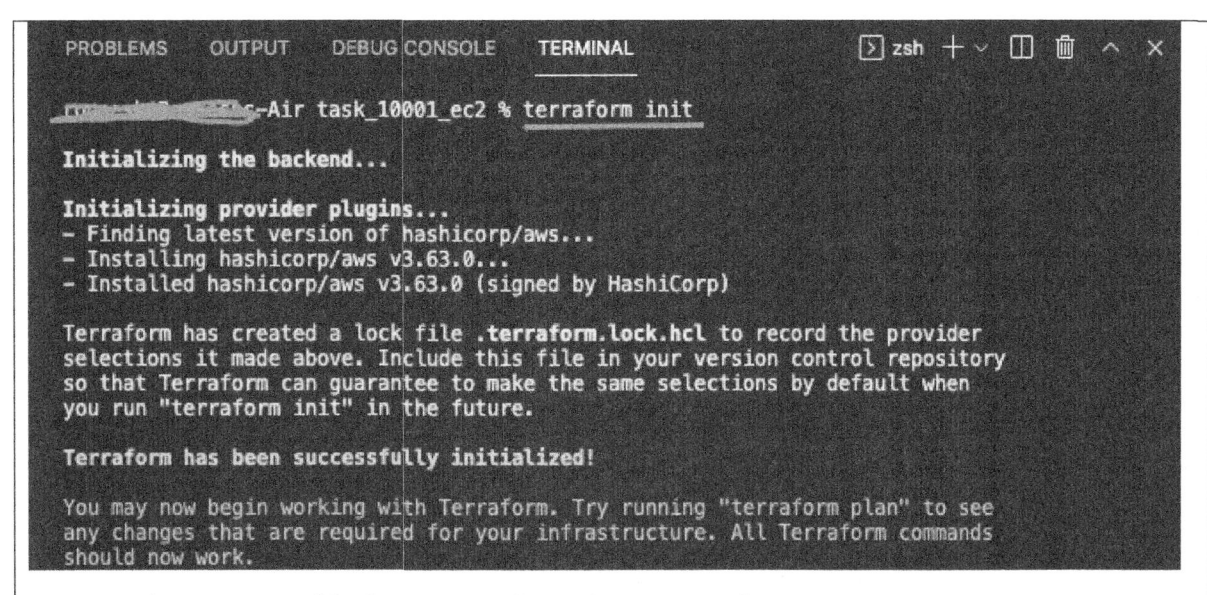

2. Run the command below to produce the action plans.

terraform plan

3. Examine the entire plan that was developed.

```
        s-MacBook-Air task_10001_ec2 % terraform plan
Terraform used the selected providers to generate the following execution plan. Resource actions are
indicated with the following symbols:
  + create

Terraform will perform the following actions:

  # aws_instance.web-server will be created
  + resource "aws_instance" "web-server" {
      + ami                          = "ami-02e136e904f3da870"
      + arn                          = (known after apply)
      + associate_public_ip_address  = (known after apply)
      + availability_zone            = (known after apply)
```

4. Run the command below to construct all of the resources specified in the main.tf configuration file.

terraform apply

5. You will be able to see the resources that will be developed, and you will be able to say yes to all of them.
6. The terraform apply command may take up to 2 minutes to develop the resources.
7. There will be a list of all the resources created by Terraform, as well as their IDs.
8. The result, i.e., the EC2 instance's Public IP, is extracted and shown. Make a copy of the public IP.

```
Do you want to perform these actions?
  Terraform will perform the actions described above.
  Only 'yes' will be accepted to approve.

  Enter a value: yes

aws_security_group.web-server: Creating...
aws_security_group.web-server: Still creating... [10s elapsed]
aws_security_group.web-server: Creation complete after 13s [id=sg-0f3b1fd0693b392ae]
aws_instance.web-server: Creating...
aws_instance.web-server: Still creating... [10s elapsed]
aws_instance.web-server: Still creating... [21s elapsed]
aws_instance.web-server: Still creating... [31s elapsed]
aws_instance.web-server: Still creating... [41s elapsed]
aws_instance.web-server: Creation complete after 43s [id=i-079861878683e7128]

Apply complete! Resources: 2 added, 0 changed, 0 destroyed.

Outputs:

web_instance_ip = "3.87.96.63"
```

9. You can also write down the IDs of all the resources if you want.

Step 08: Check the HTML Page

1. We used user data in the terraform file to establish an apache server and publish an HTML website.
2. Copy the Public IP of the newly established EC2 instance into a new browser tab.
3. The page displays the HTML material created in the user data.

Welcome to Whizlabs. Happy Learning...

4. The EC2 instance has now been built with the apache server, and the HTML content has been properly published.
5. We may also confirm that HTTP incoming requests are allowed by the security group.

Step 09: Check the resources in AWS Console

1. In a new tab, open the AWS Management Console.
2. The 12 digit Account ID will be displayed by default on the AWS sign-in page.

Chapter 02: Getting Started with Terraform

3. Leave the Account ID field blank. If you remove or change the Account ID, you will be unable to complete the experiment.
4. Enter your credentials to access the AWS Console, and click Sign in.
5. Make sure you are in the us-east-1 region of the US East (N. Virginia).

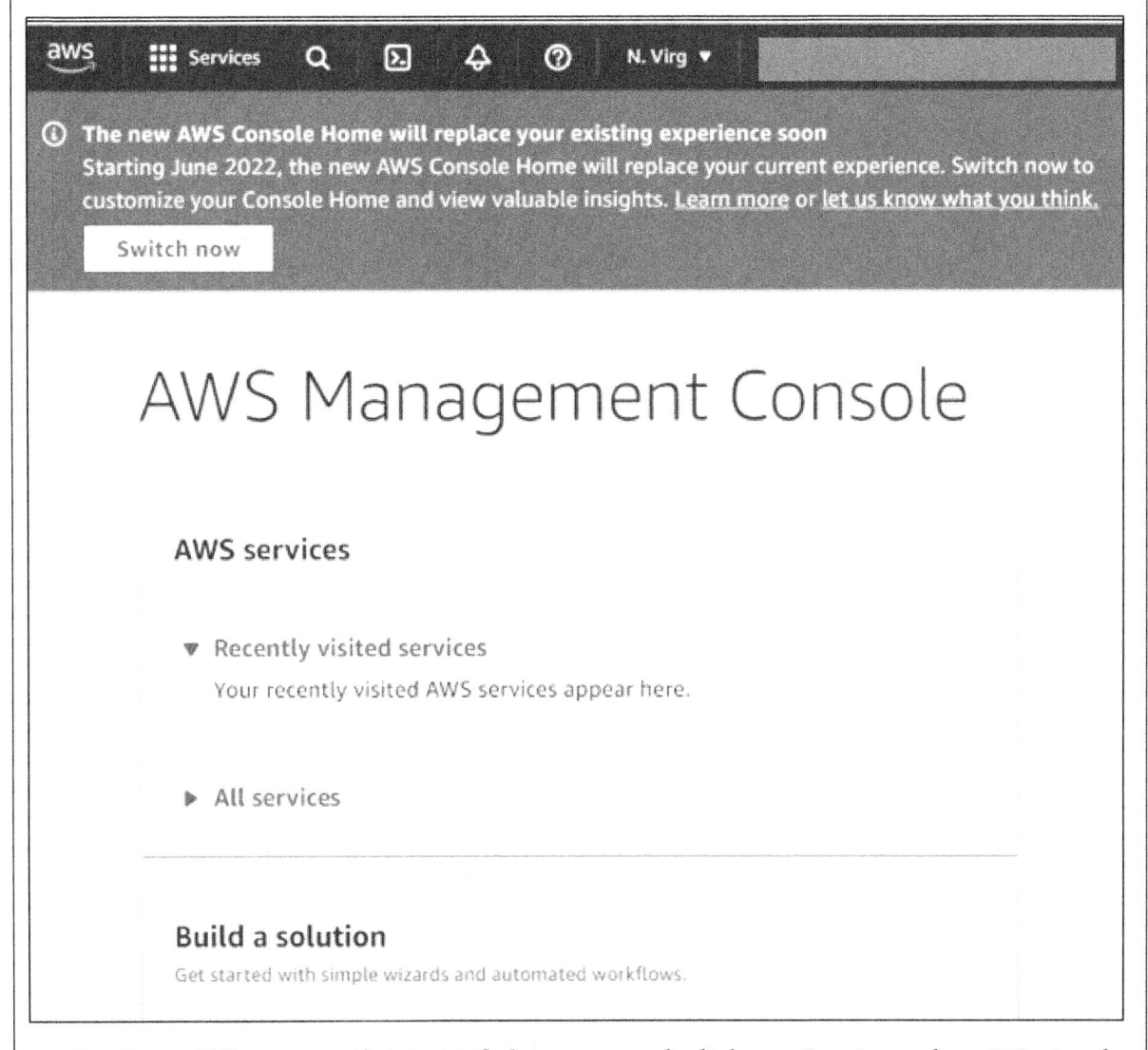

6. To go to EC2, go to the top of the page and click on Services, then EC2 in the Compute section.

Chapter 02: Getting Started with Terraform

	Name ▽	Security group ID ▽	Security group name ▽	VPC ID ▽
☑	–	sg-0f3b1fd0693b392ae	web-server	vpc-8be73cf6
☐	–	sg-33502905	default	vpc-8be73cf6

Security Groups (1/2) Info

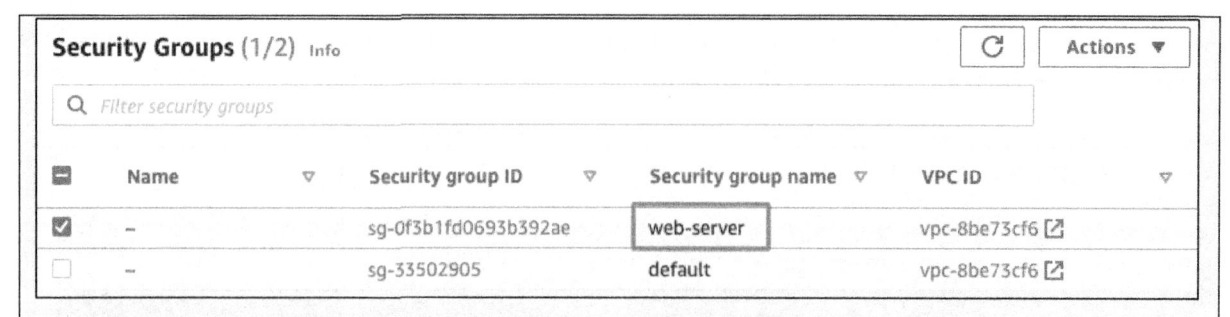

7. On the left side, go to Security Groups under Network & Security.
8. You will be able to view the security group we created with the name web-server.

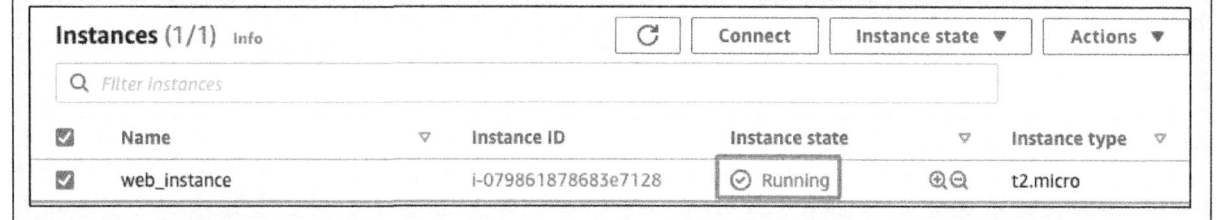

Instances (1/1) Info

	Name ▽	Instance ID	Instance state ▽	Instance type ▽
☑	web_instance	i-079861878683e7128	⊘ Running	t2.micro

Step 10: Validate

1. Please click the button on the left side panel once you have completed the lab instructions.
2. This will check the resources in your AWS account and show you whether or not you completed the lab successfully.

Step 11: Delete AWS Resources

1. Reopen Terminal to delete the resources.
2. To delete all resources, use the command below.

terraform destroy

3. To confirm the deletion, type yes.

```
Do you really want to destroy all resources?
  Terraform will destroy all your managed infrastructure, as shown above.
  There is no undo. Only 'yes' will be accepted to confirm.

  Enter a value: yes

aws_instance.web-server: Destroying... [id=i-079861878683e7128]
aws_instance.web-server: Still destroying... [id=i-079861878683e7128, 10s elapsed]
aws_instance.web-server: Still destroying... [id=i-079861878683e7128, 20s elapsed]
aws_instance.web-server: Still destroying... [id=i-079861878683e7128, 30s elapsed]
aws_instance.web-server: Destruction complete after 39s
aws_security_group.web-server: Destroying... [id=sg-0f3b1fd0693b392ae]
aws_security_group.web-server: Destruction complete after 3s

Destroy complete! Resources: 2 destroyed.
```

4. The AWS Console can be used to confirm resource deletion.

Chapter 02: Getting Started with Terraform

Instances (1) Info					
Name	Instance ID	Instance state		Instance type	Status
web_instance	i-0b822a38ba3e99440	⊖ Terminated	⊕⊖	t2.micro	–

Summary

- The Visual Studio Code editor has been configured.
- The variables.tf and terraform.tfvars are two files you have produced.
- A main.tf file has been created by you.
- You have created the resources by running the terraform configuration procedures.
- By opening the Console, you have checked all of the resources created.
- You have gone through and erased everything

Mind Map

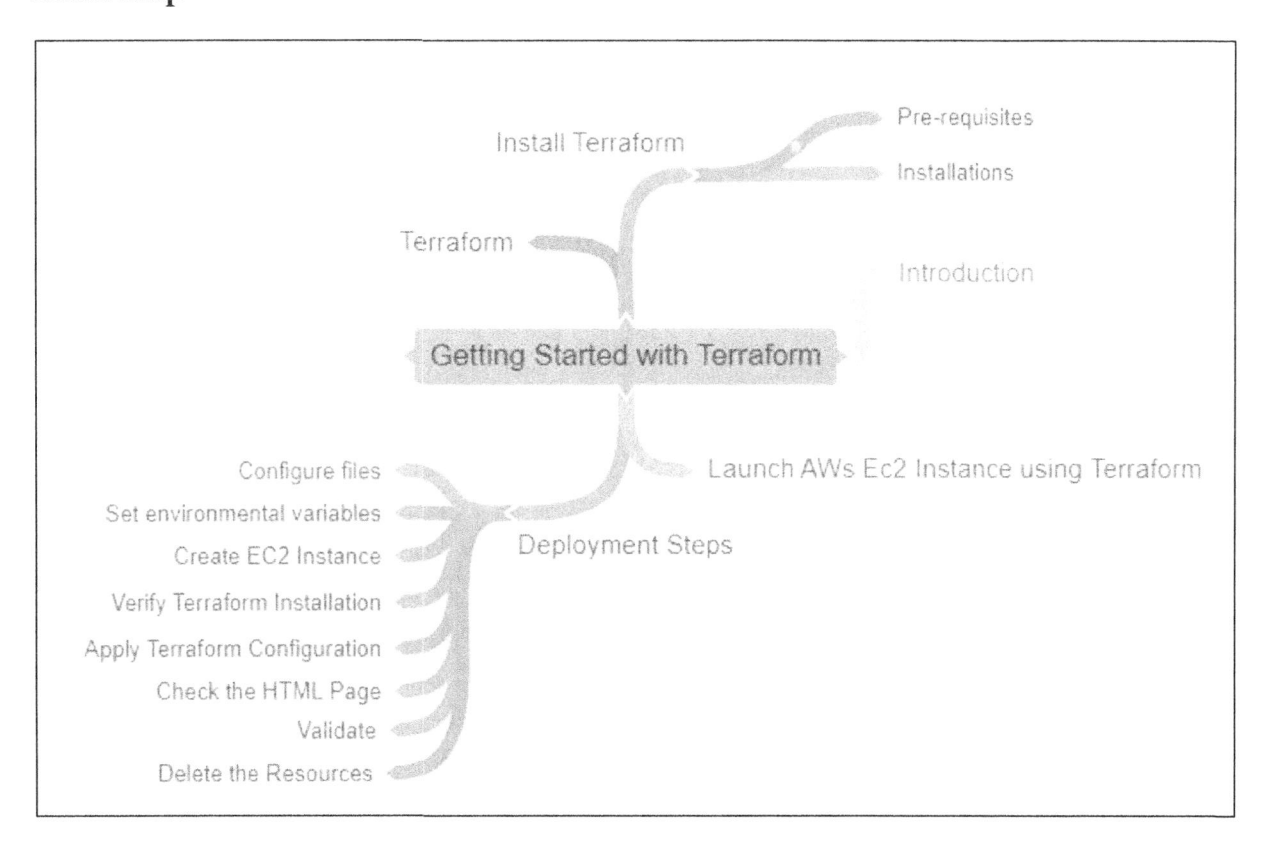

Figure 2-02: Mind Map

Practice Questions

1. Terraform is a fantastic suite of tools for automating infrastructure in _____ cloud environments.

A. Public
B. Private
C. Both A and B
D. Community

2. Terraform is distributed as a binary package by HashiCorp.

A. False
B. True

3. Which of the following command can be used to verify the Terraform installation?
A. terraform init
B. terraform -help
C. terraform destroy
D. terraform --version

4. Which of the following command can be used to build the deployment strategy?
A. terraform plan
B. terraform destroy
C. terraform init
D. terraform --version

5. What is the main purpose of Terraform?
A. Provide Infrastructure
B. Project management
C. Software Developement
D. None of the above

Chapter 03: Understanding Infrastructure As Code

Introduction

Infrastructure as Code (IaC)

Infrastructure as Code (IaC) refers to the method of provisioning and managing infrastructure using code rather than a manual approach. Because infrastructure is defined as code, users may quickly update and share configurations while guaranteeing that the infrastructure remains in the desired condition.

In simple terms, **IaC is the process of using simple lines of code to replace the manual labor necessary for IT resource management and provisioning.**

Infrastructure as code (IaC) tools let you control your infrastructure through configuration files rather than a graphical user interface. By defining resource configurations that you can version, reuse, and share, IaC allows you to develop, change, and manage your infrastructure securely, consistently, and repeatable.

HashiCorp's infrastructure as a code tool is Terraform. It maintains the lifespan of your infrastructure and allows you to define resources and infrastructure in human-readable, declarative configuration files. Using Terraform instead of manually maintaining your infrastructure has various benefits:

Terraform is capable of managing infrastructure across a variety of cloud platforms.

- The human-readable configuration language speeds up the development of infrastructure code.
- Terraform's state feature allows you to keep track of resource changes throughout your deployments.
- To cooperate on infrastructure safely, you can commit your configurations to version control.

IaC solves real-time problems

Infrastructure as Code was created to address the issue of release pipeline environment drift. Without IaC, teams are responsible for maintaining the settings of each deployment environment. Each environment evolves into a snowflake, a one-of-a-kind arrangement that cannot be replicated automatically. During deployments, inconsistency among environments causes problems. Snowflakes need manual operations that are difficult to track and contribute to errors in infrastructure administration and maintenance.

Infrastructure as Code follows the idea of idempotence. Idempotence is the property that a deployment command always configures the target environment in the same way, regardless of the environment's beginning state. Idempotency is achieved by either automatically setting an existing target or dismissing the existing target and starting over.

As a result, using IaC, teams modify the environment description and version the configuration model, which is often written in well-documented code formats like JSON. The model is run in the release pipeline to setup target environments. If changes are required, the team edits the source rather than the target.

Why is IaC important for DevOps?

Implementing DevOps principles and continuous integration/continuous delivery (CI/CD) requires IaC. IaC relieves developers of the majority of provisioning effort by allowing them to run a script to have their infrastructure ready to go.

Application deployments would not be held up while the infrastructure is built, and sysadmins would not have to deal with time-consuming manual operations.

CI/CD relies on continuous automation and monitoring throughout the application lifecycle, from integration and testing to delivery and deployment.

An environment must be consistent in order for it to be automated. When the development team delivers applications or configures environments one way and the operations team deploys and configures environments another, it's impossible to automate application deployments.

DevOps aligns development and operations teams, resulting in fewer errors, manual deployments, and inconsistencies.

IaC supports a DevOps approach by allowing both development and operations teams to share the same description of the application deployment.

A consistent environment is required for automation to work. When the development team delivers applications or configures environments one way and the operations team deploys and configures environments in a different method, it's impossible to automate application deployments.

Using a DevOps methodology to align development and operations teams results in fewer errors, manual deployments, and inconsistencies.

Since both teams can utilize the same description of the application deployment, IaC aids in the alignment of development and operations, allowing for a DevOps approach.

Every environment, including your production environment, should employ the same deployment process. Every time IaC is utilized, it creates the same environment.

IaC also eliminates the requirement for individual deployment environments with distinct configurations that cannot be replicated automatically, ensuring that the production environment is consistent.

Infrastructure in IaC is also subjected to DevOps best practices. Infrastructure code can go through the same CI/CD pipeline as applications during software development, allowing for the same testing and version control.

IaC techniques

Declarative and imperative IaC techniques are the two types of IaC methods. You specify the desired end state in the declarative approach, and the system ensures that you obtain the desired result. To achieve the intended end state, the imperative approach requires you to explicitly define each step in the process.

For the majority of the IaC tools, the code is declarative, which means that you basically declare what you want without being concerned about what underlying functions or API calls will need to be made to deploy that infrastructure. When code is written this way, anyone who reads can easily make sense of what is being deployed, and the code can be a form of documentation of the deployment itself. Less human intervention during deployment means fewer chances of security flaws, creating extra resources by mistake.

Using a consistent IaC tool such as Terraform, one can ensure that your code is uploaded to Git, tracked, and always consistent. No matter how many times you deploy it, it is always deployed with the same inputs and the same expected output.

Here is an IaC, more specifically, a Terraform code example, which is written in HashiCorp configuration language. You will be writing in a much easier-to-read-and-understand declarative language. In this example, we are using AWS cloud to deploy a VPC and notice that we are declaring everything in sequence. In the example below, you can see we have provided all the details essential to creating a VPC, such as the CIDR range.

```
 1    #declare provider
 2    provider "aws" {}
 3
 4    #Create VPC in us-east-1
 5    resource "aws_vpc" "vpc_master" {
 6      cidr_block          = "10.0.0.0/16"
 7      enable_dns_support  = true
 8      enable_dns_hostnames = true
 9      tags = {
10        Name = "master-vpc-jenkins"
11      }
12    }
13
```

Figure 3-01: Terraform Code Snippet

> **EXAM TIP:** The exam will not test you on writing full-fledged Terraform code deployments but might test you on small snippets and how to manipulate variables and logical control via Terraform.

Manage any Infrastructure

Terraform uses providers to interact with cloud platforms and other services through their application programming interfaces (APIs). HashiCorp and the Terraform community have built over 1,000 providers to manage resources on Amazon Web Services (AWS), Azure, Google Cloud Platform (GCP), Kubernetes, Helm, GitHub, Splunk, and DataDog, to mention a few. In the Terraform Registry, you may find providers for many of the platforms and services you already use. If you cannot locate the service you need, you can create your own.

Standardize your deployment workflow

Individual elements of infrastructure, such as computing instances or private networks, are defined as resources by providers. You may combine resources from several suppliers into reusable Terraform configurations known as modules, which you can manage using a common language and workflow.

In contrast to procedural programming languages, which require step-by-step instructions to complete operations, Terraform's configuration language is declarative, which means it expresses the desired end-state for your infrastructure. Terraform providers calculate resource dependencies automatically so that they can be created or destroyed in the correct sequence.

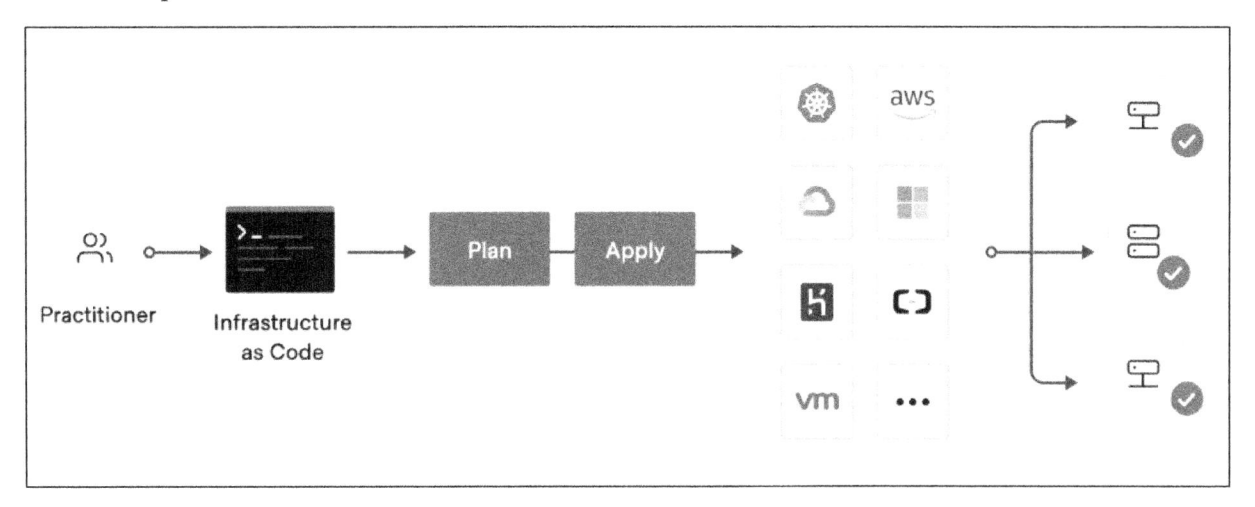

Figure 3-02: Deployment Workflow

Terraform is used to deploy infrastructure.

- **Scope** - Determine the scope of your project's infrastructure.
- **Author** - Create the infrastructure setup.
- **Initialize** - Install the Terraform plugins required to manage the infrastructure.
- **Plan** - See how Terraform will adapt your configuration to reflect your preferences.
- **Implement** - Make the desired adjustments.

Track your Infrastructure

Terraform keeps track of your real infrastructure in a state file that serves as your environment's source of truth. Terraform uses the state file to figure out what modifications need to be made to your infrastructure to match your setup.

Collaborate

Terraform's remote state backends allow you to collaborate on your infrastructure. You can securely share your state with your peers, offer a stable environment for Terraform to execute in, and eliminate race situations when multiple individuals make configuration changes at once when you use Terraform Cloud (free for up to five users).

Terraform Cloud can also be connected to version control systems (VCSs) such as GitHub, GitLab, and others, allowing it to suggest infrastructure modifications immediately when you commit configuration changes to the VCS. This allows you to manage changes to your infrastructure using version control in the same way that you would manage application code.

Benefits of IaC

Let's take a closer look at what IaC can do for your company:

Faster speed and consistency

The purpose of IaC is to make things faster by removing manual processes and slack in the system. A code-based approach allows you to accomplish more in less time. There's no need to wait for the IT Admin to finish the current task manually before moving on to the next. This also means you will be able to iterate faster and more frequently. Another important feature of IaC is consistency. You do not have to be concerned about duties not getting performed because it is the weekend or your administrator is preoccupied with something else. You can also make global changes while maintaining the same version.

Software Development Lifecycle

IaC puts the power in the hands of the developer, allowing for a more efficient software development lifecycle. Developers can begin to focus more on application development as infrastructure provisioning becomes more dependable and consistent. They can also script once and use the same code several times, saving time and effort while maintaining full control.

Reduced Management Overhead

Admins were required in the datacenter to govern and manage storage, networking, computing, and other hardware and middleware layers. These various jobs are no longer required with IaC. Those administrators can now concentrate on determining the next intriguing technology to install.

Key Challenges for IaC

There are two sides to every coin. While IaC provides a lot of value to the IT environment, it does come with some drawbacks that must be addressed. Remember to take into account your specific IT circumstances, which may make the following information more or less applicable (like organization size, state, and your technology adoption lifecycle).

Dependency on Coding

IaC is more code-dependent; thus, you will need to be a coding guru. If you do not have a development bench, the learning curve for this will be longer. JSON, HashiCorp Configuration Languages (HCL), YAML, Ruby, and other languages are utilized in IaC. The lack of certain skill sets can limit your ability to use IaC. Is it also your plan to shift away from development and toward serverless solutions? Before you go into IaC, consider the strategic path you are taking. If your end goal is different, perhaps IaC is a pit stop you can skip.

Security-based Analysis

In the new world of IaC, your traditional security technologies and processes might not be enough. It is possible that you will have to manually verify that the supplied resources are functioning and being used by the appropriate apps. Although the manual inspection is a confidence-building step, getting your old security tools adapted to IaC may require several cycles. Additionally, keep in mind that IaC is more dynamic than your current provisioning and management methods. It can be used to its full potential or abused even more quickly. As a result, you may need to take extra precautions to ensure that complete governance is established.

Cloud Agonistic IaC with Terraform

Infrastructure as Code (IaC) allows you to think of infrastructure as a software module that you can manage programmatically with scripts. Cloud platforms can use this to swiftly provision virtual infrastructure components such as computation, storage, network, security, and databases.

Cloud native templates (like AWS CloudFormation, Azure Resource Manager, and Google Deployment Manager templates) and cloud-agnostic templates are two types of Infrastructure as Code (IaC) templates.

Cloud native templates are adaptable to the native platform and may be simply integrated with any native service. Cloud-agnostic templates are appropriate for multi-cloud application services so that infrastructure scripts are consistent across cloud service providers, reducing rework in IaC script activities. Choose cloud-agnostic templates, for example, if you wish to install a Web application and API services in the AWS platform with disaster recovery services (active-passive deployment).

Cloud Foundation Toolkit (CFT) is a Google Cloud Platform (GCP) native template service that offers a set of reference templates that may be used as is or customized to your IaC needs. The deployment manager templates (GCP native) and Terraform templates are the reference templates accessible in CFT (cloud-agnostic). They are straightforward Python scripts that can be readily customized.

Providers

Terraform Cloud is a platform for running Terraform runs to provide infrastructure on-demand or react to events. It is intimately connected with Terraform's processes and data, unlike a general-purpose continuous integration (CI) system, allowing it to make Terraform substantially more convenient and powerful.

To interface with cloud providers, SaaS providers, and other APIs, Terraform uses plugins called "providers."

Terraform configurations must specify the providers they need in order for Terraform to install and use them. Some providers also require setup (such as endpoint URLs or cloud regions) before they may be used.

Terraform can be used to modify the configuration for SDNs. This opens up new possibilities for developers to think of networks in terms of code, thereby enabling DevOps. Interacts and takes care of the communication with control layer APIs with ease. Terraform does not care what cloud or infrastructure deployment method you are using. The library of Cloud and infrastructure vendors that Terraform support is growing by the day. You do not have to rely on one vendor for high availability. You can use terraform domains in highly available solutions across two public clouds and achieve high availability beyond what a single vendor can offer.

Head down to the providers' page on Terraform's official website and go to Major Cloud Providers.

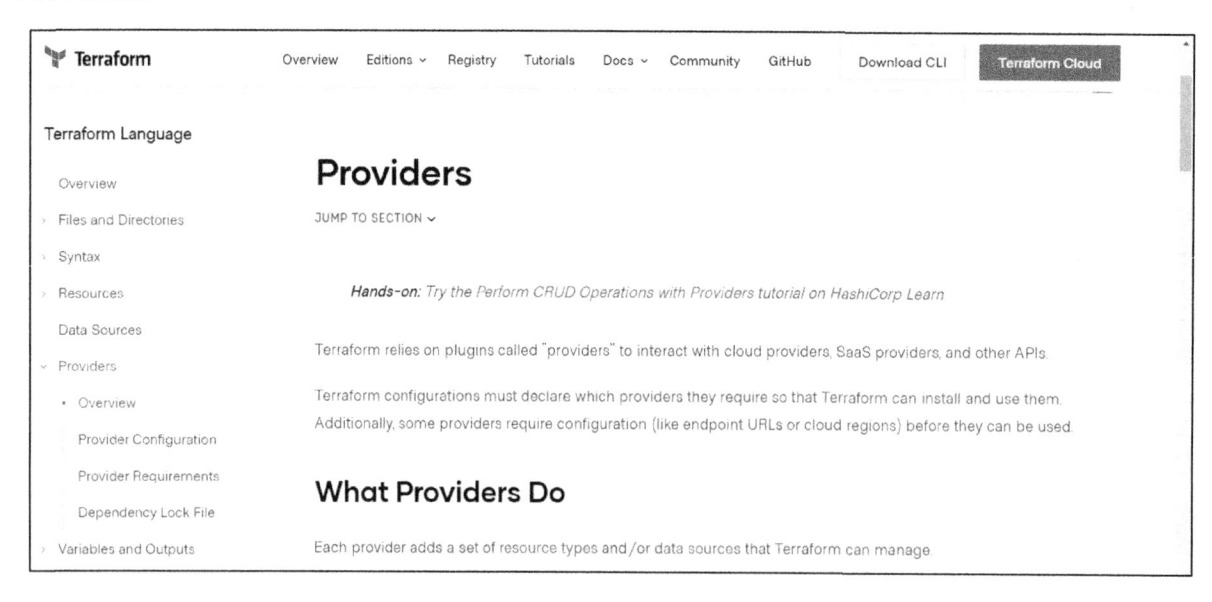

Figure 3-03: Terraform Providers Page

What Provider Do?

Terraform may manage a set of resource types and/or data sources that each provider contributes.

A provider implements each resource type; Terraform would be unable to manage any infrastructure without them.

The majority of service providers set up a specific infrastructure platform (either cloud or self-hosted). Providers can offer local utilities, such as generating random numbers for unique resource names.

You will notice that Terraform has providers for all the major public clouds.

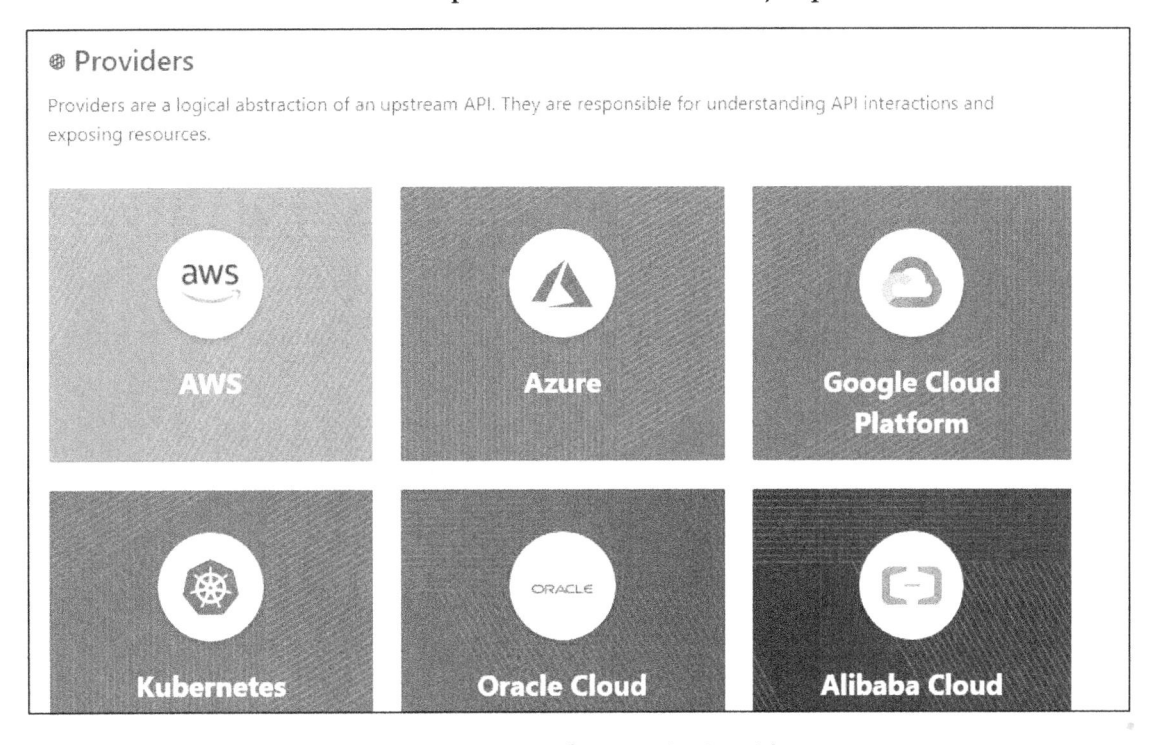

Figure 3-04: Terraform Major Providers

The Cloud has options for all sorts of cloud providers, not only popular ones.

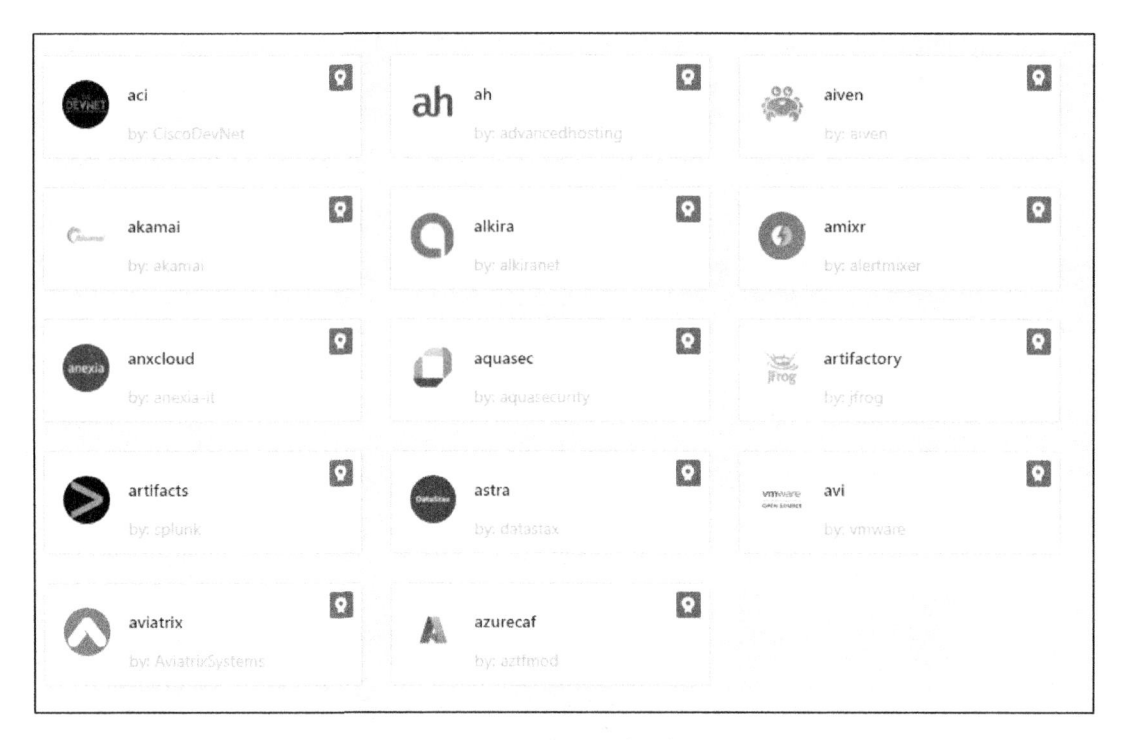

Chapter 03: Understanding Infrastructure As Code

Figure 3-05: Terraform Cloud Providers

If you go inside database providers, you will notice that Terraform has providers for interfacing with MySQL and Influx DB.

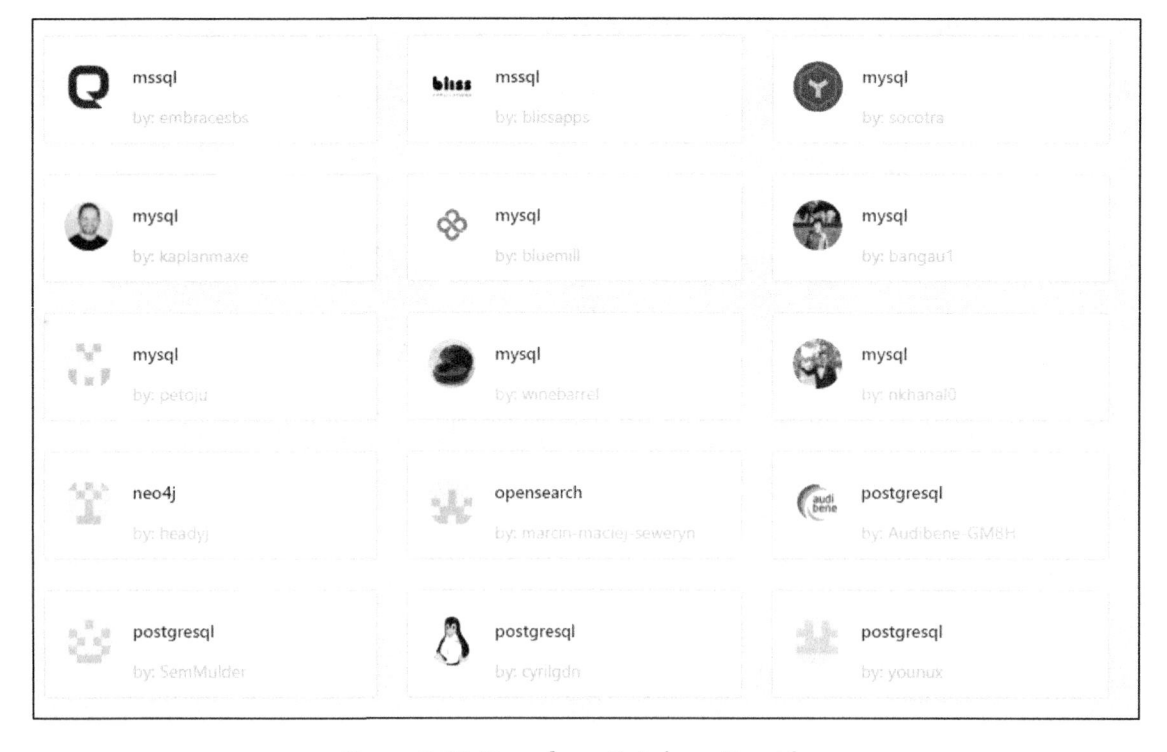

Figure 3-06: Terraform Database Providers

Terraform state tracking mechanism takes away the worry of dependency and resource tracking by keeping it all in one place. The changes made in Terraform deployed infrastructure is handled by Terraform itself. You need to know what you want to modify using Terraform code configuration. For example, suppose you change the operating system image for a cloud. In that case, VM Terraform automatically handles the deletion of a VM with the old image and spins up a new one.

Mind Map

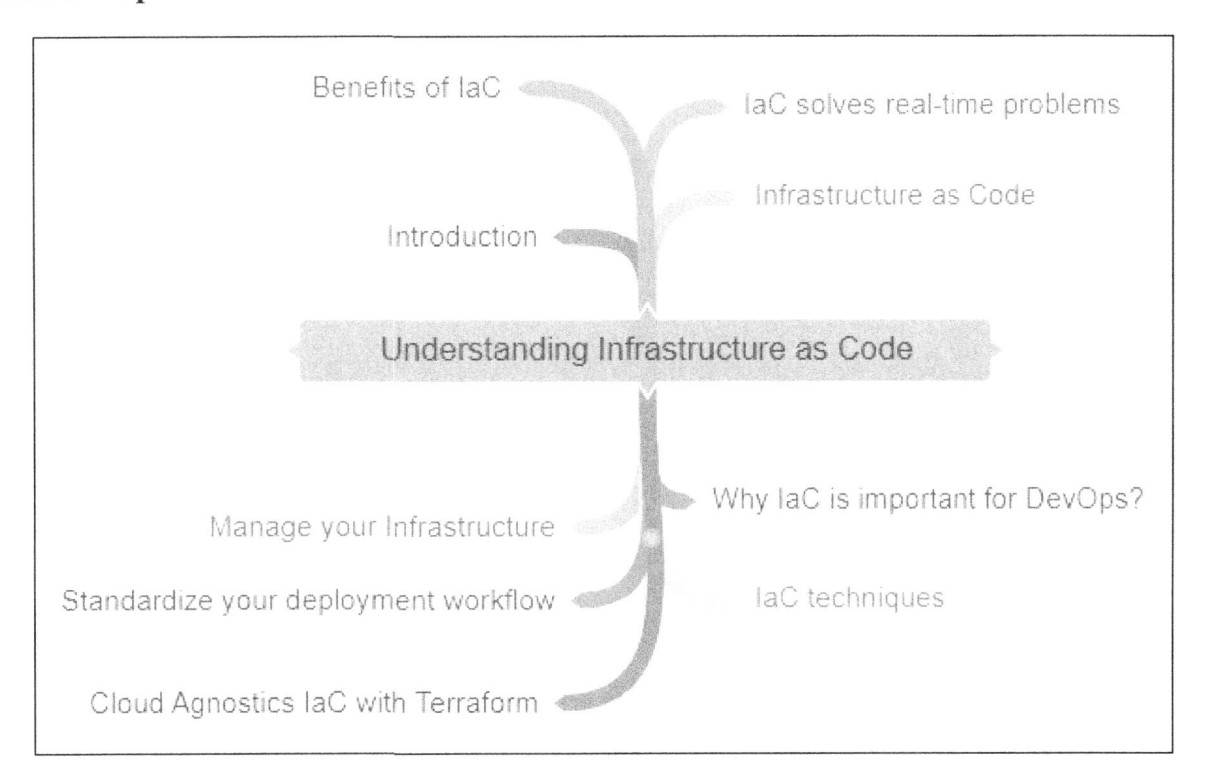

Figure 3-07: Mind Map

Practice Questions

1. IaC is also sometimes known as _____

A. Manual Infrastructure
B. Infrastructure as a Service
C. Built-in Infrastructure
D. Programmable Infrastructure

2. _____ arrangement is faster than manual arrangement.

A. Automated
B. Detailed
C. Hybrid
D. None of the mentioned

3. IaC makes job of _____ easier.

A. Technician
B. Project Engineers
C. IT Staff
D. None

4. Terraform is written in which of the following languages?

A. Go
B. Ruby
C. Python
D. HCL

5. What is the main purpose of Terraform?

A. Software development
B. Project management
C. Provide infrastructure
D. None of the above

6. Terraform is a product of _____.
A. Amazon
B. Google
C. HashiCorp
D. None of the above

7. Terraform supports which of the following cloud providers?
A. AWS
B. Oracle
C. GCP
D. All of the above

8. Terraform is declarative language. True or false?

A. True
B. False

9. IaC automates which of the following processes?
A. Testing process
B. Recovery process
C. Deployment process
D. Both B and C

10. Which of the following is not an advantage of Terraform?
A. Managing multiple cloud providers
B. Human readable configurations
C. Track resources
D. None of the above

11. Which of the following is the disadvantage of IaC?
A. Requires additional tools
B. Fast spread of errors
C. Both A and B
D. None of the above

12. What is meant by Cloud agnostic?
A. A way for developing and supporting your app on a single cloud provider
B. A group of cloud evangelists who are unconcerned about a specific cloud technology
C. When a technology is not tied to a single cloud and can function similarly across a variety of cloud environments
D. A technology that is embedded in a single public cloud and can only be used with that Cloud

13. IaC allows organization to _____.
A. Enables better DevOps methods
B. DevOps managers will be able to hire better engineers for their teams as a result of this tool
C. Allows engineers to deploy resources using the AWS Management Console as a graphical interface
D. Provides a solution for enterprises to reduce the number of people working in DevOps departments.

Chapter 03: Understanding Infrastructure As Code

14. What is IaC?
A. On Linux-based systems, a DevOps methodology for optimizing performance
B. You write this type of code to recover from production outages
C. A method for aligning all load balancers in a datacenter in the United States
D. A way for deploying resources in the Cloud and elsewhere using human-readable code

15. Kubernetes is IaC. True or false?
A. True
B. False

Chapter 04: IaC with Terraform

Introduction

Infrastructure as code (IaC) tools let you control infrastructure through configuration files instead of a graphical user interface. By defining resource configurations that you can version, reuse, and share, IaC allows you to develop, change, and manage your infrastructure securely, consistently, and repeatable.

HashiCorp's infrastructure as code tool is Terraform. It maintains your infrastructure's lifespan and allows you to define resources and infrastructure in human-readable, declarative configuration files. Using Terraform instead of manually maintaining your infrastructure has various benefits:

- Terraform is capable of managing infrastructure across a variety of cloud platforms.
- The human-readable configuration language aids in the rapid development of infrastructure code.
- Terraform's state feature allows you to keep track of resource changes as they happen throughout your deployments.
- To cooperate on infrastructure safely, you can commit your configurations to version control.

What is the Terraform Workflow?

In the Terraform workflow, we first write the code, then review the changes the code will make, and then deploy the code to real infrastructure. We are generally starting either with a version control system as a best practice or a flat file working individually in the writing phase. Version control is considered best practice so you and your team can collaborate over the issues within your code. Planning and reviewing changes that our code will make is an important step because, at this point, we are not deploying any infrastructure. Still, you can see in detail what changes the code will make within our actual environment. After reviewing the code, you can go back and modify it. Finally, you deploy changes to the actual environment and create real resources in the cloud. Whether working as a team or as an individual, this workflow will yield the best results and best efficiency.

terraform init

The terraform init is a command written as terraform in it. It initializes the working directory that contains your Terraform. The first step that terraform init does is download the supporting or ancillary components required code to work. Such as providers that provide the libraries and code for your resources to make API calls to the infrastructure you are deploying. It also sets up the backend for storing data from state files. The state file is a mechanism by which Terraform tracks resources to know when to deploy and destroy resources depending on how you change code. Terraform command is a critical command to any project because it is the first command you will run when you write your initial code. This command fetches the providers, also known as plugins, that will provide resources that your Terraform code is going to use. The terraform init can either download modules or plugins from Terraform public registry over the internet or from your custom URLs where you have uploaded your custom modules written for Terraform.

Terraform Key Concepts: Plan, Apply and Destroy

Plan, apply, and destroy are terraform commands. We know that according to the Terraform workflow, we first write code. We review the code by using the Terraform plan command, and we can do any number of iterations between the write and plan phases of our project. Finally, when we are satisfied with the code, we apply that code to the actual infrastructure.

terraform plan

The plan command reads the code and then creates and shows a "plan" of deployment. It allows the user to review the action plan before executing anything. You can look at this plan as a team or individually and decide on the final execution. At this point, Terraform also authenticates with the credentials of the platform that you are trying to deploy. It is an important command because, as an individual, you might want to look at the resources that your code is going to deploy. As a team, you might want to share your deployment plan with other teams.

> **Note:** Plan command is a sort of read-only command. It makes API calls in the backend with your preferred platform, but it does not change your environment.

terraform apply

The terraform apply is the final command to realize your code into real infrastructure being deployed. It also updates the deployment state tracking mechanism known as "state file." Terraform Apply creates this state file essential to Terraform working because subsequent commands will come back and look at the state file before making changes to your Terraform infrastructure.

> **EXAM TIP:** State file keeps track of all the resources and details that the code is creating into a single flat file called a state file. The name of this file is terraform. tfstate by default which you can change later.

terraform destroy

The terraform destroy command looks at the recorded, stored state file created during deployment and destroys all the resources created by your code. Use this command with caution as it is a non-reversible command. It is best to take backups and be sure that you want to delete the infrastructure before you use this command.

These three key concepts also comply with the Terraform code workflow and lifecycle of the resources that Terraform creates.

Resources Addressing in Terraform: Understanding Terraform Code

Terraform abstracts away all the API calls using providers. Every cloud vendor has its provider. Terraform needs to fetch a plugin so that your code can interact with different platforms.

The code in the figure below fetches AWS providers. The configuration parameters help define the arguments for the AWS provider. These will vary according to the provider we use.

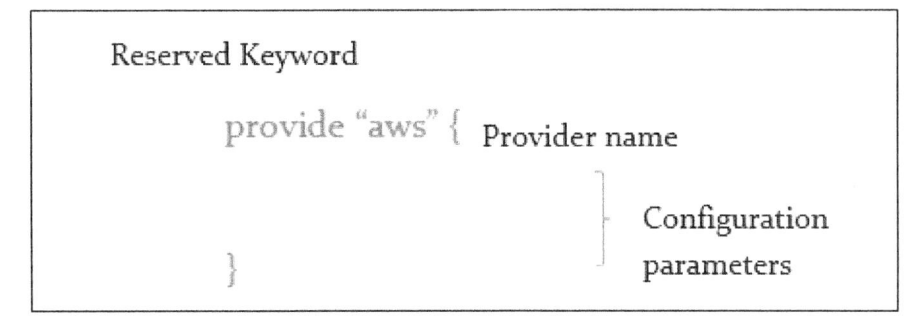

Figure 4-01: AWS Provider

The code in the figure below fetches the GCP provider. We are once again following the same structure telling keywords to fetch Google provider and then providing arguments it needs to set up authentication and environment for GCP.

```
provider "google"{         Built-in function


}
```

Figure 4-02: GCP Provider

Below is the snippet of the resource block in Terraform code. With this, Terraform creates and starts tracking resources from scratch. The resource configuration arguments change according to which resources you are creating. In this case, we are providing Amazon Machine ID (AMI) and instance type. To access the resource, we will use aws_instance.web.

```
Reserved keyword   Resource provided by Terraform provider
                                                    User        provider
resource = "aws_instance" "web"                     arbitrary name

    Ami = "ami-a1b2c3d4"

    Instance_type= "t2.micro"

}
```

Figure 4-03: Resource Block

The snippet below is the data source block through which Terraform fetches data of an already existing resource environment. The main difference between a data source and a resource block is that a data source block fetches and tracks details of already existing resources. A resource block creates resources from scratch. To access the resource, we will use data.aws_instance.my-vm.

```
                    Resource     provided     by
                    Terraform provider
   Reserved        ┌─────┴─────┐                User-provided
   keyword     data "aws_instance" "my-vm"{ ──▶ resource name

                    instance_id = "i-123456a0"

               }
```

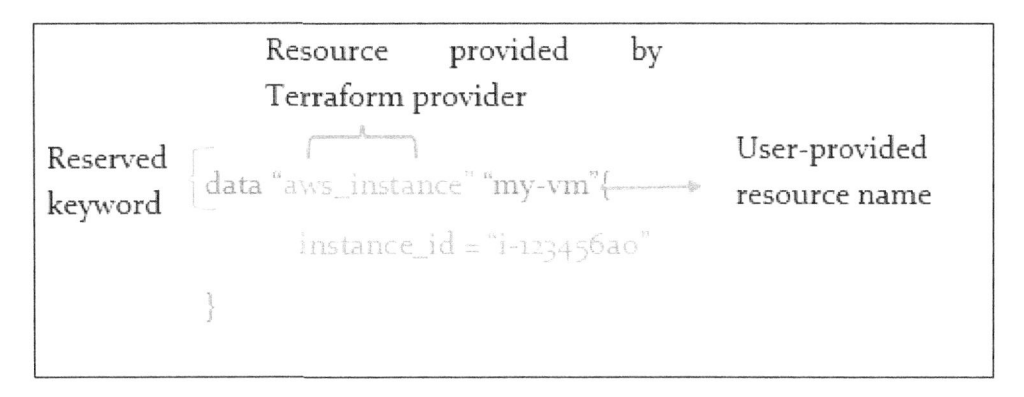

Figure 4-04: Data Source Block

Terraform executes code in files with the .tf extension. Make sure to put your code in .tf files so that Terraform can detect them automatically. Terraform looks for providers in Terraform providers registry. Providers can also be sourced locally and referenced within your Terraform code.

CDK for Terraform

The Cloud Development Kit for Terraform (CDKTF) allows you to define and provision infrastructure using conventional programming languages. This offers you access to the full Terraform ecosystem without having to learn HashiCorp Configuration Language (HCL), and allows you to use your existing toolchain for testing, dependency management, and other tasks.

TypeScript, Python, Java, C#, and Go are presently supported (experimental).

Chapter 04: IaC with Terraform

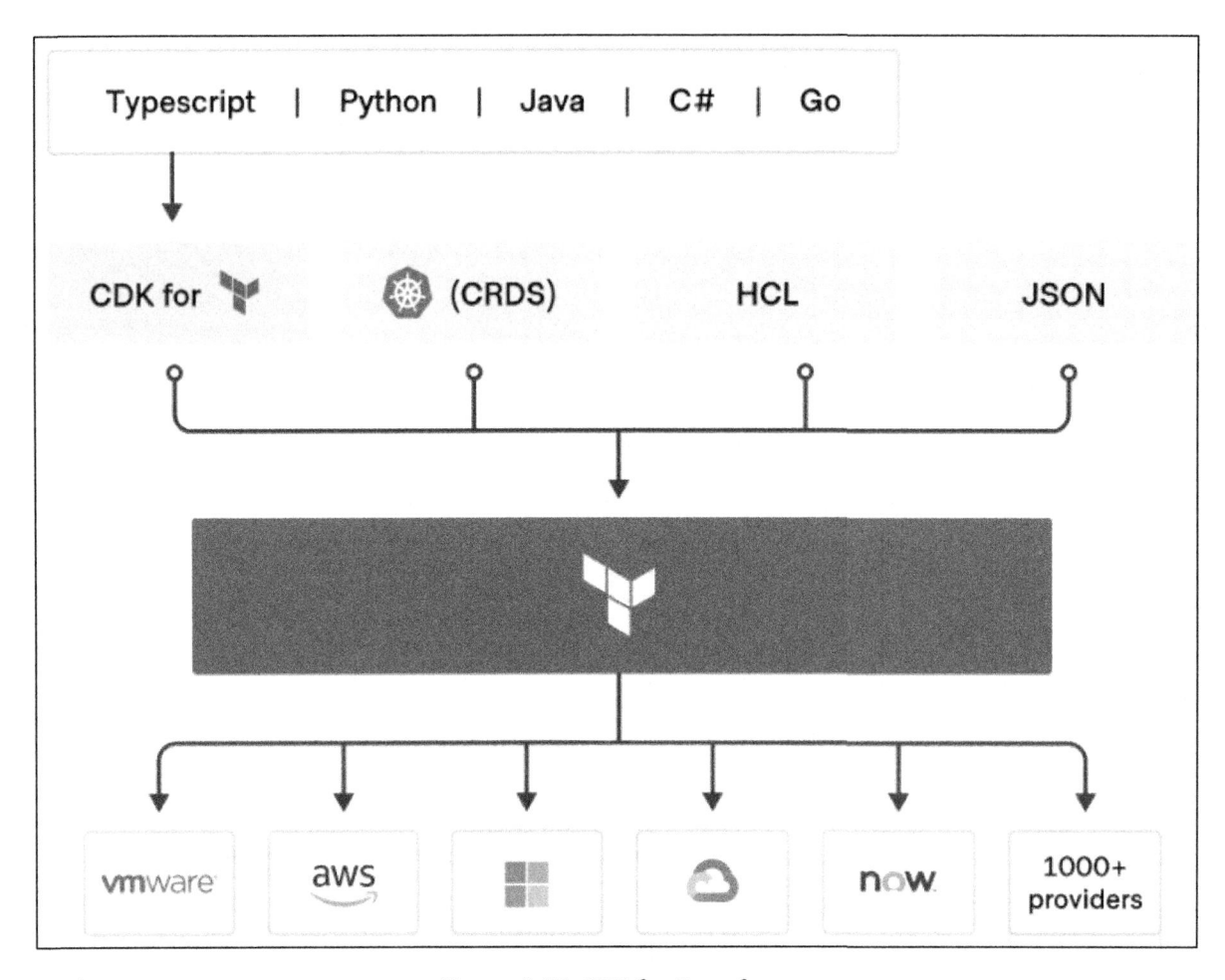

Figure 4-05: CDK for Terraform

How does CDK for Terraform work?

CDK for Terraform uses the AWS Cloud Development Kit's concepts and libraries to convert your code into Terraform infrastructure configuration files.

At a high level, you will be able to:

- **Make an application**: To scaffold a project in your chosen language, use a built-in or custom template.
- **Define Infrastructure:** Define the infrastructure you want to offer to one or more providers using your preferred language. To produce the appropriate classes for your application, CDKTF automatically extracts the schema from Terraform providers and modules.
- **Deploy:** To provision infrastructure with Terraform, utilize the cdktf CLI commands or synthesize your code into a JSON configuration file that others can use directly with Terraform.

You can utilize CDKTF with Terraform Cloud, Terraform Enterprise, and HashiCorp's policy as code framework, Sentinel, as well as every Terraform provider and module accessible on the Terraform Registry.

When to use CDK for Terraform?

Although CDKTF has numerous advantages, it is not appropriate for every project. When:

- You prefer or need to define infrastructure using procedural language.
- To manage complexity, you will need to construct abstractions. For instance, suppose you want to describe a reusable infrastructure design using constructs with many resources and convenience methods.
- You can troubleshoot on your own and do not need professional help.
- Since CDK for Terraform integrates with current Terraform providers and modules, you can make this decision for each team and project.

Demo 4-01: Create Terraform Infrastructure with Docker

> This demonstration will give the understanding about the use of Terraform in a hosted terminal to build and destroy a Docker container. You can try this demo using the following open-source link.
>
> https://learn.hashicorp.com/tutorials/terraform/infrastructure-as-code?in=terraform/aws-get-started
>
> 1. Open the main.tf file in the "Code Editor" tab. Add the following configuration. Click the icon next to the filename above the editing window to save your changes.
>
> terraform {
>   required_providers {
>   docker = {
>   source = "kreuzwerker/docker"
>   version = "~> 2.15.0"
>   }
>   }
> }

```
provider "docker" {}


resource "docker_image" "nginx" {
  name         = "nginx:latest"
  keep_locally = false
}


resource "docker_container" "nginx" {
  image = docker_image.nginx.latest
  name  = "tutorial"
  ports {
    internal = 80
    external = 8000
  }
}
```

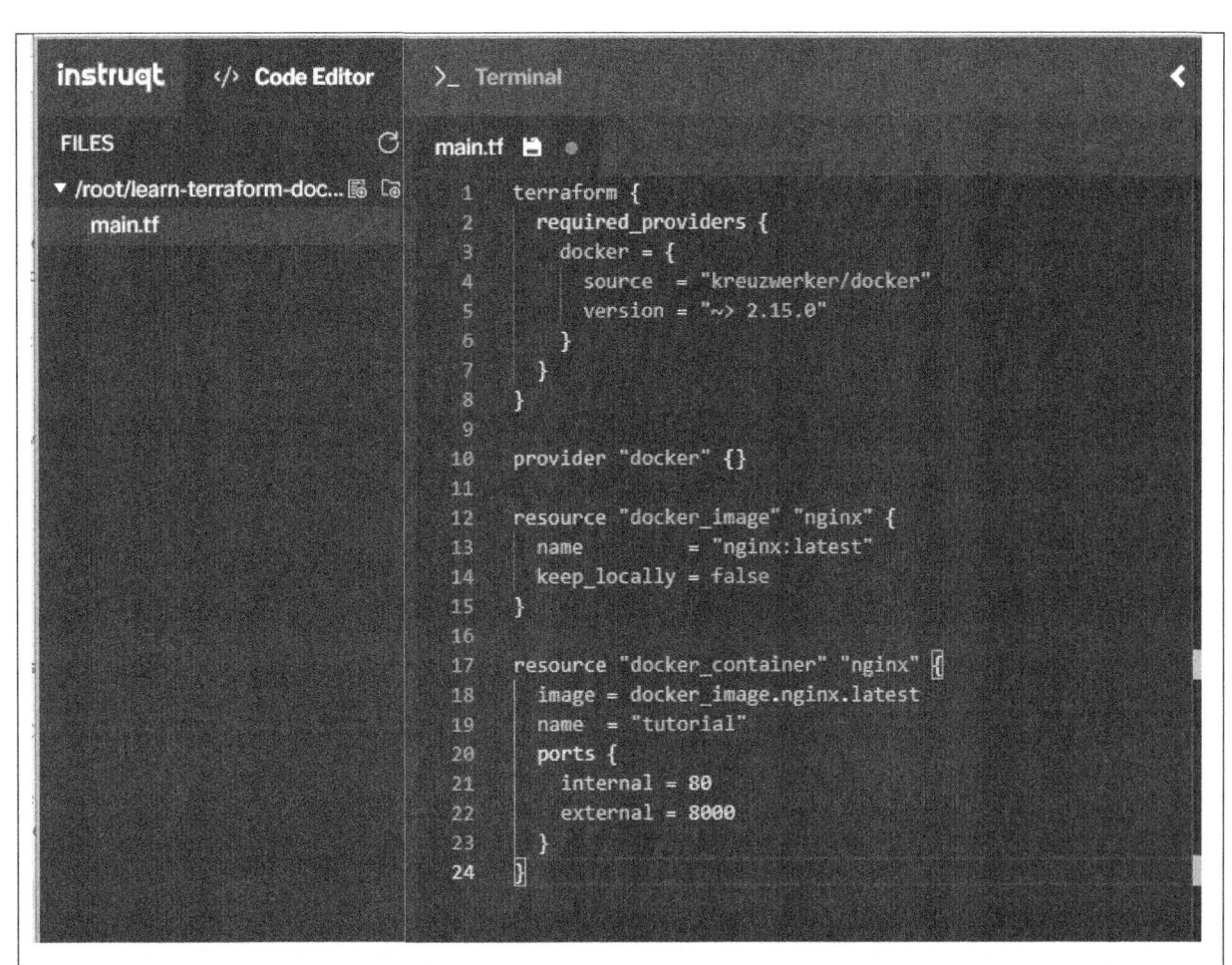

Chapter 04: IaC with Terraform

```
main.tf
1   terraform {
2     required_providers {
3       docker = {
4         source  = "kreuzwerker/docker"
5         version = "~> 2.15.0"
6       }
7     }
8   }
9
10  provider "docker" {}
11
12  resource "docker_image" "nginx" {
13    name         = "nginx:latest"
14    keep_locally = false
15  }
16
17  resource "docker_container" "nginx" {
18    image = docker_image.nginx.latest
19    name  = "tutorial"
20    ports {
21      internal = 80
22      external = 8000
23    }
24  }
```

2. Initialize the project on the "Terminal" tab, which downloads a plugin that allows Terraform to interact with Docker.

terraform init

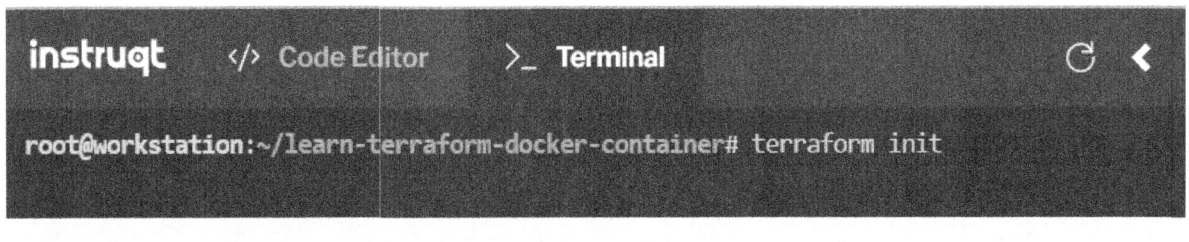

```
root@workstation:~/learn-terraform-docker-container# terraform init
```

3. The following output will appear.

Chapter 04: IaC with Terraform

```
root@workstation:~/learn-terraform-docker-container# terraform init

Initializing the backend...

Initializing provider plugins...

Terraform has been successfully initialized!

You may now begin working with Terraform. Try running "terraform plan" to see
any changes that are required for your infrastructure. All Terraform commands
should now work.

If you ever set or change modules or backend configuration for Terraform,
rerun this command to reinitialize your working directory. If you forget, other
commands will detect it and remind you to do so if necessary.
root@workstation:~/learn-terraform-docker-container#
```

4. Apply to provision the NGINX server container. Type yes and press ENTER when Terraform asks for confirmation.

terraform apply

```
root@workstation:~/learn-terraform-docker-container# terraform apply

No changes. Your infrastructure matches the configuration.

Terraform has compared your real infrastructure against your configuration and fo
root@workstation:~/learn-terraform-docker-container#
```

Verify Webserver instance

5. To see the NGINX container in Docker using Terraform, run the following command.

Docker ps

```
root@workstation:~/learn-terraform-docker-container# docker ps
CONTAINER ID        IMAGE               COMMAND             CREATED             S
TATUS               PORTS               NAMES
root@workstation:~/learn-terraform-docker-container#
learn-terraform-docker-co
```

Destory resources

6. Run **terraform destroy** to stop the container and destroy the resources developed in this tutorial. Type yes and press ENTER when Terraform asks for confirmation.

Chapter 04: IaC with Terraform

```
root@workstation:~/learn-terraform-docker-container# terraform destroy
No changes. No objects need to be destroyed.
Either you have not created any objects yet or the existing objects were already deleted outside of Terraform.
```

Note: Terraform has now provisioned and terminated an NGINX webserver.

Mind Map

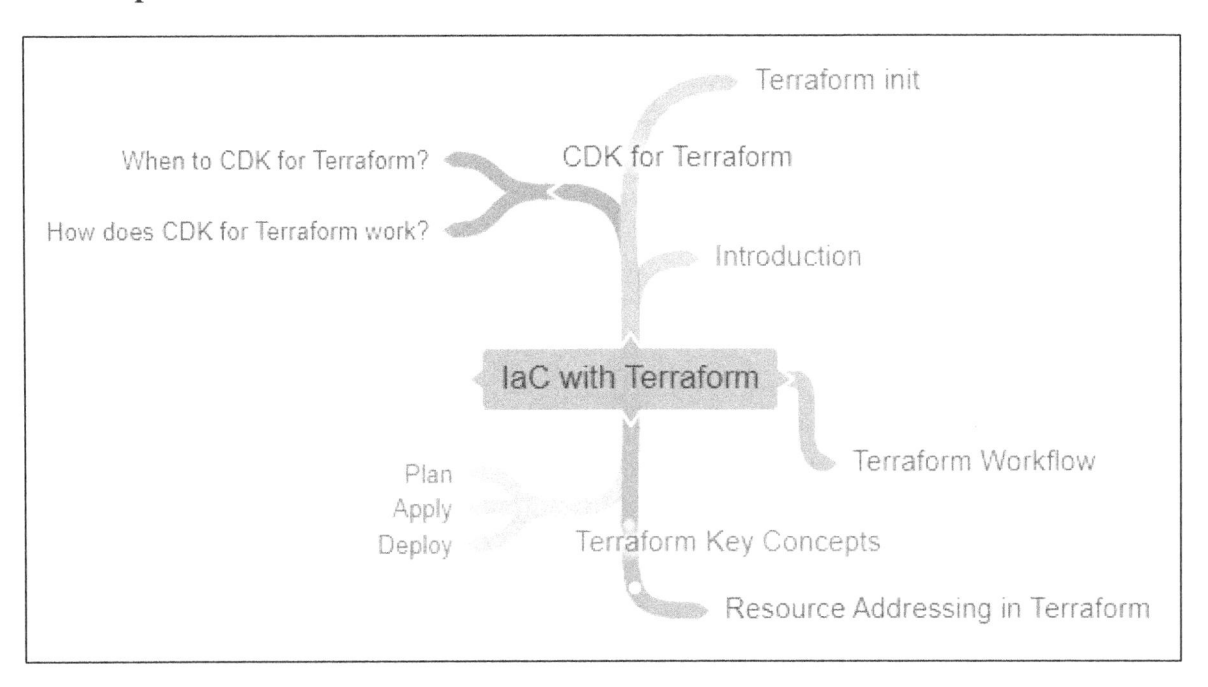

Figure 4-06: Mind Map

Practice Questions

1. Which of the following is the correct sequence of Terraform workflow?

A. Write>Plan>Apply
B. Plan>Write>Apply
C. Plan>Apply>Write
D. Apply>Plan>Write

2. Which of the following is considered best practice in the writing phase?

A. Flat file
B. Store files locally on the system

Chapter 04: IaC with Terraform

C. Version control system
D. None of the mentioned

3. According to Terraform, workflow code, once written, cannot be modified. True or false?

A. True
B. False

4. In which of the following phases of the Terraform workflow do we deploy changes defined by code to the actual environment?

A. Write
B. Apply
C. Plan
D. Destroy

5. What of the following commands initializes terraform directory?

A. terraform apply
B. terraform plan
C. terraform destroy
D. terraform init

6. Which of the following is the first step performed by terraforming init?

A. Downloads supporting components.
B. Sets up the backend
C. Connects to user
D. None of the above

7. The terraform init can only download modules from Terraform public registry. True or false?

A. True
B. False

8. With Terraform plan command, we can do _____ iteration/s between the write and plan phase of our project/

A. Single
B. Any number of
C. Three
D. All of the above

9. Which of the following commands reads the code and then creates and shows a deployment plan?

A. terraform plan
B. terraform apply
C. terraform destroy
D. terraform init

10. Which of the following commands is a read-only command?

A. terraform plan
B. terraform apply
C. terraform destroy
D. terraform init

11. Which of the following commands is used to deploy code into real infrastructure?

A. terraform plan
B. terraform apply
C. terraform destroy
D. terraform init

12. Which of the following commands is used to remove deployed infrastructure?

A. terraform plan
B. terraform apply
C. terraform destroy
D. terraform init

13. With data block, Terraform creates resources from scratch. True or false?

Chapter 04: IaC with Terraform

A. True
B. False

14. With _____ Terraform creates and starts tracking resources from scratch.

A. Provider
B. Keyword
C. Arguments
D. Resource block

15. Terraform executes code in files with the _____ extension.

A. .tf
B. .txt
C. .py
D. None

Chapter 05: Terraform Fundamentals

Introduction

Terraform allows you to safely and predictably generate, change, and expand infrastructure.

HashiCorp Terraform is an infrastructure as code tool that allows you to describe both cloud and on-premises resources in human-readable configuration files that you can version, reuse, and share. You can then use a reliable workflow to provision and manage all your infrastructures throughout their lifecycle. Terraform can manage low-level components like compute, storage, and networking resources and high-level components like DNS entries and SaaS features.

Installing Terraform and Terraform Providers

There are two methods to install Terraform. Method 1 is more manual, while method 2 is more guided with the help of Linux repositories.

In method 1, you download the zip binary file from the HashiCorp website. You unzip the zip file to expose the Terraform binary, and then as a best practice, you place it in a path on your system, which is accessible system-wide so that your Terraform binary can be used and invoked.

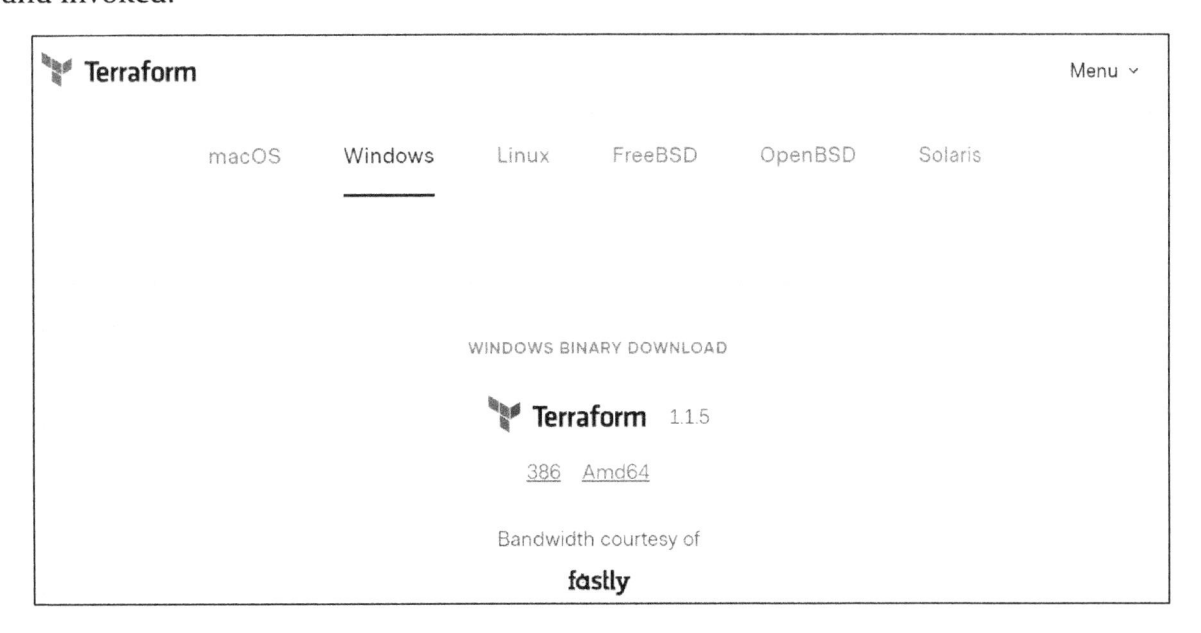

Figure 5-01: Method 01

The second method is a bit more guided. You set up the Terraform repository on your system, and it is only available for Linux systems, such as Debian, Red Hat, and Amazon Linux. You then guide your package manager to install the Terraform binary using the repository that you have set up, and then the system takes care of downloading and installing the Terraform binary in the appropriate path.

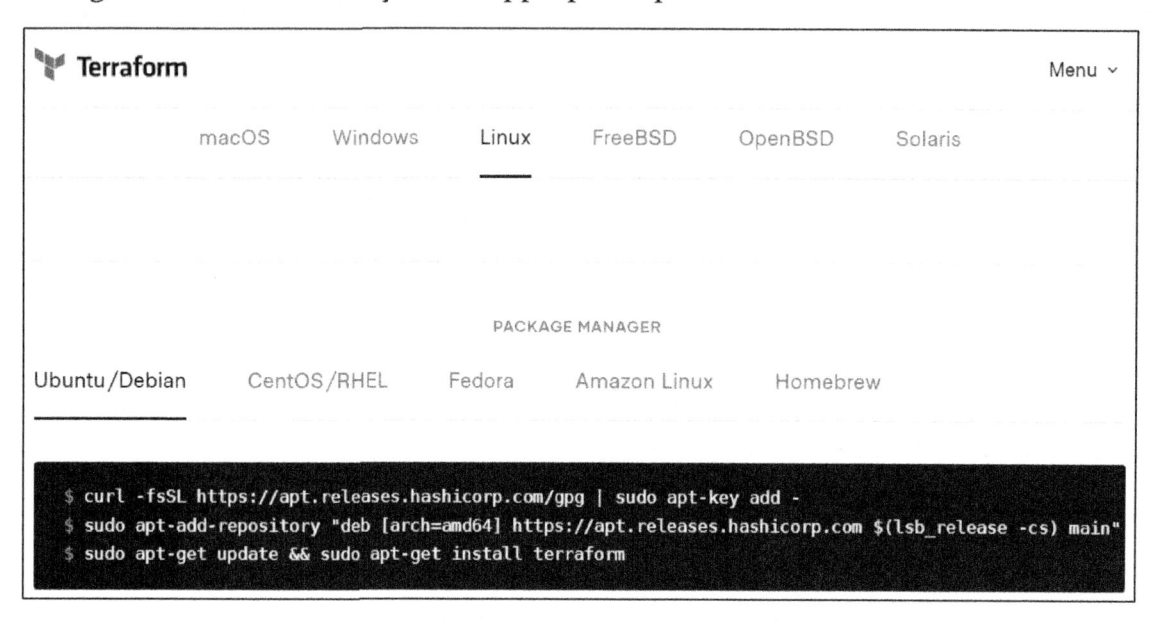

Figure 5-02: Method 02

Method 1

For method 1, head to the Terraform install page on the official HashiCorp website and follow the manual installation method. You will need to go to the pre-compiled binary and follow the link to the appropriate packages for downloading for your system. Right click on 64-bit, copy the link location, and head to the shell of your system. Use a download agent such as wget or curl, and if you do not have one of these agents installed, go ahead and install it using yam or apt package manager, depending on whatever Linux OS you are using. Unzip this file using the unzip command. If you do not have the unzip command installed, you can install it using yum or apt package manager. Unzip the Terraform zip file and clear the screen. You have got the Terraform binary here. So now, to make this binary generally accessible across the system, move it inside one of the path's directories, which is system-wide available. Echo the path variable, which contains a list of folders that are system-wide accessible, and move the Terraform binary to the bin folder. Issue the command move Terraform bin and ensure that Terraform is not in this folder anymore because it got moved out. If you start typing Terraform and then press the tab, the tab auto-completion points to the fact that the system can find the binary inside the bin folder.

Test if the binary is working correctly and issue a Terraform command. The help output from this command ensures that the Terraform binary was downloaded and installed successfully.

Method 2

Remove the binary you just placed inside the bin folder. Also, delete the zip file and head back to the Terraform official installation page. Head over to Linux and follow the instructions for CentOS Red Hat. You need to have the yum-utils package installed. Copy the command and execute it. It looks like you already had that packet installed. Next, copy the second command. You may need to execute the command as the sudo user. Then press Enter, and the repository will be saved. The last step is to show the **yum - y installed terraform** command. Before you do that, just confirm that Terraform was successfully deleted from the previous method's demonstration. If you try to tab-complete this, it will not work, and even if you try to type the command out and press Enter, you will see that there is no such file. First, clear the screen; it should have the command **yum –y install terraform.** You have Terraform installed successfully through the Linux repository for CentOS 7. Clear the screen and test it out; it should be successful now. Issue a Terraform command and ensure that the Terraform binary was successfully installed and is working. This was a quick run-through of how to download and install Terraform.

> **Note:** There are various ways, and depending on how you want to automate your system, you can either use manual installation or Linux.

Terraform Providers

Terraform abstracts away all the API calls it makes under the hood using providers. Every cloud vendor has its provider. Terraform, by default, looks for providers in the Terraform provider's registry, the link for additional and below. However, providers can also be sourced locally or internally and referenced within your Terraform code. Providers are plugins. Terraform downloads them and uses them on the go. Providers are not released and updated on the same schedule as Terraform, so each provider has its series of versions. In essence, each provider is a pre-compiled chunk of code, which defines resources used by Terraform to interact with the respective vendor, such as Alibaba Cloud, AWS, and the likes. You can even write your custom providers. However, it goes to show the flexibility that Terraform offers. Terraform pulls down the providers when you initialize your different projects, using the terraform init command.

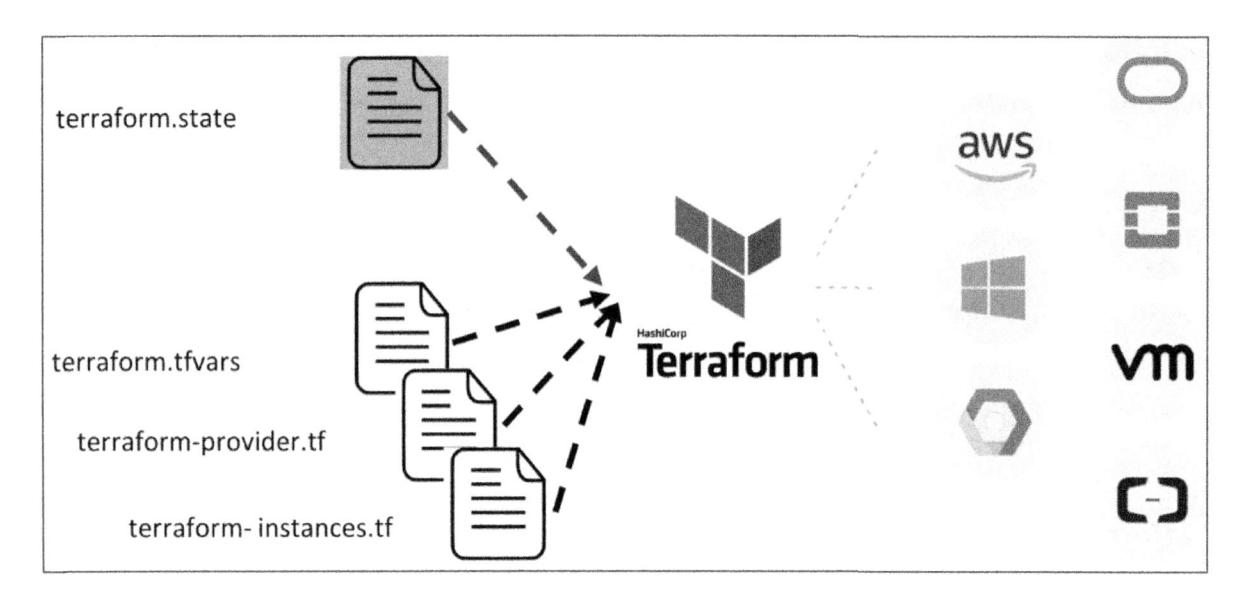

Figure 5-03: Terraform

The best practice for working with providers in production is to fix the version of Terraform providers in your code -- the reason being that because providers are updated and released independent of Terraform versions, any changes across provider versions may break your Terraform deployment.

Terraform State: The Concept

It is a functionality through which Terraform can operate the way it does, and without it, there would be no Terraform. It is a mechanism for Terraform to keep tabs on what has been deployed, and it is critical to Terraform because of the various lifecycles of deploying infrastructure through Terraform.

Chapter 05: Terraform Fundamentals

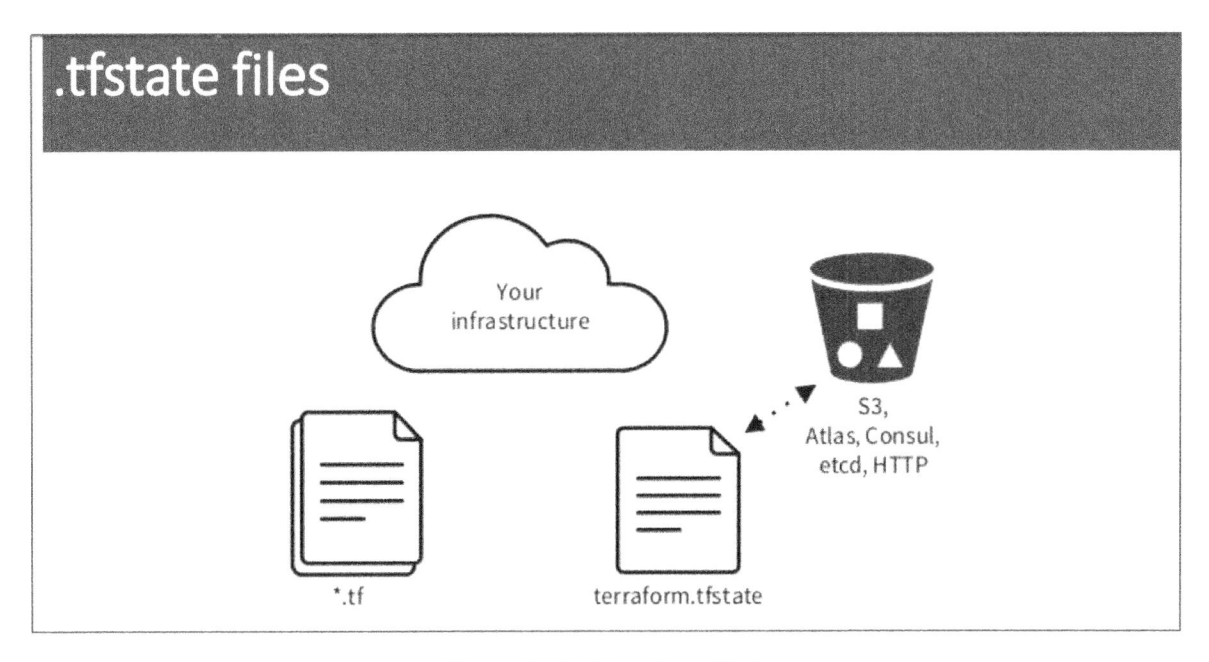

Figure 5-04: Terraform State

Terraform needs to refer to the state of deployed resources before deciding whether resources need to be created from scratch, modified, or destroyed. You have your Terraform configuration or code, and you have deployed the code into managed infrastructure platforms. Terraform state file helps Terraform map the resources in code to the resources in the team. This file is a JSON dump containing all the metadata about your Terraform deployment and details about its deployed resources. For example, if you want to delete all the resources you created, you would just issue the Terraform destroy command instead of separately writing code to delete everything. Terraform will look at the state file and know exactly what resources to destroy. Terraform state is stored in flat files as JSON data. It is usually stored locally in the same directory where your Terraform code resides. However, it can also be stored remotely for better integrity and availability. The state file helps Terraform calculate deployment deltas. This is the difference between what was deployed previously via Terraform and the current code records. The plan provided by the Terraform plan command is compared to the state file for calculating this delta and reconciling and deploying the actual changes into the environment. You do not want to lose it because you will have no codified way to go back and make changes to our infrastructure, which is deployed through Terraform, because manually deleting or trying to make changes to complex infrastructures can be a real pain. Also, you would not want the state file to fall into the wrong hands because it may contain sensitive data and details about the resources deployed through Terraform.

Terraform Variables and Outputs

In this section, you will be learning about Terraform Variables and Outputs. You first have the reserved keyword variable. Next, you have the user-provided arbitrary name for the variable, and between the curly braces, you have the configuration parameters for the variable, such as description, the type of variable, and the default value for it in case the user does not provide one explicitly. However, all the config parameters within the curly braces are optional for just declaring the variables.

```
output "vpc_id" {
  description = "ID of project VPC"
  value       = module.vpc.vpc_id
}

output "lb_url" {
  description = "URL of load balancer"
  value       = "http://${module.elb_http.this_elb_dns_name}/"
}

output "web_server_count" {
  description = "Number of web servers provisioned"
  value       = length(module.ec2_instances.instance_ids)
}
```

Figure 5-05: Terraform Variables and Outputs

Variables can help make your code versatile and reusable. Although variables can be in germane Terraform code files, the best practice is to gather them in a separate file just picked up by default. This file is called terraform.tfvars.

Variable Validation

Variable validation allows you to set a criterion for allowed values for a variable. For example, the validation block checks to ensure that this variable will only store values of the typed string if the number of correctors in the string is greater than four. Otherwise, it will throw an error message. This is immensely useful because you do not want to find out the way that the value passed was illegal and wait for everything to roll back. Instead, terraform will stop before it deploys anything if the value for the variable does not meet the validation criteria. This feature was made generally available in Terraform version 0.13 and beyond and an experimental feature in version 0.12. Also, you can enable a config parameter known as sensitive to prevent Terraform from showing its value during Terraform execution runs, the default behavior within Terraform. This would be the case if your variable values were sensitive, and you do not want everybody to be seeing them as Terraform was executing.

> **EXAM TIP:** The syntax for using the sensitive parameter would be a Boolean value, so it can either be true or false. And by default, it is false.

There are three base variable types for Terraform variables. The first is a string, the second is a number, and the final is bool or boolean. The more complex type of variables that you can use the base type variables to create -- are list, set, map, object, and double.

Square braces present a list in many popular programming languages, such as Python. You also have an example of a complex variable type where you create a list of objects. This block defines the variable type and assigns a default value to the variable. For example, internal being a number type has a value of 8,300, whereas protocol is a string type as TCP. Another thing to note is that there is certain precedence to how variables are read at runtime. The highest precedence is given to variables passed to the operating system environment variables, the Terraform dot tfvars file, and so on.

You have the user-provided arbitrary name for the output, and in the curly braces, you have the description for the output and a value. The only mandatory field here is the value, which can be assigned to any value or even to reference values of other Terraform resources and variables. Outputs are shown on the shell or CLI after a successful Terraform application or execution. Think of output values like return values for a function in a programming language. These output values can be used to track and show pertinent details about your Terraform deployed resources and their specific details.

Terraform Provisioners: When to Use Them

Provisioners, in essence, give users a way to execute custom scripts or commands through Terraform resources. You can choose to run such scripts either locally, on the same system where the Terraform commands are running, or remotely on a newly spun up VM through Terraform. A provisioner is attached to your Terraform resource and allows custom connection parameters that can be passed to connect to the remote resources via SSH or WinRM for carrying out commands against that resource.

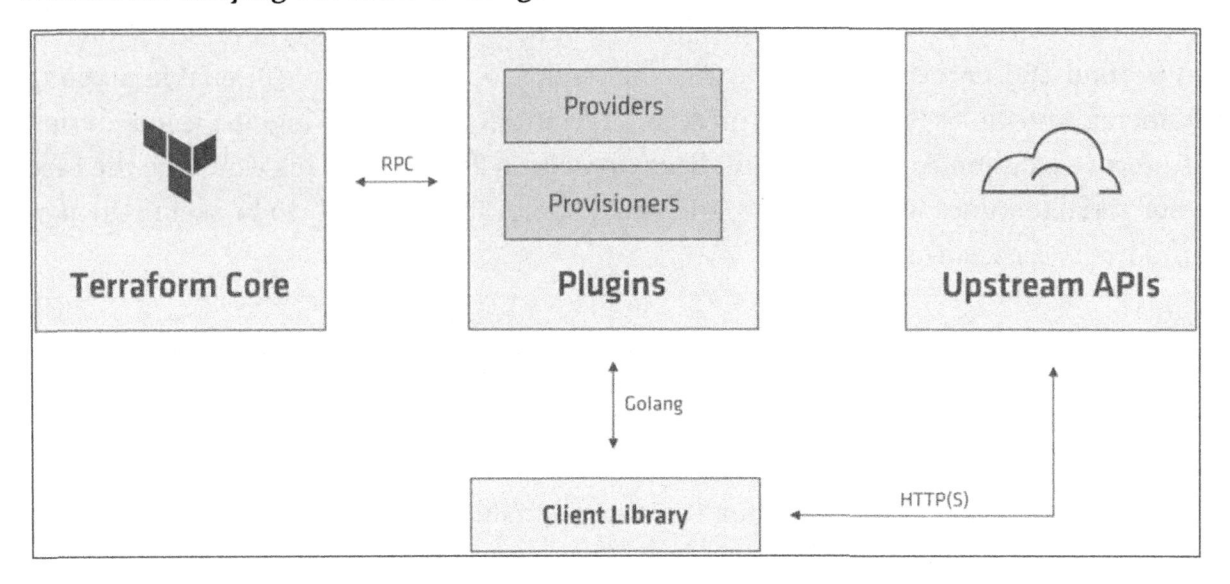

Figure 5-06: Terraform Provisioners

There are two types of provisioners, which cover two events of your Terraform resource's lifecycle. A Create-time provisioner and a Destroy-time provisioner. As evident from their names, a Create-time provisioner is run as a resource is being created, and a Destroy-time provisioner is run as a resource is being destroyed. They can come in very handy with custom one-off automation tasks.

Best Practices

Terraform is a powerful (if not the most powerful) and widely used program that allows infrastructure control using code. It gives developers a lot of freedom and does not prevent them from doing things in ways that are difficult to support or integrate.

In the case of provisioners, HashiCorp recommends using them sparingly, only when the underlying vendors, such as AWS, do not already provide a built-in mechanism for bootstrapping via custom commands or scripts. For example, AWS allows passing scripts through user data in EC2 virtual machines. If there is a better inherently available method for a resource, Hashicorp recommends using that. An important thing to note is that since provisioners can take any independent action through a script or command, Terraform cannot track them, as they break Terraform's declarative model. Terraform can be fully aware of all the custom-independent actions your one-off scripts may take. For this reason, provisioners are not tracked through Terraform state files either.

Well then, when would you have to use provisioners? Only when you want to execute actions that are not covered by Terraform's declarative model or through inherent options for the resources in available providers. Provisioners expect any custom script or commands to be executed with a return code of 0. Otherwise, it deems the execution failed and taints the resource, marking the resource against which the provisioner was to be run to be created again on the next run.

The only difference in syntax between a Create and a Destroy-time provisioner is that the Destroy-time provisioner has an option called when, which is set to destroy, and that tells it to run on a destroy of a resource. In the Destroy provisioner, you have it output the value one to the same status .txt file upon being deleted or destroyed. You can use multiple provisioners against the same resource, and they will be executed in the same sequence as they are written out. If you have five local Creation-time provisioners, they will execute in sequence, and so will the Destroy-time provisioners.

> **EXAM TIP:** Provisioners are not tracked and are independent of the Terraform state file, and there is no mention of the provisioner.

The Terraform logic first checks the state file. Notice that there is a resource that needs to be destroyed. It goes ahead and runs the Destroy-time provisioner this time, echoing the number one inside the status.txt file. If a Creation-time provisioner fails, Terraform will mark that resource as tainted, and on the next supply, it will try to delete and recreate the resource. Whereas for a Destroy-time provisioner, if the command inside or the script inside a Destroy-time provisioner fails, Terraform will try to re-run the provisioner on the next destroy attempt.

Lab 5-01: Installing Terraform and Working with Terraform Providers

Introduction

In this hands-on lab, you will go through the installation and configuration of Terraform version 13 on a Linux OS. You will also explore how to select and use a Terraform provider from among the many providers available publicly.

Problem

A provisioner is attached to your Terraform resource, and it allows custom connection parameters that can be passed to connect to the remote resources via SSH or WinRM for carrying out commands against that resource.

Chapter 05: Terraform Fundamentals

Solution

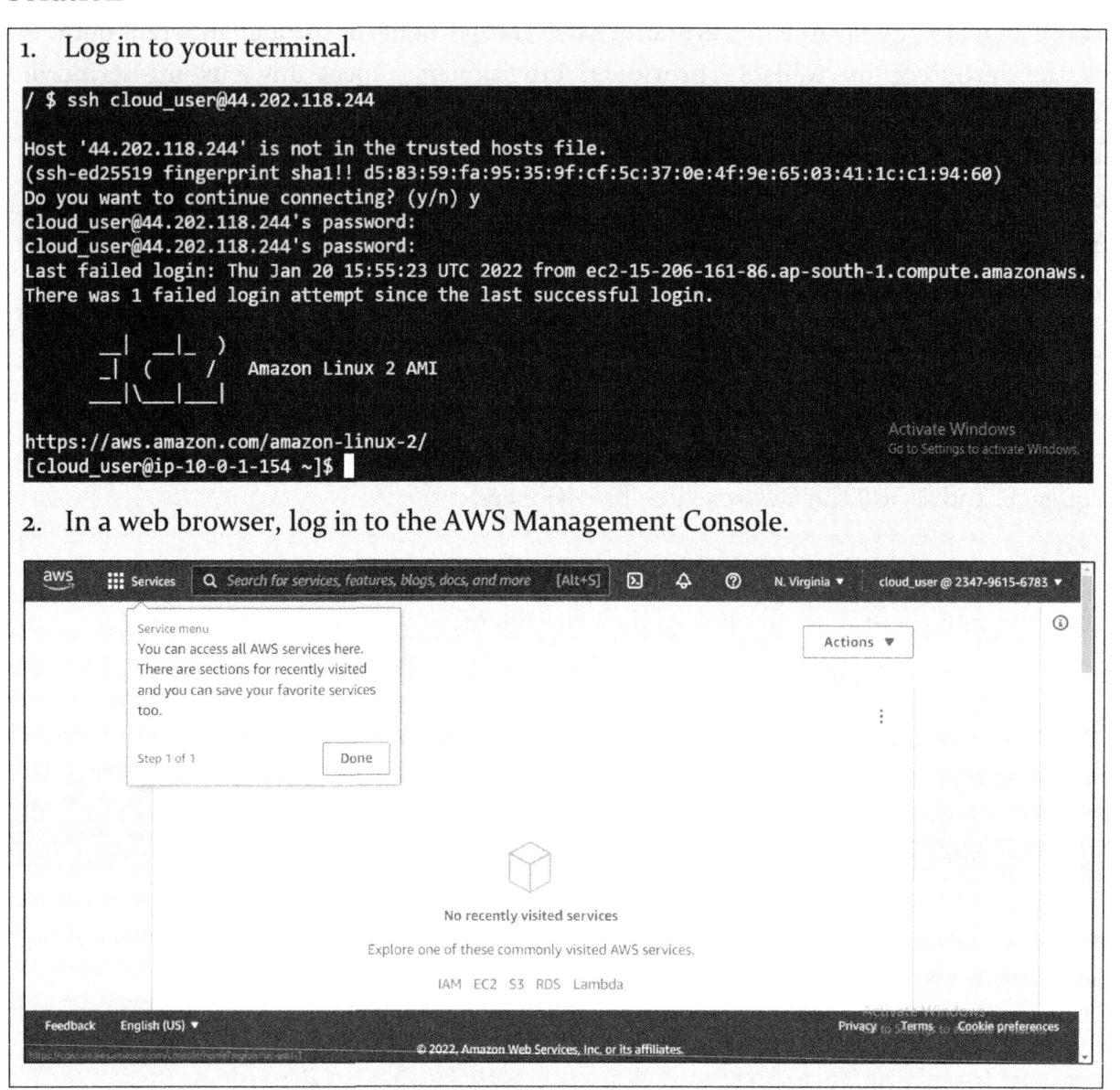

1. Log in to your terminal.

```
/ $ ssh cloud_user@44.202.118.244

Host '44.202.118.244' is not in the trusted hosts file.
(ssh-ed25519 fingerprint sha1!! d5:83:59:fa:95:35:9f:cf:5c:37:0e:4f:9e:65:03:41:1c:c1:94:60)
Do you want to continue connecting? (y/n) y
cloud_user@44.202.118.244's password:
cloud_user@44.202.118.244's password:
Last failed login: Thu Jan 20 15:55:23 UTC 2022 from ec2-15-206-161-86.ap-south-1.compute.amazonaws.
There was 1 failed login attempt since the last successful login.

       __|  __|_  )
       _|  (     /   Amazon Linux 2 AMI
      ___|\___|___|

https://aws.amazon.com/amazon-linux-2/
[cloud_user@ip-10-0-1-154 ~]$
```

2. In a web browser, log in to the AWS Management Console.

Download and Manually Install the Terraform Binary

1. Download the appropriate Terraform binary package for the provided VM (Linux 64-bit) using the wget command:

wget-c

https://releases.hashicorp.com/terraform/0.13.4/terraform_0.13.4_linux_amd64.zip

Chapter 05: Terraform Fundamentals

```
[cloud_user@ip-10-0-1-154 ~]$ wget -c https://releases.hashicorp.com/terraform/0.13.4/terraform_0.13.4_linux_amd64.zip
--2022-01-20 15:59:39--  https://releases.hashicorp.com/terraform/0.13.4/terraform_0.13.4_linux_amd64.zip
Resolving releases.hashicorp.com (releases.hashicorp.com)... 146.75.29.183, 2a04:4e42:77::439
Connecting to releases.hashicorp.com (releases.hashicorp.com)|146.75.29.183|:443... connected.
HTTP request sent, awaiting response... 200 OK
Length: 34879084 (33M) [application/zip]
Saving to: 'terraform_0.13.4_linux_amd64.zip'

100%[=========================================================>] 34,879,084  --.-K/s   in 0.1s

2022-01-20 15:59:39 (300 MB/s) - 'terraform_0.13.4_linux_amd64.zip' saved [34879084/34879084]

[cloud_user@ip-10-0-1-154 ~]$
```

2. Unzip the downloaded file:

unzip terraform_0.13.4_linux_amd64.zip

```
[cloud_user@ip-10-0-1-154 ~]$ unzip terraform_0.13.4_linux_amd64.zip
Archive:  terraform_0.13.4_linux_amd64.zip
  inflating: terraform
[cloud_user@ip-10-0-1-154 ~]$
```

3. Place the Terraform binary in the PATH of the VM operating system so the binary is accessible system-wide to all users:

sudo mv terraform /usr/sbin/

```
[cloud_user@ip-10-0-1-154 ~]$ sudo mv terraform /usr/sbin/
[sudo] password for cloud_user:
```

Note: If prompted, enter the username and password provided for the terminal.

4. Check the Terraform version information:

terraform version

```
[cloud_user@ip-10-0-1-154 ~]$ terraform version
Terraform v0.13.4
```

Since the Terraform version is returned, you have validated that the Terraform binary is installed and working properly.

Chapter 05: Terraform Fundamentals

Clone Over Code for Terraform Providers

1. Create a providers directory:

mkdir providers

```
[cloud_user@ip-10-0-1-154 ~]$ mkdir providers
```

2. Move into the provider's directory:

cd providers/

```
[cloud_user@ip-10-0-1-154 ~]$ cd providers/
[cloud_user@ip-10-0-1-154 providers]$
```

3. Create the file main.tf:

vim main.tf

```
[cloud_user@ip-10-0-1-154 providers]$ vim main.tf
```

4. Paste in the following code:

```
provider "aws" {
    alias  = "us-east-1"
    region = "us-east-1"
}

provider "aws" {
    alias  = "us-west-2"
    region = "us-west-2"
}
```

Chapter 05: Terraform Fundamentals

```
resource "aws_sns_topic" "topic-us-east" {
  provider = aws.us-east-1
  name     = "topic-us-east"
}

resource "aws_sns_topic" "topic-us-west" {
  provider = aws.us-west-2
  name     = "topic-us-west"
}
```

5. To save and exit the file, press "**Escape**" and enter **:wq**.

```
:wq
```

```
"main.tf" [New] 19L, 338B written
[cloud_user@ip-10-0-1-154 providers]$
```

Deploy the Code with Terraform Apply

1. Enable verbose output logging for Terraform commands using TF_LOG=TRACE:

export TF_LOG=TRACE

```
[cloud_user@ip-10-0-1-154 providers]$ export TF_LOG=TRACE
[cloud_user@ip-10-0-1-154 providers]$
```

Note: You can turn off verbose logging at any time using the **export TF_LOG=** command.

2. Initialize the working directory where the code is located:

terraform init

```
The following providers do not have any version constraints in configuration,
so the latest version was installed.

To prevent automatic upgrades to new major versions that may contain breaking
changes, we recommend adding version constraints in a required_providers block
in your configuration, with the constraint strings suggested below.

* hashicorp/aws: version = "~> 3.72.0"

Terraform has been successfully initialized!

You may now begin working with Terraform. Try running "terraform plan" to see
any changes that are required for your infrastructure. All Terraform commands
should now work.

If you ever set or change modules or backend configuration for Terraform,
rerun this command to reinitialize your working directory. If you forget, other
commands will detect it and remind you to do so if necessary.
[cloud_user@ip-10-0-1-154 providers]$
```

3. Review the actions performed when you deploy the Terraform code:

terraform plan

```
      + content_based_deduplication = false
      + fifo_topic                  = false
      + id                          = (known after apply)
      + name                        = "topic-us-west"
      + name_prefix                 = (known after apply)
      + owner                       = (known after apply)
      + policy                      = (known after apply)
      + tags_all                    = (known after apply)
    }

Plan: 2 to add, 0 to change, 0 to destroy.

─────────────────────────────────────────────────────────────────────

Note: You didn't specify an "-out" parameter to save this plan, so Terraform
can't guarantee that exactly these actions will be performed if
"terraform apply" is subsequently run.

[cloud_user@ip-10-0-1-154 providers]$
```

Note: Two resources will be created, consistent with the providers configured in the provided code snippet.

4. Deploy the code:

terraform apply

5. When prompted, type yes and press "**Enter.**"

```
  + resource "aws_sns_topic" "topic-us-west" {
      + arn                         = (known after apply)
      + content_based_deduplication = false
      + fifo_topic                  = false
      + id                          = (known after apply)
      + name                        = "topic-us-west"
      + name_prefix                 = (known after apply)
      + owner                       = (known after apply)
      + policy                      = (known after apply)
      + tags_all                    = (known after apply)
    }

Plan: 2 to add, 0 to change, 0 to destroy.

Do you want to perform these actions?
  Terraform will perform the actions described above.
  Only 'yes' will be accepted to approve.

  Enter a value: yes
```

6. Verify that two resources were created with their corresponding Amazon Resource Name (ARN) IDs in the region in which they were spun up.

```
2022/01/20 16:22:45 [TRACE] vertex "root": starting visit (*terraform.nodeCloseModule)
2022/01/20 16:22:45 [TRACE] vertex "root": evaluating
2022/01/20 16:22:45 [TRACE] [walkApply] Entering eval tree: root
2022/01/20 16:22:45 [TRACE] eval: *terraform.EvalSequence
2022/01/20 16:22:45 [TRACE] eval: *terraform.EvalOpFilter
2022/01/20 16:22:45 [TRACE] eval: *terraform.evalCloseModule
2022/01/20 16:22:45 [TRACE] [walkApply] Exiting eval tree: root
2022/01/20 16:22:45 [TRACE] vertex "root": visit complete
2022/01/20 16:22:45 [TRACE] statemgr.Filesystem: no original state snapshot to back up
2022/01/20 16:22:45 [TRACE] statemgr.Filesystem: state has changed since last snapshot, so incrementing serial to 3
2022/01/20 16:22:45 [TRACE] statemgr.Filesystem: writing snapshot at terraform.tfstate

Apply complete! Resources: 2 added, 0 changed, 0 destroyed.
2022/01/20 16:22:45 [TRACE] statemgr.Filesystem: removing lock metadata file .terraform.tfstate.lock.info
2022/01/20 16:22:45 [TRACE] statemgr.Filesystem: unlocking terraform.tfstate using fcntl flock
[cloud_user@ip-10-0-1-154 providers]$
```

7. Optionally, verify that the resources were created in their respective regions within the **AWS Management Console:**

   o Navigate to the **AWS Management Console** in your browser

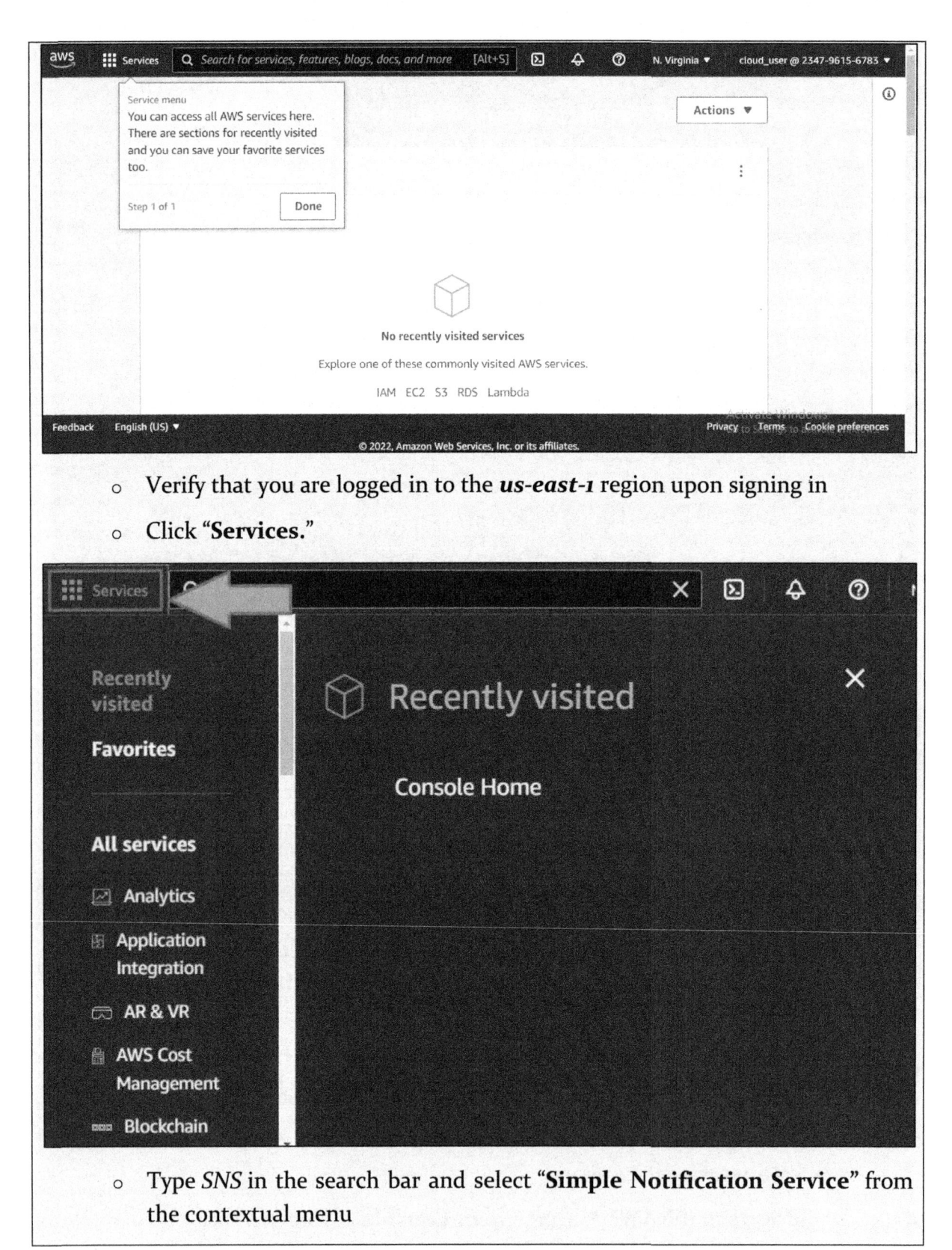

Chapter 05: Terraform Fundamentals

- Verify that you are logged in to the *us-east-1* region upon signing in
- Click "**Services.**"

- Type *SNS* in the search bar and select "**Simple Notification Service**" from the contextual menu

Chapter 05: Terraform Fundamentals

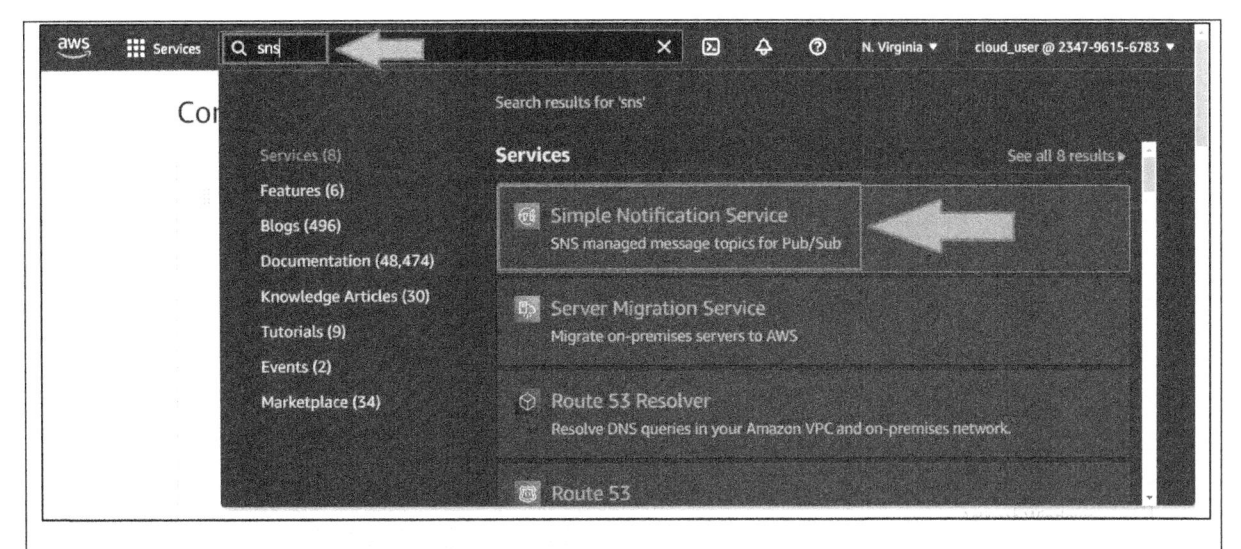

- In the menu on the left, click "**Topics**."

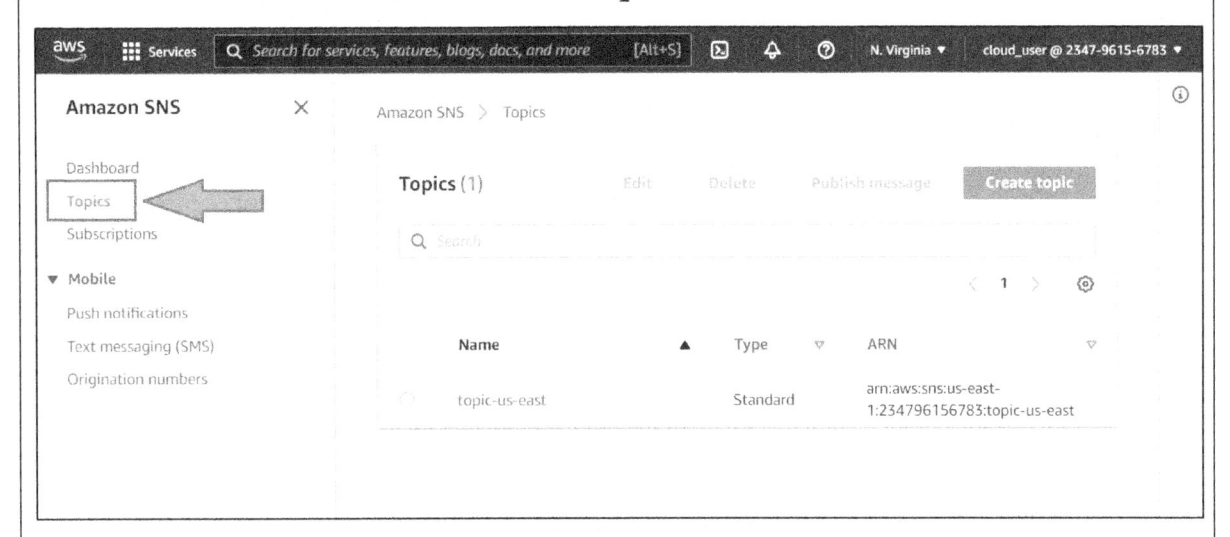

- Verify that the *topic-us-east* resource appears in the list

o At the top-right, click "**N. Virginia**" and select "**us-west-2**"

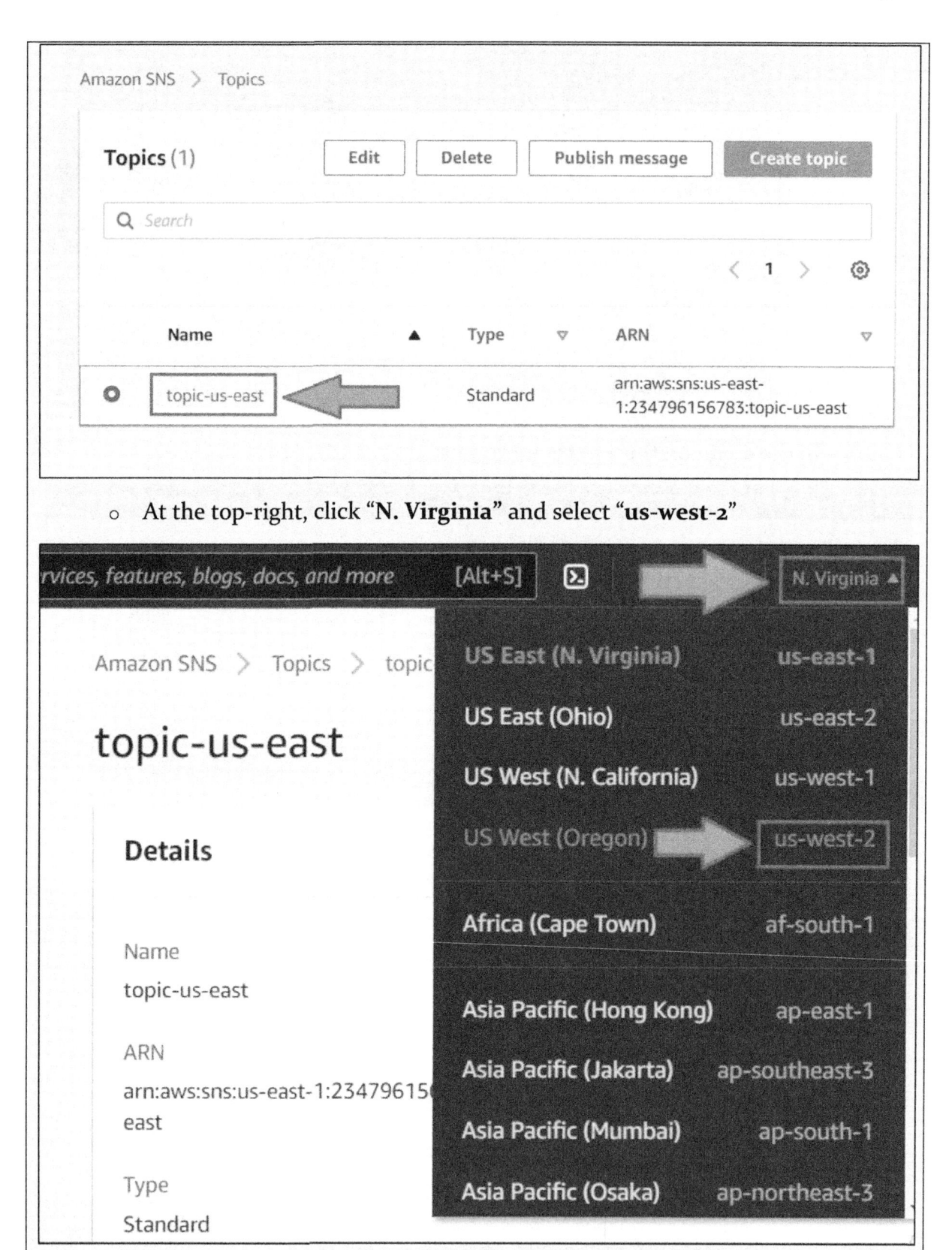

Chapter 05: Terraform Fundamentals

o Verify that the *topic-us-west* resource appears in the list.

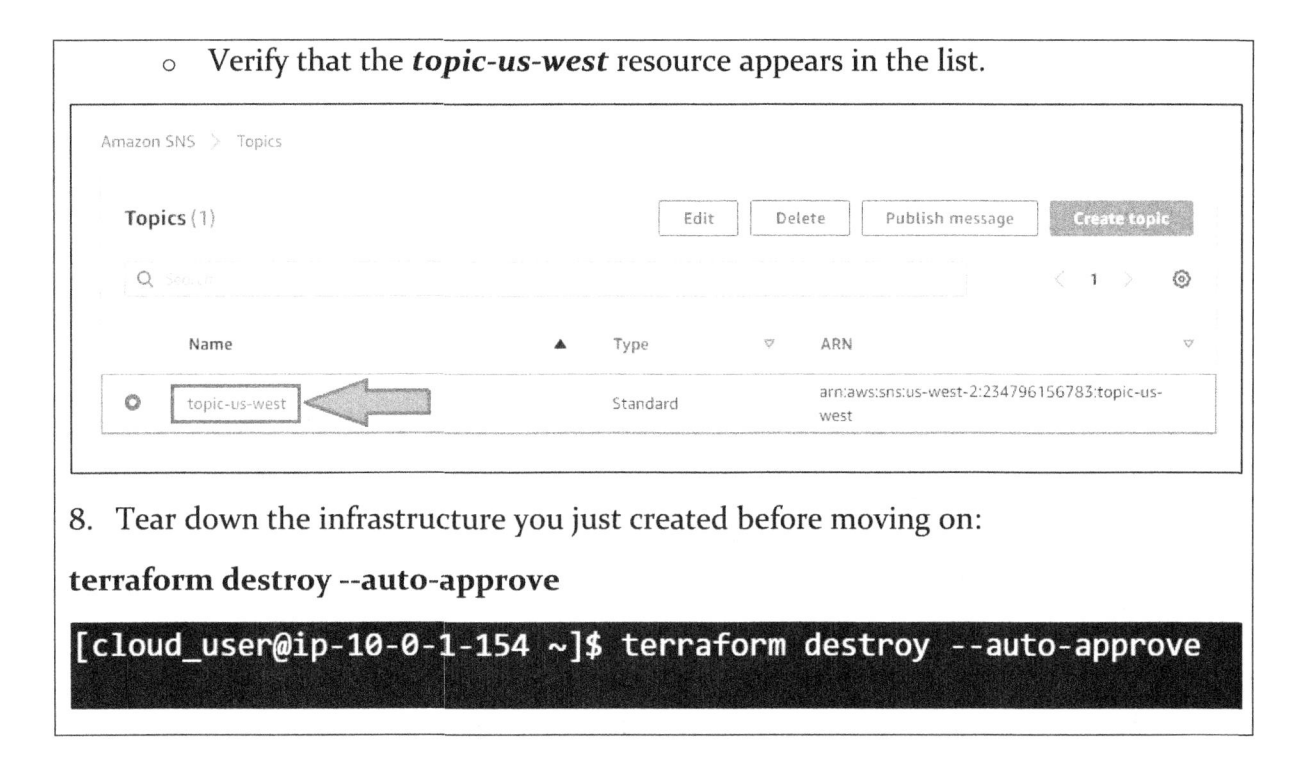

8. Tear down the infrastructure you just created before moving on:

terraform destroy --auto-approve

Lab 5-02: Using Terraform Provisioners to Set up an Apache Web Server on AWS

Introduction

In this hands-on lab, you will be using a Terraform provisioner to custom bootstrap a VM in AWS, install a webserver, and then test that the webserver is working as expected.

Problem

Provisioners run scripts on a local or remote machine as resource creation or destruction.

Solution

1. Log in to your terminal.

Chapter 05: Terraform Fundamentals

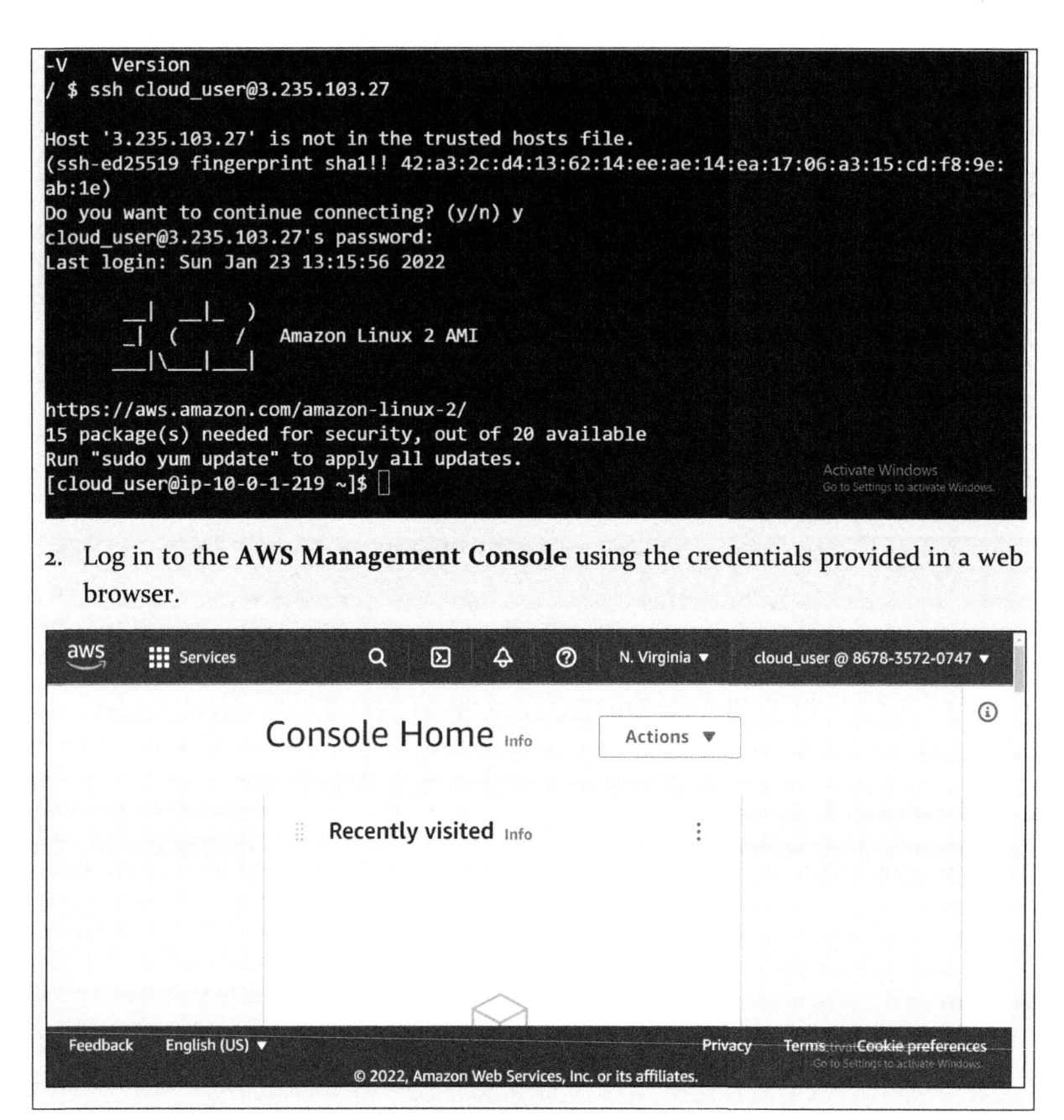

```
-V      Version
/ $ ssh cloud_user@3.235.103.27

Host '3.235.103.27' is not in the trusted hosts file.
(ssh-ed25519 fingerprint sha1!! 42:a3:2c:d4:13:62:14:ee:ae:14:ea:17:06:a3:15:cd:f8:9e:
ab:1e)
Do you want to continue connecting? (y/n) y
cloud_user@3.235.103.27's password:
Last login: Sun Jan 23 13:15:56 2022

       __|  __|_  )
       _|  (     /   Amazon Linux 2 AMI
      ___|\___|___|

https://aws.amazon.com/amazon-linux-2/
15 package(s) needed for security, out of 20 available
Run "sudo yum update" to apply all updates.
[cloud_user@ip-10-0-1-219 ~]$
```

2. Log in to the **AWS Management Console** using the credentials provided in a web browser.

Clone Code and Switch to the Directory

1. Clone the required code from the provided repository:

git clone https://github.com/12920/IPSpecialist01/blob/main/content-hashicorp-certified-terraform-associate-foundations-master%20(2).zip

Chapter 05: Terraform Fundamentals

```
       _|  _|_  )
       _|  (    /    Amazon Linux 2 AMI
       __|\___|___|

https://aws.amazon.com/amazon-linux-2/
15 package(s) needed for security, out of 20 available
Run "sudo yum update" to apply all updates.
[cloud_user@ip-10-0-1-219 ~]$ git clone https://github.com/linuxacademy/content-hashic
orp-certified-terraform-associate-foundations.git
Cloning into 'content-hashicorp-certified-terraform-associate-foundations'...
remote: Enumerating objects: 76, done.
remote: Counting objects: 100% (76/76), done.
remote: Compressing objects: 100% (67/67), done.
remote: Total 76 (delta 19), reused 59 (delta 6), pack-reused 0
Receiving objects: 100% (76/76), 2.38 MiB | 34.85 MiB/s, done.
Resolving deltas: 100% (19/19), done.
[cloud_user@ip-10-0-1-219 ~]$
```

2. Switch to the directory where the code is located:

cd content-hashicorp-certified-terraform-associate-foundations/section3-hol2/

```
[cloud_user@ip-10-0-1-219 ~]$ cd content-hashicorp-certified-terraform-associate-found
ations/section3-hol2/
[cloud_user@ip-10-0-1-219 section3-hol2]$
```

3. List the files in the directory:

ls

```
[cloud_user@ip-10-0-1-219 section3-hol2]$ ls
main.tf   README.md   setup.tf
[cloud_user@ip-10-0-1-219 section3-hol2]$
```

The files in the directory should include the main.tf, README.md, and setup.tf.

Examine the Code in the main.tf File

1. View the contents of the main.tf file using the cat command.

cat main.tf

Chapter 05: Terraform Fundamentals

```
[cloud_user@ip-10-0-1-219 section3-hol2]$ cat main.tf
#Create and bootstrap webserver
resource "aws_instance" "webserver" {
  ami                         = data.aws_ssm_parameter.webserver-ami.value
  instance_type               = "t3.micro"
  key_name                    = aws_key_pair.webserver-key.key_name
  associate_public_ip_address = true
  vpc_security_group_ids      = [aws_security_group.sg.id]
  subnet_id                   = aws_subnet.subnet.id
  provisioner "remote-exec" {
    inline = [
      "sudo yum -y install httpd && sudo systemctl start httpd",
      "echo '<h1><center>My Test Website With Help From Terraform Provisioner</center></h1>' > index.html",
      "sudo mv index.html /var/www/html/"
    ]
    connection {
```

2. Examine the code in the resource block and note the following:

- You are creating an AWS EC2 instance (virtual machine) named webserver

- You are passing several parameters for the resource, such as the AMI that the VM will be spun up as, the instance type, the private key that the instance will be used, the public IP attached to the instance, the security group applied to the instance, and the subnet ID where the VM will be spun up

```
[cloud_user@ip-10-0-1-219 section3-hol2]$ cat main.tf
#Create and bootstrap webserver
resource "aws_instance" "webserver" {
  ami                         = data.aws_ssm_parameter.webserver-ami.value
  instance_type               = "t3.micro"
  key_name                    = aws_key_pair.webserver-key.key_name
  associate_public_ip_address = true
  vpc_security_group_ids      = [aws_security_group.sg.id]
  subnet_id                   = aws_subnet.subnet.id
  provisioner "remote-exec" {
    inline = [
      "sudo yum -y install httpd && sudo systemctl start httpd",
      "echo '<h1><center>My Test Website With Help From Terraform Provisioner</center></h1>' > index.html",
      "sudo mv index.html /var/www/html/"
    ]
    connection {
```

Note: All of these resources are being created via the setup.tf file, which you can view if desired.

3. Examine the code in the provisioner block and note the following:

Chapter 05: Terraform Fundamentals

- o The remote-exec keyword tells us that this is a remote provisioner, which invokes a script on a remote resource after it is created
- o The provisioner uses the parameters configured in the embedded connection block to connect to the AWS EC2 instance is created
- o The provisioner will then issue the commands configured in the inline-block to install Apache web server on CentOS through the yum package manager, start up the Apache server, create a single web page called *My Test Website With Help From Terraform Provisioner* as an index.html file, and move that file into the data directory of the webserver to be served out globally

```
provisioner "remote-exec" {
  inline = [
    "sudo yum -y install httpd && sudo systemctl start httpd",
    "echo '<h1><center>My Test Website With Help From Terraform Provisioner</center></h1>' > index.html",
    "sudo mv index.html /var/www/html/"
  ]
  connection {
    type        = "ssh"
    user        = "ec2-user"
    private_key = file("~/.ssh/id_rsa")
    host        = self.public_ip
  }
}
tags = {
  Name = "webserver"
}
}
```

Deploy the Code and Access the Webserver

1. Initialize the Terraform working directory, and download the required providers:

terraform init

```
so the latest version was installed.

To prevent automatic upgrades to new major versions that may contain breaking
changes, we recommend adding version constraints in a required_providers block
in your configuration, with the constraint strings suggested below.

* hashicorp/aws: version = "~> 3.73.0"

Terraform has been successfully initialized!

You may now begin working with Terraform. Try running "terraform plan" to see
any changes that are required for your infrastructure. All Terraform commands
should now work.

If you ever set or change modules or backend configuration for Terraform,
rerun this command to reinitialize your working directory. If you forget, other
commands will detect it and remind you to do so if necessary.
[cloud_user@ip-10-0-1-219 section3-hol2]$
```

2. Validate the code to look for any errors in syntax, parameters, or attributes within Terraform resources that may prevent it from deploying correctly:

terraform validate

```
[cloud_user@ip-10-0-1-219 section3-hol2]$ terraform validate
Success! The configuration is valid.

[cloud_user@ip-10-0-1-219 section3-hol2]$
```

You should receive a notification that the configuration is valid.

3. Review the actions that will be performed when you deploy the Terraform code:

terraform plan

```
[cloud_user@ip-10-0-1-219 section3-hol2]$ terraform plan
Refreshing Terraform state in-memory prior to plan...
The refreshed state will be used to calculate this plan, but will not be
persisted to local or remote state storage.

data.aws_availability_zones.azs: Refreshing state...
data.aws_ssm_parameter.webserver-ami: Refreshing state...

-----------------------------------------------------------------------
```

In this case, it will create seven resources as configured in the Terraform code.

4. Deploy the code:

terraform apply

Chapter 05: Terraform Fundamentals

```
[cloud_user@ip-10-0-1-219 section3-hol2]$ terraform apply
data.aws_ssm_parameter.webserver-ami: Refreshing state...
data.aws_availability_zones.azs: Refreshing state...

An execution plan has been generated and is shown below.
Resource actions are indicated with the following symbols:
  + create
 <= read (data resources)
```

5. When prompted, type *yes* and press "**Enter**."

```
Plan: 7 to add, 0 to change, 0 to destroy.

Do you want to perform these actions?
  Terraform will perform the actions described above.
  Only 'yes' will be accepted to approve.

  Enter a value: yes
```

6. As the code is being deployed, you will notice that the Terraform provisioner will try to connect to the EC2 instance, and once that connection is established, it will run the bootstrapping that was configured in the provisioner block against the instance.

7. When complete, it will output the public IP for the Apache webserver as the Webserver-Public-IP value.

```
aws_instance.webserver (remote-exec):    apr.x86_64 0:1.7.0-9.amzn2
aws_instance.webserver (remote-exec):    apr-util.x86_64 0:1.6.1-5.amzn2.0.2
aws_instance.webserver (remote-exec):    apr-util-bdb.x86_64 0:1.6.1-5.amzn2.0.2
aws_instance.webserver (remote-exec):    generic-logos-httpd.noarch 0:18.0.0-4.amzn2
aws_instance.webserver (remote-exec):    httpd-filesystem.noarch 0:2.4.52-1.amzn2
aws_instance.webserver (remote-exec):    httpd-tools.x86_64 0:2.4.52-1.amzn2
aws_instance.webserver (remote-exec):    mailcap.noarch 0:2.1.41-2.amzn2
aws_instance.webserver (remote-exec):    mod_http2.x86_64 0:1.15.19-1.amzn2.0.1

aws_instance.webserver (remote-exec): Complete!
aws_instance.webserver: Creation complete after 26s [id=i-0f5abd39eabea5229]

Apply complete! Resources: 7 added, 0 changed, 0 destroyed.

Outputs:

Webserver-Public-IP = 34.200.252.2
[cloud_user@ip-10-0-1-219 section3-hol2]$
```

8. Copy the IP address, paste it in a new browser window or tab, and press "**Enter**."

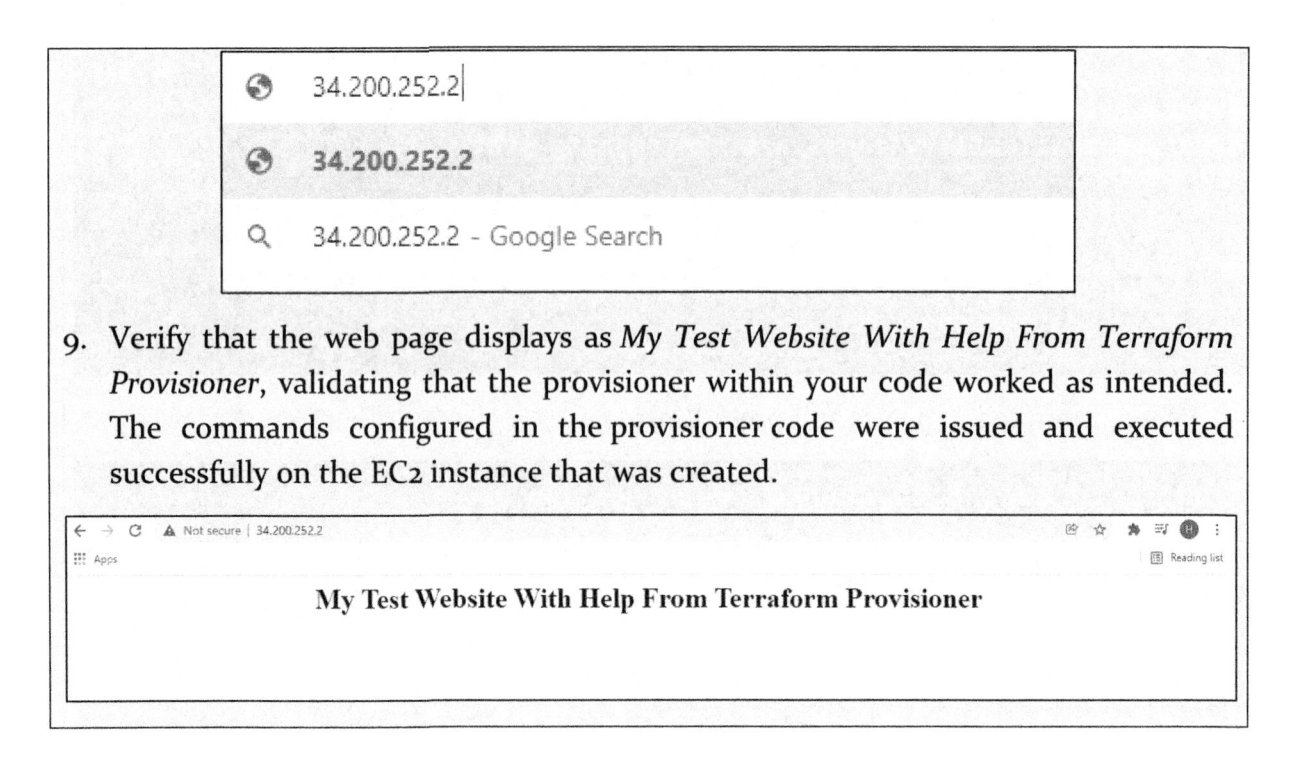

Chapter 05: Terraform Fundamentals

> 34.200.252.2
>
> 34.200.252.2
>
> 34.200.252.2 - Google Search

9. Verify that the web page displays as *My Test Website With Help From Terraform Provisioner*, validating that the provisioner within your code worked as intended. The commands configured in the provisioner code were issued and executed successfully on the EC2 instance that was created.

My Test Website With Help From Terraform Provisioner

Mind Map

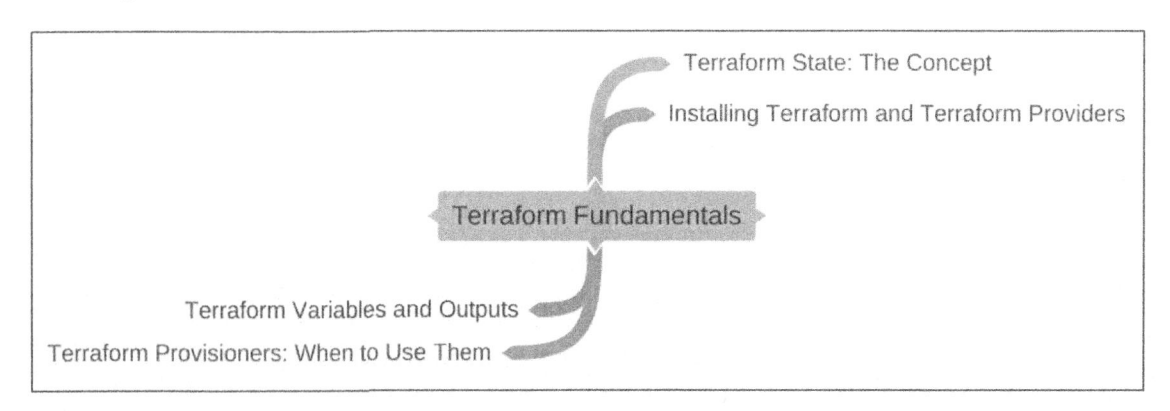

Terraform Fundamentals
- Terraform State: The Concept
- Installing Terraform and Terraform Providers
- Terraform Variables and Outputs
- Terraform Provisioners: When to Use Them

Figure 5-07: Mind Map

Chapter 05: Terraform Fundamentals

Practice Questions

1. There are _____ methods to install Terraform.
A. 1
B. 2
C. 3
D. 4

2. The syntax for using the sensitive parameter would be a Boolean value, and by default, it is _____.
A. True
B. False
C. Null
D. None of the above

3. There are _____ base variable types for Terraform variables.
A. 1
B. 2
C. 3
D. 4

4. In the curly braces, you have the description for the _____ and a value.
A. Input
B. Output
C. Both of the above
D. None of the above

5. There are _____ types of provisioners.
A. 1
B. 2

C. 3
D. 4

6. In the Destroy provisioner, you are having _____ the value one to the same status.txt file upon being deleted or getting destroyed.
A. Input
B. Output
C. Both of the above
D. None of the above

7. Provisioners are _____ of the Terraform state file.
A. Independent
B. Dependent
C. Both of the above
D. None of the above

8. You set up the Terraform repository on your system, and it is only available for _____ systems.
A. Windows
B. Linux
C. Both of the above
D. None of the above

9. Between the _____ braces, you have the configuration parameters for the variable.
A. Square
B. Curly
C. Both of the above
D. None of the above

10. Providers can be sourced _____ and referenced within your Terraform code.
A. Locally
B. Internally
C. Both of the above
D. None of the above

11. Method _____ is a bit more guided with the help of Linux repositories.
A. 1
B. 2
C. Both of the above
D. None of the above

12. Terraform pulls down the providers when you initialize your different projects using the Terraform _____ command.
A. wget
B. init
C. Both of the above
D. None of the above

13. Terraform state is stored into flat files as _____ data.
A. SQL
B. JSON
C. Both of the above
D. None of the above

14. The _____ file helps Terraform calculate deployment deltas.
A. State
B. Resource
C. Both of the above

Chapter 05: Terraform Fundamentals

D. None of the above

15. All the config parameters within the _____ braces are optional for declaring the variables.

A. Curly
B. Square
C. Round
D. None of the above

Chapter 06: Terraform CLI

Introduction

The command-line interface to Terraform is through the terraform command, which receives a variability of subcommands such as terraform init or terraform plan.

This vocabulary is often used to differentiate it from other components you might use in the Terraform product family, such as Terraform Cloud or the numerous Terraform providers, which are established and released separately from Terraform CLI.

Terraform CLI can be organized with some global settings separate from any Terraform configuration and apply across all working directories.

Terraform CLI

To provision infrastructure, Terraform Cloud uses Terraform CLI.

Terraform is accessed from the command line via the terraform command, which accepts a number of subcommands such as terraform init and terraform plan. The navigation section of this page has a complete list of all supported subcommands.

The terraform command-line tool is referred to as "Terraform CLI" throughout the documentation. This terminology is frequently used to distinguish it from other Terraform product family components such as Terraform Cloud and Terraform providers, which are developed and distributed independently of Terraform CLI.

Terraform Cloud provides a team-oriented remote Terraform process that is easy to understand for new Terraform users and comfortable for established Terraform users. Remote Terraform execution, a workspace-based organizational model, version control integration, command-line integration, remote state management with cross-workspace data sharing, and a private Terraform module registry serve as the basis for this workflow.

Initializing Working Directories

Terraform requires to be called from a working directory containing Terraform-compatible configuration files. Terraform uses this directory to store configuration content, as well as settings, cached plugins and modules, and sometimes state data.

Terraform cannot do anything in a working directory until it's been initialized (like provisioning infrastructure or modifying state).

Working Directory Content

Typical contents of a Terraform working directory are:

- A Terraform configuration that describes the resources that Terraform should look after. This arrangement is likely to vary over time.
- Terraform uses a hidden.terraform directory to manage cached provider plugins and modules, keep track of which workspace is active, and keep track of the last known backend configuration in case it needs to migrate state on the next run. Terraform creates this directory during initialization and manages it automatically.
- If the setup utilizes the default local backend, state data is stored. If the directory only uses the default workspace, Terraform manages this in a terraform.tfstate file or a terraform.tfstate.d directory (if the directory uses multiple workspaces).

Initialization

To create a working directory with a Terraform configuration, use the terraform init command. Other commands, such as terraform plan and terraform apply, will be available after setup.

If you try to run a command that requires initialization without first doing so, it will fail with an error and tell you that you need to run init.

Initialization prepares a directory by accessing state in the configured backend, downloading and installing provider plugins, and downloading modules, among other things. It may prompt the user for instruction or confirmation under certain circumstances (typically when switching from one backend to another).

Reinitialization

Certain Terraform configuration modifications may necessitate reinitialization before normal operations can resume. Changes to provider needs, module sources or version constraints, and backend configurations are all examples of this.

Running terraform init again will reinitialize a directory. You can really reinitialize at any moment; the init command is idempotent, meaning it has no effect if no modifications are required.

Any commands that rely on initialization will fail with an error and notify you if reinitialization is required.

Remote Terraform Execution

By default, Terraform Cloud uses disposable virtual machines in its own cloud infrastructure to run Terraform. Terraform Cloud Agents can be used to run Terraform on isolated, private, or on-premises infrastructure. "Remote operations" is a term used to describe the execution of Terraforms from afar.

Critical provisioning operations benefit from remote execution because it ensures consistency and visibility. Sentinel policy enforcement, cost estimation, notifications, version control integration, and more are all possible with it.

Demo 6-01: Initialize Terraform Configuration

After you have written your Terraform setup, there are three primary steps in the Terraform workflow:

- **Initialize** - Initialize sets up the working directory for Terraform to use while running the configuration.
- **Plan** - Plan allows you to see how your changes will look before you make them.
- **Apply** - To create, update, or destroy resources, apply makes the modifications indicated by your Terraform configuration.

Terraform configures the backend, installs all providers and modules referenced to in the Terraform project, and creates a lock file if one does not already exist when it initializes your working directory. You can also use the init command to upgrade your project's providers and modules. These procedures guarantee Terraform creates, updates, or destroys your resources using the correct state, modules, and providers.

In this demo, you will create a Terraform setup that includes both local and remote modules, look through the .terraform directory, and update your provider and module versions. You will discover more about the init command's importance in the Terraform workflow in the process.

> **Step 01: Clone the repository**
>
> 1. Open the Linux terminal, clone the repository using the following command.
>
> **git clone https://github.com/hashicorp/learn-terraform-init**

Chapter 06: Terraform CLI

```
root@workstation:~/learn-terraform-docker-container# git clone https://github.com/hashicorp/learn-terraform-init
Cloning into 'learn-terraform-init'...
remote: Enumerating objects: 22, done.
remote: Counting objects: 100% (22/22), done.
remote: Compressing objects: 100% (21/21), done.
remote: Total 22 (delta 6), reused 14 (delta 1), pack-reused 0
Unpacking objects: 100% (22/22), done.
root@workstation:~/learn-terraform-docker-container#
```

2. Navigate to the cloned repository.

cd learn-terraform-init

```
root@workstation:~/learn-terraform-docker-container# cd learn-terraform-init
root@workstation:~/learn-terraform-docker-container/learn-terraform-init#
```

Step 02: Initialize the configuration

3. Run the following command to initialize the Terraform configuration.

terraform init

```
root@workstation:~/learn-terraform-docker-container# cd learn-terraform-init
root@workstation:~/learn-terraform-docker-container/learn-terraform-init# terraform init
Initializing modules...
Downloading joatmon08/hello/random 3.0.1 for hello...
- hello in .terraform/modules/hello
- nginx-pet in nginx

Initializing the backend...

Initializing provider plugins...
- Finding hashicorp/random versions matching "3.1.0"...
- Finding kreuzwerker/docker versions matching "~> 2.16.0"...
- Installing hashicorp/random v3.1.0...
- Installed hashicorp/random v3.1.0 (signed by HashiCorp)
- Installing kreuzwerker/docker v2.16.0...
```

Note: When you initialize your configuration, the output specifies the actions Terraform takes.

- Terraform downloads the configuration's referenced modules. It recognizes the hello module as a remote module and downloads it from the Terraform Registry. It also understands that the "nginx-pet" module block makes use of the local nginx module.
- The backend is initialized via Terraform. Terraform defaults to the local backend because the terraform block lacks a cloud or backend block.

Chapter 06: Terraform CLI

- Terraform gets the providers specified in the configuration and downloads them. Terraform downloads the docker and random providers provided in versions.tf because the configuration does not yet contain a lock file.
- Terraform saves the versions and hashes of the providers used in this run in a lock file. Terraform will download the versions recorded in the lock file for subsequent runs, ensuring consistent Terraform runs in various environments.

```
Downloading joatmon08/hello/random 3.0.1 for hello...
- hello in .terraform/modules/hello
- nginx-pet in nginx

Initializing the backend...

Initializing provider plugins...
- Finding hashicorp/random versions matching "3.1.0"...
- Finding kreuzwerker/docker versions matching "~> 2.16.0"...
- Installing hashicorp/random v3.1.0...
- Installed hashicorp/random v3.1.0 (signed by HashiCorp)
- Installing kreuzwerker/docker v2.16.0...
- Installed kreuzwerker/docker v2.16.0 (self-signed, key ID BD080C4571C6104C)

Partner and community providers are signed by their developers.
If you'd like to know more about provider signing, you can read about it here:
https://www.terraform.io/docs/cli/plugins/signing.html

Terraform has created a lock file .terraform.lock.hcl to record the provider
selections it made above. Include this file in your version control repository
so that Terraform can guarantee to make the same selections by default when
you run "terraform init" in the future.

Terraform has been successfully initialized!

You may now begin working with Terraform. Try running "terraform plan" to see
any changes that are required for your infrastructure. All Terraform commands
should now work.

If you ever set or change modules or backend configuration for Terraform,
rerun this command to reinitialize your working directory. If you forget, other
commands will detect it and remind you to do so if necessary.
root@workstation:~/learn-terraform-docker-container/learn-terraform-init#
```

Step 03: Validate the configuration

4. Run the following command to validate the Terraform configuration.

terraform validate

Chapter 06: Terraform CLI

```
root@workstation:~/learn-terraform-docker-container/learn-terraform-init# terraform validate
Success! The configuration is valid.

root@workstation:~/learn-terraform-docker-container/learn-terraform-init#
```

Explore the lock file.

5. Open the .terraform.lock.hcl file.

.terraform.lock.hcl

\# This file is maintained automatically by "terraform init".
\# Manual edits may be lost in future updates.

provider "registry.terraform.io/hashicorp/random" {
  version   = "3.1.0"
  constraints = "3.1.0"
  hashes = [
    "h1:rKYu5ZUbXwrLG1w81k7H3nce/Ys6yAxXhWcbtk36HjY=",
    \#\# ...
    "zh:f7605bd1437752114baf601bdf6931debe6dc6bfe3006eb7e9bb9080931dca8a",
  ]
}

provider "registry.terraform.io/kreuzwerker/docker" {
  version   = "2.16.0"
  constraints = "~> 2.16.0"
  hashes = [
    "h1:FyU8TUgpwfu+O+k+Uu5N58I/JWlEZk2PzQLJMluuaIQ=",
    \#\# ...
    "zh:fd634e973eb2b6483a1ce9251801a393d04cb496f8e83ffcf3f0c4cad8c18f4c",
  ]
}

Chapter 06: Terraform CLI

```
# This file is maintained automatically by "terraform init".
# Manual edits may be lost in future updates.

provider "registry.terraform.io/hashicorp/random" {
  version     = "3.1.0"
  constraints = "3.1.0"
  hashes = [
    "h1:rKYu5ZUbXwrLG1w81k7H3nce/Ys6yAxXhWcbtk36HjY=",
    ## ...
    "zh:f7605bd1437752114baf601bdf6931debe6dc6bfe3006eb7e9bb9
  ]
}

provider "registry.terraform.io/kreuzwerker/docker" {
  version     = "2.16.0"
  constraints = "~> 2.16.0"
  hashes = [
    "h1:FyU8TUgpwfu+O+k+Uu5N58I/JWlEZk2PzQLJMluuaIQ=",
    ## ...
    "zh:fd634e973eb2b6483a1ce9251801a393d04cb496f8e83ffcf3f0
  ]
}
```

Explore the modules.json

6. Open the modules.json file. The setup employs three modules, according to this file: the root module, the remote hello module, and the local nginx-pet module.

modules.json

```
{
 "Modules": [
   {
    "Key": "",
    "Source": "",
    "Dir": "."
   },
   {
    "Key": "hello",
    "Source": "registry.terraform.io/joatmon08/hello/random",
    "Version": "3.0.1",
    "Dir": ".terraform/modules/hello"
   },
   {
    "Key": "nginx-pet",
    "Source": "./nginx",
    "Dir": "nginx"
```

Chapter 06: Terraform CLI

```
    }
  ]
}
```

```
FILES                                    main.tf  ×   main.tf  ×    .terraform.lock.hcl     modules.json
▼ /root/learn-terraform-doc...      1   {
  ▼ learn-terraform-init             2     "Modules": [
    ▶ .git                           3       {
    ▼ .terraform                     4         "Key": "",
      ▼ modules                      5         "Source": "",
        ▶ hello                      6         "Dir": "."
          modules.json               7       },
      ▶ providers                    8       {
    ▼ nginx                          9         "Key": "hello",
        main.tf                     10         "Source": "registry.terraform.io/joatmon08/hello/random",
        variables.tf                11         "Version": "3.0.1",
        versions.tf                 12         "Dir": ".terraform/modules/hello"
      .gitignore                    13       },
      .terraform.lock.hcl           14       {
      README.md                     15         "Key": "nginx-pet",
      main.tf                       16         "Source": "./nginx",
      versions.tf                   17         "Dir": "nginx"
    main.tf                         18       }
                                    19     ]
                                    20   }
```

Step 04: Update provider and module version

7. Update the random provider's version to 3.0.1 in versions.tf.

```
terraform {
 required_providers {
  ## ..
  random = {
   source = "hashicorp/random"
   version = "3.0.1"
  }
 }
}
```

```
:S                              C      main.tf  ×    main.tf  ×    .terraform.lock.hcl  💾
ot/learn-terraform-doc...              1    terraform {
earn-terraform-init                    2      required_providers {
 .git                                  3        ## ..
 .terraform                            4        random = {
 ▼ modules                             5          source  = "hashicorp/random"
   ▶ hello                             6          version = "3.0.1"
     modules.json                      7        }
 ▶ providers                           8      }
 nginx                                 9    }
   main.tf                            10
   variables.tf
   versions.tf
 .gitignore
 .terraform.lock.hcl
 README.md
 main.tf
 versions.tf
nain.tf
```

8. Update the version of the hello module in main.tf to 3.1.0.

module "hello" {
 source = "joatmon08/hello/random"
 version = "3.1.0"

 hello = random_pet.dog.id

 secret_key = "secret"
}

Chapter 06: Terraform CLI

```
module "hello" {
  source  = "joatmon08/hello/random"
  version = "3.1.0"

  hello = random_pet.dog.id

  secret_key = "secret"
}
```

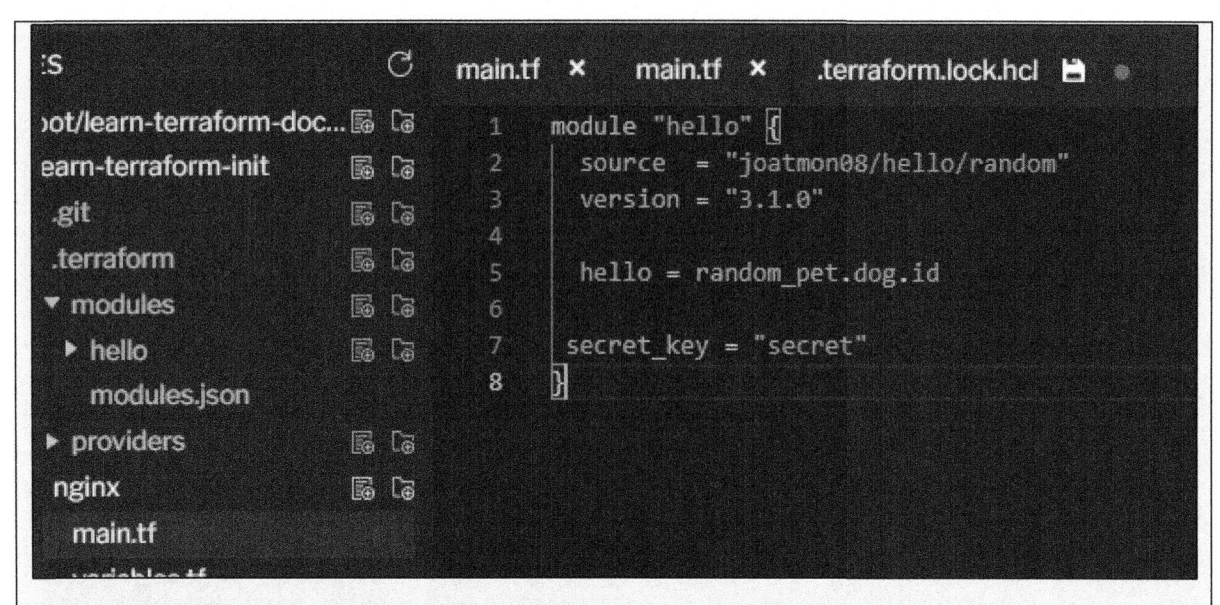

Step 05: Reinitialize the configuration

9. Run the following command to reinitialize the configuration.

terraform init

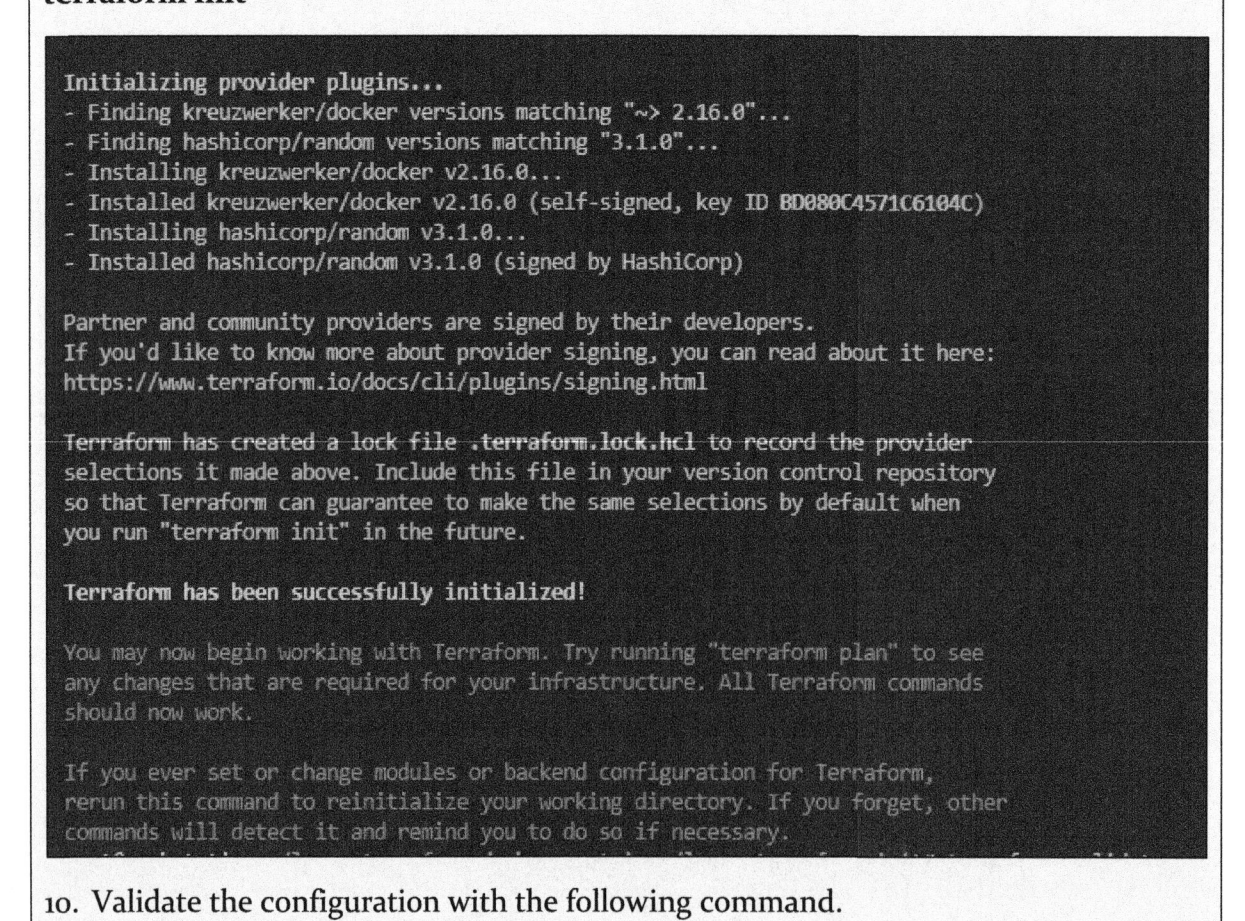

```
Initializing provider plugins...
- Finding kreuzwerker/docker versions matching "~> 2.16.0"...
- Finding hashicorp/random versions matching "3.1.0"...
- Installing kreuzwerker/docker v2.16.0...
- Installed kreuzwerker/docker v2.16.0 (self-signed, key ID BD080C4571C6104C)
- Installing hashicorp/random v3.1.0...
- Installed hashicorp/random v3.1.0 (signed by HashiCorp)

Partner and community providers are signed by their developers.
If you'd like to know more about provider signing, you can read about it here:
https://www.terraform.io/docs/cli/plugins/signing.html

Terraform has created a lock file .terraform.lock.hcl to record the provider
selections it made above. Include this file in your version control repository
so that Terraform can guarantee to make the same selections by default when
you run "terraform init" in the future.

Terraform has been successfully initialized!

You may now begin working with Terraform. Try running "terraform plan" to see
any changes that are required for your infrastructure. All Terraform commands
should now work.

If you ever set or change modules or backend configuration for Terraform,
rerun this command to reinitialize your working directory. If you forget, other
commands will detect it and remind you to do so if necessary.
```

10. Validate the configuration with the following command.

Chapter 06: Terraform CLI

terraform validate

```
root@workstation:~/learn-terraform-docker-container/learn-terraform-init# terraform validate
Success! The configuration is valid.
```

11. In case of error, you can upgrade the configuration using the command.

```
root@workstation:~/learn-terraform-docker-container/learn-terraform-init# terraform init -upgrade
Upgrading modules...
Downloading joatmon08/hello/random 3.0.1 for hello...
- hello in .terraform/modules/hello
- nginx-pet in nginx

Initializing the backend...

Initializing provider plugins...
- Finding hashicorp/random versions matching "3.1.0"...
- Finding kreuzwerker/docker versions matching "~> 2.16.0"...
- Using previously-installed hashicorp/random v3.1.0
- Using previously-installed kreuzwerker/docker v2.16.0

Terraform has been successfully initialized!

You may now begin working with Terraform. Try running "terraform plan" to see
any changes that are required for your infrastructure. All Terraform commands
should now work.

If you ever set or change modules or backend configuration for Terraform,
rerun this command to reinitialize your working directory. If you forget, other
commands will detect it and remind you to do so if necessary.
root@workstation:~/learn-terraform-docker-container/learn-terraform-init#
```

Note: With the -upgrade flag, you can reset your setup. This instructs Terraform to get the latest provider version and update the lock file's version and signature.

Step 06: Reconcile Configuration

12. Check that your setup is still valid now that your provider and module versions have been updated.

A new mandatory argument is expected in the new version of the hello module. To the hello module, add the second hello mandatory argument.

main.tf

module "hello" {
  source = "joatmon08/hello/random"
  version = "3.1.0"

```
hello = random_pet.dog.id
second_hello = random_pet.dog.id

secret_key = "secret"
}
```

```
main.tf  ×    .terraform.lock.hcl        modules.json

1   module "hello" {
2       source  = "joatmon08/hello/random"
3       version = "3.1.0"
4
5       hello = random_pet.dog.id
6       second_hello = random_pet.dog.id
7
8       secret_key = "secret"
9   }
10
```

13. After that, run the following command to validate your configuration.

terraform validate

```
root@workstation:~/learn-terraform-docker-container/learn-terraform-init# terraform validate
```

```
root@workstation:~/learn-terraform-docker-container/learn-terraform-init# terraform validate
Success! The configuration is valid.

root@workstation:~/learn-terraform-docker-container/learn-terraform-init#
root@workstation:~/learn-terraform-docker-container/learn-terraform-init#
```

Terraform fmt, taint, and import Commands

Terraform is measured through an easy-to-use Command Line Interface (CLI). This application takes a subcommand such as "apply" or "plan."

The Terraform CLI is a command-line application. In inaccurate cases, a non-zero exit status will be reverted. It also replies to -h and --help.

fmt Command

This command helps make your code beautiful-looking and consistent by formatting it to a standard. It makes the code consistent, easy to maintain, and read through on version control systems. It only modifies the look of the code, but it does not change anything else otherwise. Its command syntax is terraform space format, and by default, it expects no arguments. It looks for all the files ending in dot tf extension and formats them, outputting any files fixed for syntax and consistency.

Before pushing your code to a version control system, so that your teams can collaborate on it better, and after upgrading Terraform or its modules in case Terraform or HashiCorp changes the syntax or the way a certain block of code is written or any time you made changes to the code. If you made many changes and did not take care of the syntax, just save the file, run the Terraform format command on it and let the Terraform command work its magic of making your code look synchronized.

Usage

The command-line flags are all optional. The list of available flags are:

- -list=false – Do not list the files containing formatting inconsistencies
- -write=false – Do not overwrite the input files
- -diff - Display diffs of formatting changes
- -check - Check if the input is formatted

taint Command

Terraform receives notification from the terraform taint command that a specific item has been degraded or damaged. This is represented in Terraform by labeling the object as "tainted" in the Terraform state, and Terraform will suggest replacing it in the next plan you generate.

This command does not change the infrastructure, but it does change the state file to mark a resource as contaminated. Once a resource has been tagged as contaminated, the next plan will show that it will be destroyed and regenerated, and the following application will carry out this change.

Forcing a resource's recreation is handy when you desire a certain side effect of recreation that is not obvious in the resource's properties. Re-running provisioners, for example, will result in a different node, and rebooting the system from a base image will result in new startup scripts running.

It is worth noting that tainting a resource for recreational purposes may have an impact on resources that rely on the tainted resource. A DNS resource that utilizes a server's IP address, for example, may need to be updated to reflect a tainted server's potentially new IP address. If this is the case, the plan command will display it.

untaint Command

The terraform untaint unmark a resource as tainted manually to restore it as the state's primary instance. This removes either a manual 'terraform taint' or the outcome of resource provisioners failing.

There will be no changes to your infrastructure as a result of this. To unmark a resource as tainted, use this command to alter your status. Reverting the state backup file made by this command or running 'terraform taint' on the resource will undo it.

Usage

This command accepts the following options:

> - -allow-missing - If stated, the command will succeed (exit code 0) even if the resource is missing
> - -lock=false - Restricts Terraform's default behavior of trying to take a read/write lock on the state for the duration of the operation
> - -lock-timeout=DURATION - Unless locking is inactivated with -lock=false, instructs Terraform to retry acquiring a lock for a while before recurring an error

Import Command

This command takes an existing resource that Terraform manages and maps it to a resource within Terraform code using an ID. The ID referred here depends on the vendor infrastructure from where you are trying to import the resource. For example, to import an AWS EC2 virtual machine, you need its instance ID. You cannot import the same real-world resource against multiple Terraform configuration resources in your Terraform code. Terraform itself makes sure that there is one-to-one mapping for all real-world and Terraform resources. However, it cannot control that when you import something from external systems, and so it is up to you to make sure you are not importing a resource more than once within the same configuration, as that can cause unknown behavior in Terraform. The syntax you are using in the command is terraform import resource underscore address (this is the resource name that you want to map to the real-world infrastructure resource) and, finally, the ID of the real-world resource.

You should use this command when you need to work with existing resources and bring them into the Terraform fold, or when you are not allowed to create new resources in an environment, or when you are not in control of the creation process of infrastructure and are only allowed to manage it once it has been created already.

Usage

The command-line flags are all optional. The list of available flags are:

- -config=path - Path to the directory of Terraform configuration files that configure the provider for import
- -input=true - Whether to ask for input for provider configuration
- -lock=false – Do not hold a state lock during the operation
- -lock-timeout=0s - Duration to retry a state lock
- -no-color - If specified, the output would not contain any color
- -provider=provider - Deprecated Override the provider configuration to use when importing the object
- -var 'foo=bar' - Set a variable in the Terraform configuration

Terraform Block

The configuration block only allows constant values, and you cannot use named resources or variables within this block. It allows you to configure various things concerning Terraform workflows, such as configuring the backend where your state files are stored, and specifying a required version of Terraform against which your code will run (otherwise, it will error out). This block also specifies the required versions of a Terraform provider with which your code works and makes it a requirement, enabling and testing the features Terraform releases with each release and passing metadata to providers and modules.

In the configuration block, you put in a couple of constraints, requiring that Terraform only run if the Terraform binary version is greater than version 13. You are doing it to this line -- the required underscore version is equal to -- and then you are passing in a regular expression. The other constraint is that our code should only run if the Terraform AWS provider version is greater than version 3. If any of these requirements are not met, you would not be able to deploy infrastructure with code in which this Terraform block exists.

> **EXAM TIP:** A number of settings relevant to Terraform's behavior can be found in each terraform block. Only constant values may be used within a terraform block; arguments may not relate to named objects such as resources, input variables, or other variables and may not use any of the Terraform language's built-in functions.

Terraform Workspaces

Terraform workspaces are also known as CLI workspaces and are alternate state files within the same working directory. You know by now that state files are extremely crucial to Terraform's workflow, and it is Terraform's source of truth. If you have ever used Terraform and never created additional workspaces, you can use the default workspace that Terraform provides.

> **Note:** Each workspace tracks a separate independent copy of the state file against Terraform code in that directory.

Terraform Workspaces Subcommand

The new terraform workspace subcommand creates a workspace for you when you pass in the workspace name. The **terraform workspace select** command selects or switches to the workspace of your choice that already exists. Among the many available, these are two common commands that you will find yourself using. Each workspace tracks a separate independent copy of the state file, which means that Terraform will deploy a new environment for each workspace. You can test different environments using the same code. It can be modeled against branches in version control, such as Git. For example, you could have various workspaces, each of which refers to a different environment, and you can even commit the state files for those workspaces into Git and keep track of them. Workspaces are good for sharing resources and enabling collaboration between teams. For example, the developers in a team can spin up separate workspaces to test out the code in a different environment and not mess with the default workspace for a production environment, thereby leaving the state file untouched. Your Terraform code can leverage the workspaces by using the terraform dot workspace variable readily available to you when you start working with Terraform. Using this variable, you can name your resources to easily identify them, and additionally, using logic within your code, you can even instruct Terraform to take a unique action depending on the workspace you are currently in.

You have your Terraform controller node on which you are running your Terraform commands, and you choose to create a workspace. You set the workspace name as 'developer.' When you switch to the developer workspace using the workspace command, the terraform workspace's name will populate the dot workspace variable. Using this variable and some clever logic within Terraform, you can instruct it to deploy it to that developer account so that the production or default workspace is not affected or a state file is not affected. Terraform will go out and create independent new shared files for the developer workspace, and you can modify it to your heart's liking without impacting the state files for the production account or the default account. Once you are happily testing the infrastructure using the developer workspace, you can switch to the default workspace and deploy it using the normal Terraform to apply the workflow.

Terraform Dot Workspace

If the terraform dot workspace variable has the value default when the Terraform applies is executed, it will spin up to five instances. However, if the workspace is not default, then only one instance will be spun up, as evident in this logic. If your workspace is named default, the name of the bucket you just created would be XYZ bucket dash default. These are a couple of use cases of terraform dot workspace variables.

Debugging Terraform

Troubleshooting is an inevitable part of the software. In Terraform, the tf underscore log is an environment variable that enables verbose logging for Terraform and, by default, sends the logs to standard error output or your screen. It allows five levels of verbosity. The most verbose of them is the trace option. However, it is also the most reliable one, as per HashiCorp, and provides Terraform internal logs and backend API calls made to providers. You can also redirect the output logs to a file using the tf_log_ path, which takes a file as an input. By default, the tf_log is disabled. You can use the export command in Linux to set its value. It spins up a container using the Docker provider. It returns you many attributes, such as the configuration file paths, the versions for Terraform and Golang, and many other ancillary features, which help enable the terraform init command to work. It is also looking for various files and the workspace it is working in. If you ever were to raise an issue with HashiCorp, these are the logs you would be sending them, which is what they would be expecting.

Lab 6-01: Terraform CLI Commands

Introduction

In this hands-on lab, you will be working with the Terraform fmt, taint, and import commands to help you understand when you may need to use them in your everyday work with Terraform.

Problem

Chapter 06: Terraform CLI

Terraform has become common across the world to improve and transform infrastructure. Terraform offers a command-line interface called Terraform CLI.

Solution

Log in to the terminal.

```
Do you want to continue connecting? (y/n) y
cloud_user@3.235.126.209's password:
Last login: Sat Jan 29 16:46:46 2022

       __|  __|_  )
       _|  (     /   Amazon Linux 2 AMI
      ___|\___|___|

https://aws.amazon.com/amazon-linux-2/
15 package(s) needed for security, out of 20 available
Run "sudo yum update" to apply all updates.
[cloud_user@ip-10-0-1-51 ~]$
```

Clone Terraform Code and Switch to the Proper Directory

1. Clone the required code from the provided repository:

git clone https://github.com/12920/IPSpecialist/blob/main/content-hashicorp-certified-terraform-associate-foundations-master%20(2).zip

```
[cloud_user@ip-10-0-1-51 ~]$ git clone https://github.com/linuxacademy/content-hashico
rp-certified-terraform-associate-foundations.git
Cloning into 'content-hashicorp-certified-terraform-associate-foundations'...
remote: Enumerating objects: 76, done.
remote: Counting objects: 100% (76/76), done.
remote: Compressing objects: 100% (67/67), done.
remote: Total 76 (delta 19), reused 59 (delta 6), pack-reused 0
Receiving objects: 100% (76/76), 2.38 MiB | 33.89 MiB/s, done.
Resolving deltas: 100% (19/19), done.
[cloud_user@ip-10-0-1-51 ~]$
```

2. Switch to the directory where the code is located:

cd content-hashicorp-certified-terraform-associate-foundations/section4-hol1

```
[cloud_user@ip-10-0-1-51 ~]$ cd content-hashicorp-certified-terraform-assoc
tions/section4-hol1
```

3. List the files in the directory:

ls

```
[cloud_user@ip-10-0-1-51 section4-hol1]$ ls
main.tf   README.md   setup.tf
[cloud_user@ip-10-0-1-51 section4-hol1]$
```

The files in the directory should include the main.tf, README.md, and setup.tf. The main.tf file contains the code used to spin up an AWS EC2 instance (virtual machine) and the setup.tf contains the code for the resources that support the creation of the VM.

Use the fmt Command to Format Any Unformatted Code Before Deployment

1. View the contents of the main.tf file using the cat command:

cat main.tf

```
[cloud_user@ip-10-0-1-51 section4-hol1]$ cat main.tf
#Create and bootstrap webserver
resource "aws_instance" "webserver" {
        ami                       = data.aws_ssm_parameter.webserver-ami.value
    instance_type            = "t3.micro"
                key_name               = aws_key_pair.webserver-key.key_name
        associate_public_ip_address = true
        vpc_security_group_ids    = [aws_security_group.sg.id]
    subnet_id                = aws_subnet.subnet.id
  provisioner "remote-exec" {
        inline = [
      "sudo yum -y install httpd && sudo systemctl start httpd
```

Notice that the code in the file is pretty messy and improperly formatted, with issues like inconsistent indentation, making it hard to read.

2. Use the terraform fmt command to format the code in any file in the directory in which Terraform finds formatting issues:

terraform fmt

Chapter 06: Terraform CLI

```
[cloud_user@ip-10-0-1-51 section4-hol1]$ terraform fmt main.tf
```

3. View the contents of the main.tf file again:

cat main.tf

```
[cloud_user@ip-10-0-1-51 section4-hol1]$ cat main.tf
#Create and bootstrap webserver
resource "aws_instance" "webserver" {
            ami                          = data.aws_ssm_parameter.webserver-ami.value
    instance_type                = "t3.micro"
                        key_name         = aws_key_pair.webserver-key.key_name
        associate_public_ip_address = true
        vpc_security_group_ids     = [aws_security_group.sg.id]
    subnet_id                    = aws_subnet.subnet.id
 provisioner "remote-exec" {
        inline = [
        "sudo yum -y install httpd && sudo systemctl start httpd"
```

Notice that the code has now been formatted cleanly and consistently.

4. Initialize the Terraform working directory and fetch any required providers:

terraform init

```
* hashicorp/aws: version = "~> 3.74.0"

Terraform has been successfully initialized!

You may now begin working with Terraform. Try running "terraform plan" to see
any changes that are required for your infrastructure. All Terraform commands
should now work.

If you ever set or change modules or backend configuration for Terraform,
rerun this command to reinitialize your working directory. If you forget, other
commands will detect it and remind you to do so if necessary.
[cloud_user@ip-10-0-1-51 section4-hol1]$
```

5. Deploy the code:

terraform apply

Chapter 06: Terraform CLI

```
[cloud_user@ip-10-0-1-51 section4-hol1]$ terraform apply
data.aws_availability_zones.azs: Refreshing state...
data.aws_ssm_parameter.webserver-ami: Refreshing state...

An execution plan has been generated and is shown below.
Resource actions are indicated with the following symbols:
  + create
 <= read (data resources)
```

6. When prompted, type *yes* and press "**Enter**."

```
Plan: 7 to add, 0 to change, 0 to destroy.

Do you want to perform these actions?
  Terraform will perform the actions described above.
  Only 'yes' will be accepted to approve.

  Enter a value: yes
```

7. When complete, it will output the public IP for the EC2 instance hosting the webserver as the Webserver-Public-IP value.

```
Apply complete! Resources: 7 added, 0 changed, 0 destroyed.

Outputs:

Webserver-Public-IP = 44.197.181.204
```

Use the Taint Command to Replace a Resource

Modify the Provisioner Code for the aws_instance.webserver Resource

1. Using vim, open the main.tf file:

vim main.tf

Chapter 06: Terraform CLI

```
#Create and bootstrap webserver
resource "aws_instance" "webserver" {
  ami                         = data.aws_ssm_parameter.webserver-ami.value
  instance_type               = "t3.micro"
  key_name                    = aws_key_pair.webserver-key.key_name
  associate_public_ip_address = true
  vpc_security_group_ids      = [aws_security_group.sg.id]
  subnet_id                   = aws_subnet.subnet.id
  provisioner "remote-exec" {
    inline = [
      "sudo yum -y install httpd && sudo systemctl start httpd",
      "echo '<h1><center>My Website via Terraform Version 1</center></h1>' > index.html",
      "sudo mv index.html /var/www/html/"
    ]
"main.tf" 25L, 854C                                              2,1    Top
```

2. Note the name of the resource created by this code; in this case, it would be **aws_instance.webserver** as configured.

```
#Create and bootstrap webserver
resource "aws_instance" "webserver" {
  ami                         = data.aws_ssm_parameter.webserver-ami.value
  instance_type               = "t3.micro"
  key_name                    = aws_key_pair.webserver-key.key_name
  associate_public_ip_address = true
  vpc_security_group_ids      = [aws_security_group.sg.id]
  subnet_id                   = aws_subnet.subnet.id
  provisioner "remote-exec" {
    inline = [
      "sudo yum -y install httpd && sudo systemctl start httpd",
      "echo '<h1><center>My Website via Terraform Version 1</center></h1>' > index.html",
      "sudo mv index.html /var/www/html/"
    ]
"main.tf" 25L, 854C                                              2,1    Top
```

3. Inside the provisioner block, find the following line of code that outputs the content on a webpage, which currently displays *Version 1*:

echo '<h1> My Website via Terraform Version 1 </h1>'

```
      "echo '<h1><center>My Website via Terraform Version 1</center></h1>' > index.html",
```

4. In this line of code, change Version 1 to Version 2.

Chapter 06: Terraform CLI

```
"echo '<h1><center>My Website via Terraform Version 2</center></h1>' > index.html",
"sudo mv index.html /var/www/html/"
```

5. Press **Escape** and enter **:wq** to save and exit the file.

Taint the Existing aws_instance.webserver Resource

1. Use the terraform taint command and the name of the resource to tell Terraform to replace that resource and run the provisioner again upon the next deployment:

terraform taint aws_instance.webserver

```
[cloud_user@ip-10-0-1-51 section4-hol1]$ terraform taint aws_instance.webs
Resource instance aws_instance.webserver has been marked as tainted.
```

2. View the Terraform state file to verify that the resource has been tainted:

vim terraform.tfstate

```
{
  "version": 4,
  "terraform_version": "0.13.4",
  "serial": 10,
  "lineage": "4eb40196-2cd2-a92e-b11a-0362d8954640",
  "outputs": {
    "Webserver-Public-IP": {
      "value": "44.197.181.204",
      "type": "string"
    }
  },
  "resources": [
    {
      "mode": "data",
      "type": "aws_availability_zones",
"terraform.tfstate" 475L, 16159C
```

3. Search for the keyword /taint and notice that the **aws_instance** resource with the name webserver has tainted status.

4. Press **Escape** and enter **:q!** to exit the file.

135

Chapter 06: Terraform CLI

```
[cloud_user@ip-10-0-1-51 section4-hol1]$ vim terraform.tfstate
[cloud_user@ip-10-0-1-51 section4-hol1]$
```

Deploy the Code to Rerun the Provisioner and Replace the aws_instance.webserver Resource

1. Deploy the code:

terraform apply

```
[cloud_user@ip-10-0-1-51 section4-hol1]$ terraform apply
data.aws_ssm_parameter.webserver-ami: Refreshing state... [id=/aws/service/ami-amazon-linux-latest/amzn2-ami-hvm-x86_64-gp2]
data.aws_availability_zones.azs: Refreshing state... [id=us-east-1]
aws_key_pair.webserver-key: Refreshing state... [id=webserver-key]
aws_vpc.vpc: Refreshing state... [id=vpc-016ab33b39cdd970a]
data.aws_route_table.main_route_table: Refreshing state... [id=rtb-0547da9a7d2fe2569]
aws_internet_gateway.igw: Refreshing state... [id=igw-0b582d2f59dc799c5]
aws_security_group.sg: Refreshing state... [id=sg-04549b96ef3fd7c40]
aws_subnet.subnet: Refreshing state... [id=subnet-0a77868488b07ba8a]
aws_default_route_table.internet_route: Refreshing state... [id=rtb-0547da9a7d2fe2569]
```

2. Type *yes* and press **Enter** to deploy the code as planned.

```
Do you want to perform these actions?
  Terraform will perform the actions described above.
  Only 'yes' will be accepted to approve.

  Enter a value: yes
```

3. When complete, it will output the new public IP for the webserver as the **Webserver-Public-IP** value.

```
Apply complete! Resources: 1 added, 0 changed, 1 destroyed.

Outputs:

Webserver-Public-IP = 3.236.190.210
```

4. Use the curl command to view the contents of the webpage using the IP address provided:

curl http://<WEBSERVER-PUBLIC-IP>

```
[cloud_user@ip-10-0-1-51 section4-hol1]$ curl http://3.236.190.210
<h1><center>My Website via Terraform Version 2</center></h1>
```

Note: Alternately, you could open the IP address in a web browser to view the webpage's contents.

> My Website via Terraform Version 2

Use the Import Command to Import a Resource

Add the VM as a Resource Named aws_instance.webserver2 in Your Code

1. View the contents of the resource_ids.txt file:

cat /home/cloud_user/resource_ids.txt

```
[cloud_user@ip-10-0-1-51 section4-hol1]$ cat /home/cloud_user/resource_ids
.txt
import_server: i-0b9e9b4a625e0fcdc
```

2. Copy the EC2 instance ID displayed in the contents of the file.

3. Open the **main.tf** file to modify it:

vim main.tf

4. At the bottom of the code, insert a new line and add the associated resource named **aws_instance.webserver2** into your main Terraform code:

resource "aws_instance" "webserver2" {

ami = data.aws_ssm_parameter.webserver-ami.value

instance_type = "t3.micro"

```
resource "aws_instance" "webserver2" {
    ami = data.aws_ssm_parameter.webserver-ami.value
    instance_type = "t3.micro"
```

Chapter 06: Terraform CLI

> 5. Press **Escape** and enter **:wq** to save and exit the file.

Import the aws_instance.webserver2 Resource to Your Terraform Configuration

1. Use the terraform import command, the name of the resource in your main code, and the EC2 instance ID to tell Terraform which resource to import:

terraform import aws_instance.webserver2 <COPIED-EC2-INSTANCE-ID>

```
[cloud_user@ip-10-0-1-51 section4-hol1]$ terraform import aws_instance.webserver2 i-0
b9e9b4a625e0fcdc
aws_instance.webserver2: Importing from ID "i-0b9e9b4a625e0fcdc"...
aws_instance.webserver2: Import prepared!
  Prepared aws_instance for import
aws_instance.webserver2: Refreshing state... [id=i-0b9e9b4a625e0fcdc]

Import successful!

The resources that were imported are shown above. These resources are now in
your Terraform state and will henceforth be managed by Terraform.
```

2. View the Terraform state file to verify that the resource has been imported:

vim terraform.tfstate

```
        "vpc_id": "vpc-016ab33b39cdd970a"
      }
    }
  ]
},
{
  "mode": "data",
  "type": "aws_ssm_parameter",
  "name": "webserver-ami",
  "provider": "provider[\"registry.terraform.io/hashicorp/aws\"]",
  "instances": [
    {
      "schema_version": 0,
      "attributes": {
        "arn": "arn:aws:ssm:us-east-1::parameter/aws/service/ami-amazon-linux-lat
est/amzn2-ami-hvm-x86_64-gp2",
        "id": "/aws/service/ami-amazon-linux-latest/amzn2-ami-hvm-x86_64-gp2",
"terraform.tfstate" 599L, 20580C                                        117,1          18%
```

3. Search for the keyword /webserver2 and notice that the **aws_instance** resource with the name webserver2 is listed and has a mode of management.

4. Press '**Escape**' and enter **:q!** to exit the file.

Chapter 06: Terraform CLI

Modify the aws_instance.webserver2 Resource

1. Open the **main.tf file** to modify it:

vim main.tf

2. At the bottom of the file, replace the existing code for the **aws_instance.webserver2 resource** with the following:

resource "aws_instance" "webserver2" {

  ami = data.aws_ssm_parameter.webserver-ami.value

  instance_type = "t3.micro"

}

```
resource "aws_instance" "webserver2" {
    ami = data.aws_ssm_parameter.webserver-ami.value
    instance_type = "t3.micro"
}
```

3. As a best practice, format the code before deployment:

terraform fmt

```
[cloud_user@ip-10-0-1-51 section4-hol1]$ terraform fmt
main.tf
```

4. Deploy the updated code:

terraform apply

```
[cloud_user@ip-10-0-1-51 section4-hol1]$ terraform apply
data.aws_ssm_parameter.webserver-ami: Refreshing state... [id=/aws/service
/ami-amazon-linux-latest/amzn2-ami-hvm-x86_64-gp2]
data.aws_availability_zones.azs: Refreshing state... [id=us-east-1]
aws_key_pair.webserver-key: Refreshing state... [id=webserver-key]
aws_vpc.vpc: Refreshing state... [id=vpc-016ab33b39cdd970a]
aws_instance.webserver2: Refreshing state... [id=i-0b9e9b4a625e0fcdc]
data.aws_route_table.main_route_table: Refreshing state... [id=rtb-0547da9
a7d2fe2569]
aws_security_group.sg: Refreshing state... [id=sg-04549b96ef3fd7c40]
aws_internet_gateway.igw: Refreshing state... [id=igw-0b582d2f59dc799c5]
aws_subnet.subnet: Refreshing state... [id=subnet-0a77868488b07ba8a]
aws_default_route_table.internet_route: Refreshing state... [id=rtb-0547da
9a7d2fe2569]
```

Chapter 06: Terraform CLI

5. Type *yes* and press **Enter** to deploy the code as planned.

```
Do you want to perform these actions?
  Terraform will perform the actions described above.
  Only 'yes' will be accepted to approve.

  Enter a value: yes
```

6. Tear down the infrastructure you just created before moving on:

terraform destroy

```
[cloud_user@ip-10-0-1-51 section4-hol1]$ terraform destroy
data.aws_ssm_parameter.webserver-ami: Refreshing state... [id=/aws/service
/ami-amazon-linux-latest/amzn2-ami-hvm-x86_64-gp2]
data.aws_availability_zones.azs: Refreshing state... [id=us-east-1]
aws_vpc.vpc: Refreshing state... [id=vpc-016ab33b39cdd970a]
aws_key_pair.webserver-key: Refreshing state... [id=webserver-key]
data.aws_route_table.main_route_table: Refreshing state... [id=rtb-0547da9
a7d2fe2569]
aws_internet_gateway.igw: Refreshing state... [id=igw-0b582d2f59dc799c5]
aws_security_group.sg: Refreshing state... [id=sg-04549b96ef3fd7c40]
aws_subnet.subnet: Refreshing state... [id=subnet-0a77868488b07ba8a]
aws_default_route_table.internet_route: Refreshing state... [id=rtb-0547da
9a7d2fe2569]
```

7. When prompted, type *yes* and press **Enter**.

```
Do you really want to destroy all resources?
  Terraform will destroy all your managed infrastructure, as shown above.
  There is no undo. Only 'yes' will be accepted to confirm.

  Enter a value: yes
```

```
aws_vpc.vpc: Destruction complete after 1s

Destroy complete! Resources: 7 destroyed.
[cloud_user@ip-10-0-1-51 section4-hol1]$
```

Lab 6-02: Using Terraform CLI Commands (workspace and state) to Manipulate a Terraform Deployment

Introduction

Chapter 06: Terraform CLI

In this hands-on lab, you will create two distinct, parallel environments against the same Terraform code using the terraform workspace command. You will also use the terraform state command to see what resources are being tracked in the state files of the different workspaces.

Problem

Terraform command-line interface uses the terraform command that takes a variety of subcommands such as terraform init or terraform plan, and it is referred to as Terraform CLI.

Solution

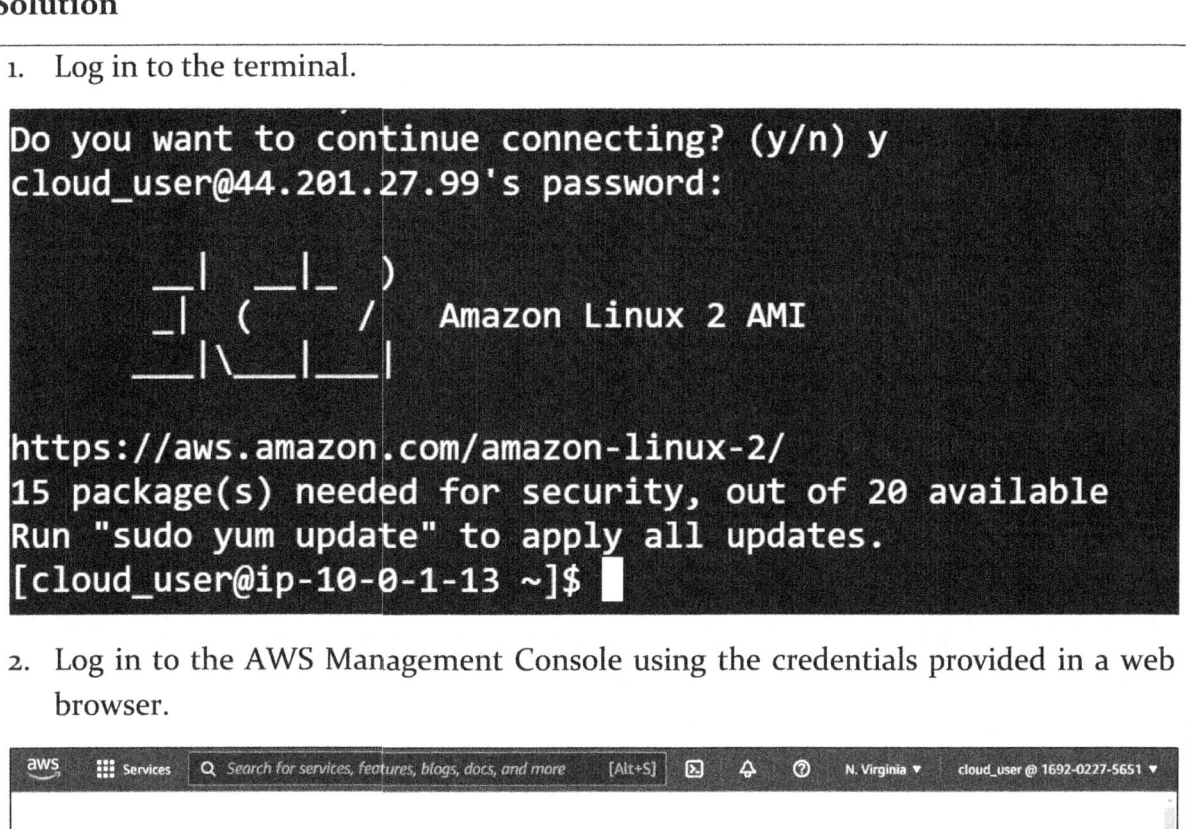

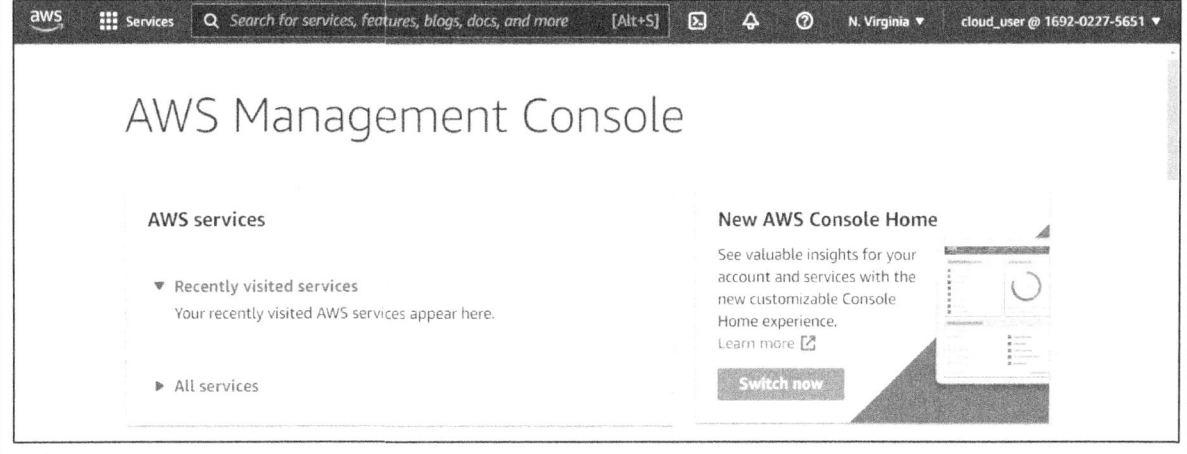

1. Log in to the terminal.

```
Do you want to continue connecting? (y/n) y
cloud_user@44.201.27.99's password:

       __|  __|_  )
       _|  (     /   Amazon Linux 2 AMI
      ___|\___|___|

https://aws.amazon.com/amazon-linux-2/
15 package(s) needed for security, out of 20 available
Run "sudo yum update" to apply all updates.
[cloud_user@ip-10-0-1-13 ~]$
```

2. Log in to the AWS Management Console using the credentials provided in a web browser.

Chapter 06: Terraform CLI

Clone Terraform Code and Switch to the Proper Directory

1. Clone the required code from the provided repository:

git clone https://github.com/12920/IPSpecialist01/blob/main/content-hashicorp-certified-terraform-associate-foundations-master%20(2).zip

```
[cloud_user@ip-10-0-1-13 ~]$ git clone https://github.com/linuxacademy/content-hashicorp-certified-terraform-associate-foundations.git
Cloning into 'content-hashicorp-certified-terraform-associate-foundations'...
remote: Enumerating objects: 76, done.
remote: Counting objects: 100% (76/76), done.
remote: Compressing objects: 100% (67/67), done.
remote: Total 76 (delta 19), reused 59 (delta 6), pack-reused 0
Receiving objects: 100% (76/76), 2.38 MiB | 29.39 MiB/s, done.
Resolving deltas: 100% (19/19), done.
```

2. Switch to the directory where the code is located:

cd content-hashicorp-certified-terraform-associate-foundations/section4-lesson3/

```
[cloud_user@ip-10-0-1-13 ~]$ cd content-hashicorp-certified-terraform-associate-foundations/section4-lesson3/
```

3. List the files in the directory:

ls

```
[cloud_user@ip-10-0-1-13 section4-lesson3]$ ls
main.tf   network.tf   README.md
```

The files in the directory should include **main.tf** and **network.tf**.

Create a New Workspace

1. Check that no workspace other than the default one currently exists:

terraform workspace list

```
[cloud_user@ip-10-0-1-13 section4-lesson3]$ terraform workspace list
* default
```

The output should only show the default workspace, which cannot be deleted.

Chapter 06: Terraform CLI

2. Create a new workspace named test:

terraform workspace new test

```
[cloud_user@ip-10-0-1-13 section4-lesson3]$ terraform workspace new test
Created and switched to workspace "test"!

You're now on a new, empty workspace. Workspaces isolate their state,
so if you run "terraform plan" Terraform will not see any existing state
for this configuration.
```

You will be automatically switched into the newly created test workspace upon successful completion.

Deploy Infrastructure in the Test Workspace and Confirm Deployment via AWS

1. In the test workspace, initialize the working directory and download the required providers:

terraform init

```
* hashicorp/aws: version = "~> 3.74.0"

Terraform has been successfully initialized!

You may now begin working with Terraform. Try running "terraform plan" to s
ee
any changes that are required for your infrastructure. All Terraform comman
ds
should now work.

If you ever set or change modules or backend configuration for Terraform,
rerun this command to reinitialize your working directory. If you forget, o
ther
commands will detect it and remind you to do so if necessary.
```

2. View the contents of the **main.tf file** using the cat command:

cat main.tf

Chapter 06: Terraform CLI

```
data "aws_ssm_parameter" "linuxAmi" {
  name = "/aws/service/ami-amazon-linux-latest/amzn2-ami-hvm-x86_64-gp2"
}

#Create and bootstrap EC2 in us-east-1
resource "aws_instance" "ec2-vm" {
  ami                         = data.aws_ssm_parameter.linuxAmi.value
  instance_type               = "t3.micro"
  associate_public_ip_address = true
  vpc_security_group_ids      = [aws_security_group.sg.id]
  subnet_id                   = aws_subnet.subnet.id
  tags = {
    Name = "${terraform.workspace}-ec2"
  }
}
```

3. Note the configurations in the main.tf code, particularly:

    o AWS is the selected provider

    o If the code is deployed on the default workspace, the resources will be deployed in the us-east-1 region

    o If the code is deployed on any other workspace, the resources will be deployed in the us-west-2 region

    o In the code creating the EC2 virtual machine, we have embedded the $terraform.workspace variable in the Name attribute, so we can easily distinguish those resources created within their respective workspaces by their name: **<workspace name>-ec2**

4. View the contents of the **network.tf** file:

cat network.tf

Chapter 06: Terraform CLI

```
      from_port   = 22
      to_port     = 22
      protocol    = "tcp"
      cidr_blocks = ["0.0.0.0/0"]
    }
    egress {
      from_port   = 0
      to_port     = 0
      protocol    = "-1"
      cidr_blocks = ["0.0.0.0/0"]
    }
    tags = {
      Name = "${terraform.workspace}-securitygroup"
    }
  }
}
```

5. Note the configurations in the **network.tf** code, particularly:
   - In the code creating the security group resource, we have embedded the $terraform. Workspace variable in the Name attribute; so, we can easily distinguish those resources created within their respective workspaces by their name: **<workspace name>-securitygroup**.

6. Deploy the code in the test workspace:

terraform apply --auto-approve

```
[cloud_user@ip-10-0-1-13 section4-lesson3]$ terraform apply --auto-approve
data.aws_availability_zones.azs: Refreshing state...
data.aws_ssm_parameter.linuxAmi: Refreshing state...
aws_vpc.vpc_master: Creating...
aws_vpc.vpc_master: Creation complete after 4s [id=vpc-0ed135385037501eb]
aws_subnet.subnet: Creating...
aws_security_group.sg: Creating...
aws_subnet.subnet: Creation complete after 1s [id=subnet-0004729189778317a]
aws_security_group.sg: Creation complete after 4s [id=sg-0dd685a076a08bd6a]
aws_instance.ec2-vm: Creating...
aws_instance.ec2-vm: Still creating... [10s elapsed]
aws_instance.ec2-vm: Creation complete after 15s [id=i-0cf207490c3ae31db]

Apply complete! Resources: 4 added, 0 changed, 0 destroyed.
```

Chapter 06: Terraform CLI

7. Once the code has been executed successfully, confirm that Terraform is tracking resources in this workspace:

terraform state list

```
[cloud_user@ip-10-0-1-13 section4-lesson3]$ terraform state list
data.aws_availability_zones.azs
data.aws_ssm_parameter.linuxAmi
aws_instance.ec2-vm
aws_security_group.sg
aws_subnet.subnet
aws_vpc.vpc_master
```

8. Switch over to the default workspace:

terraform workspace select default

```
[cloud_user@ip-10-0-1-13 section4-lesson3]$ terraform workspace select default
Switched to workspace "default".
```

9. Confirm that Terraform is currently not tracking any resources in this workspace, as nothing has been deployed:

terraform state list

```
[cloud_user@ip-10-0-1-13 section4-lesson3]$ terraform state list
No state file was found!

State management commands require a state file. Run this command
in a directory where Terraform has been run or use the -state flag
to point the command to a specific state location.
```

The return output should say that No state file was found for this workspace.

10. Verify that the deployment in the test workspace was successful by viewing the resources that were created in the AWS Management Console:

    o   Navigate to the AWS Management Console in your browser

Chapter 06: Terraform CLI

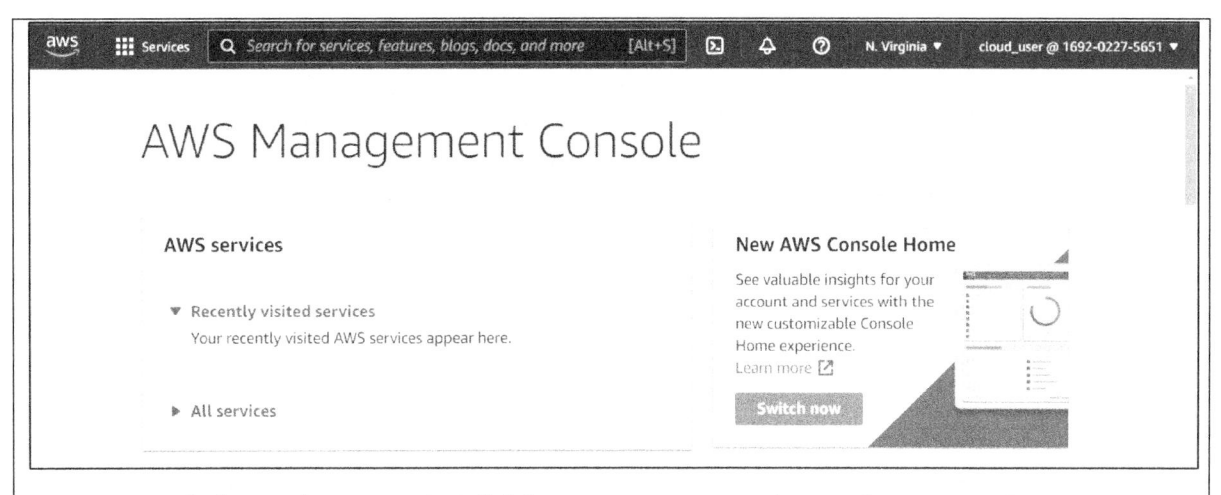

- Click on **"N. Virginia"** (the *us-east-1* region) at the top-right to engage the *Region* drop-down, and select **US West (Oregon)** or **us-west-2**.

- Expand the *Services* drop-down and select **EC2**.

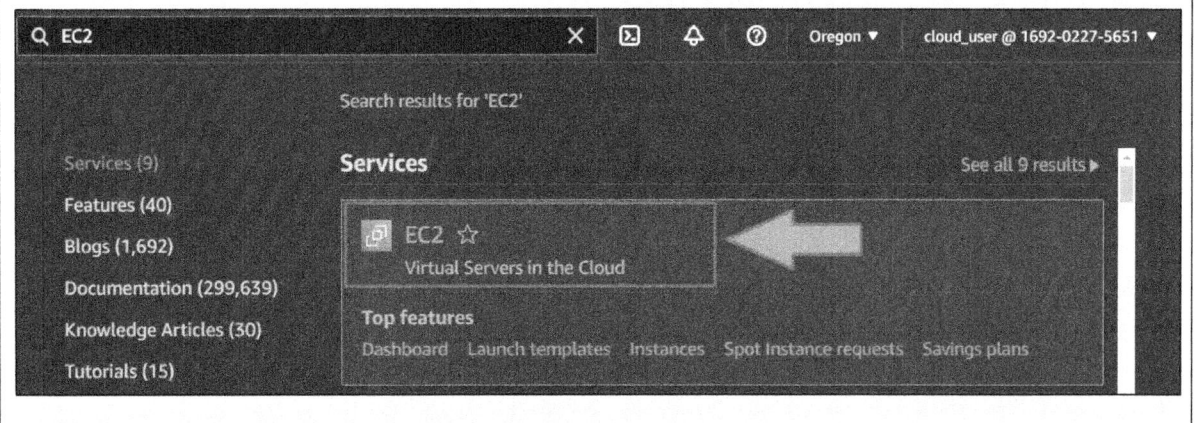

- On the *Resources* page, click **Instances**.

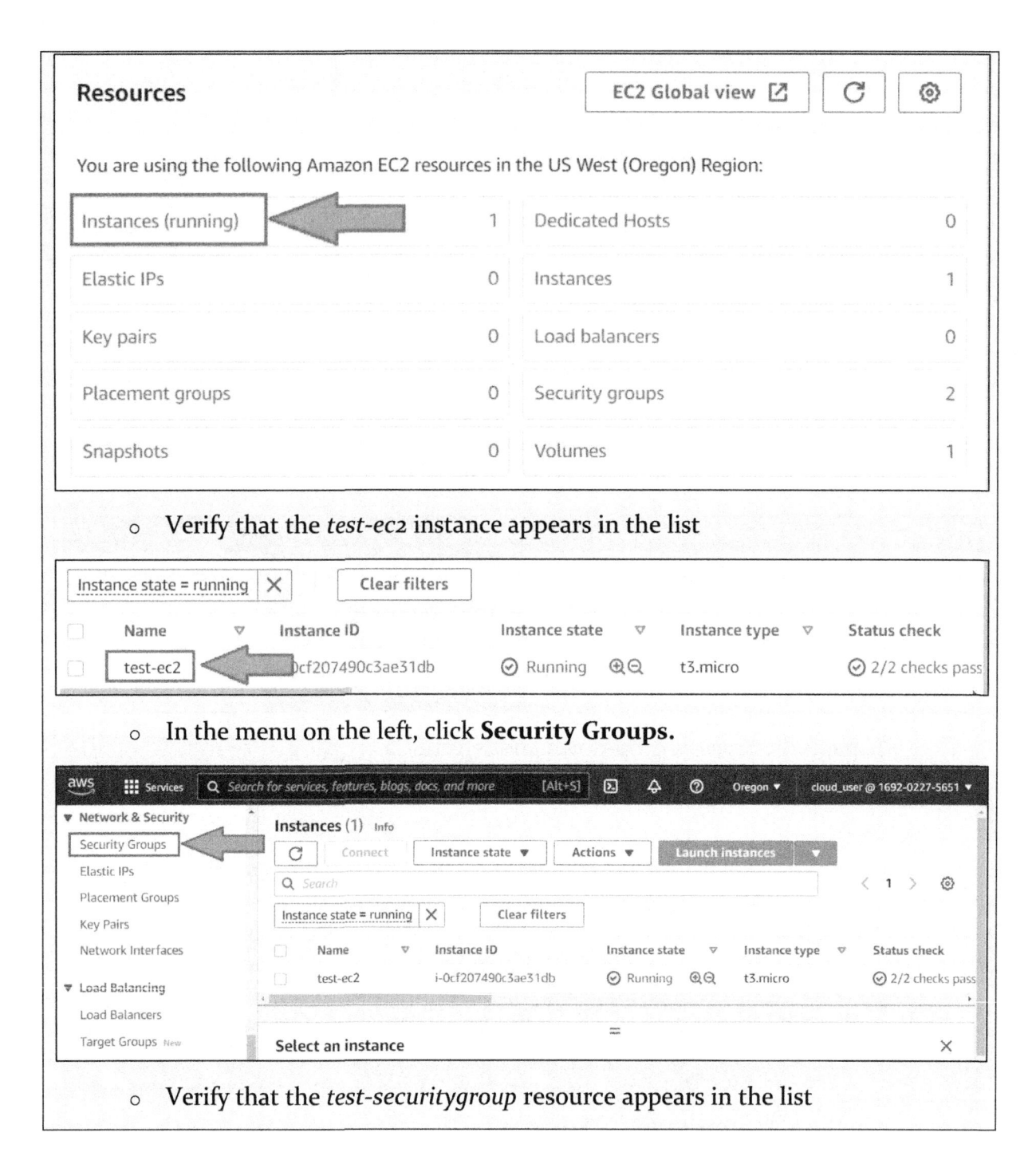

Chapter 06: Terraform CLI

Resources		EC2 Global view		

You are using the following Amazon EC2 resources in the US West (Oregon) Region:

Instances (running)	1	Dedicated Hosts	0
Elastic IPs	0	Instances	1
Key pairs	0	Load balancers	0
Placement groups	0	Security groups	2
Snapshots	0	Volumes	1

- Verify that the *test-ec2* instance appears in the list

Name	Instance ID	Instance state	Instance type	Status check
test-ec2	0cf207490c3ae31db	⊘ Running ⊕⊖	t3.micro	⊘ 2/2 checks pass

- In the menu on the left, click **Security Groups**.

▼ Network & Security
  Security Groups
  Elastic IPs
  Placement Groups
  Key Pairs
  Network Interfaces
▼ Load Balancing
  Load Balancers
  Target Groups New

Instances (1) Info

Name	Instance ID	Instance state	Instance type	Status check
test-ec2	i-0cf207490c3ae31db	⊘ Running ⊕⊖	t3.micro	⊘ 2/2 checks pass

Select an instance

- Verify that the *test-securitygroup* resource appears in the list

148

Chapter 06: Terraform CLI

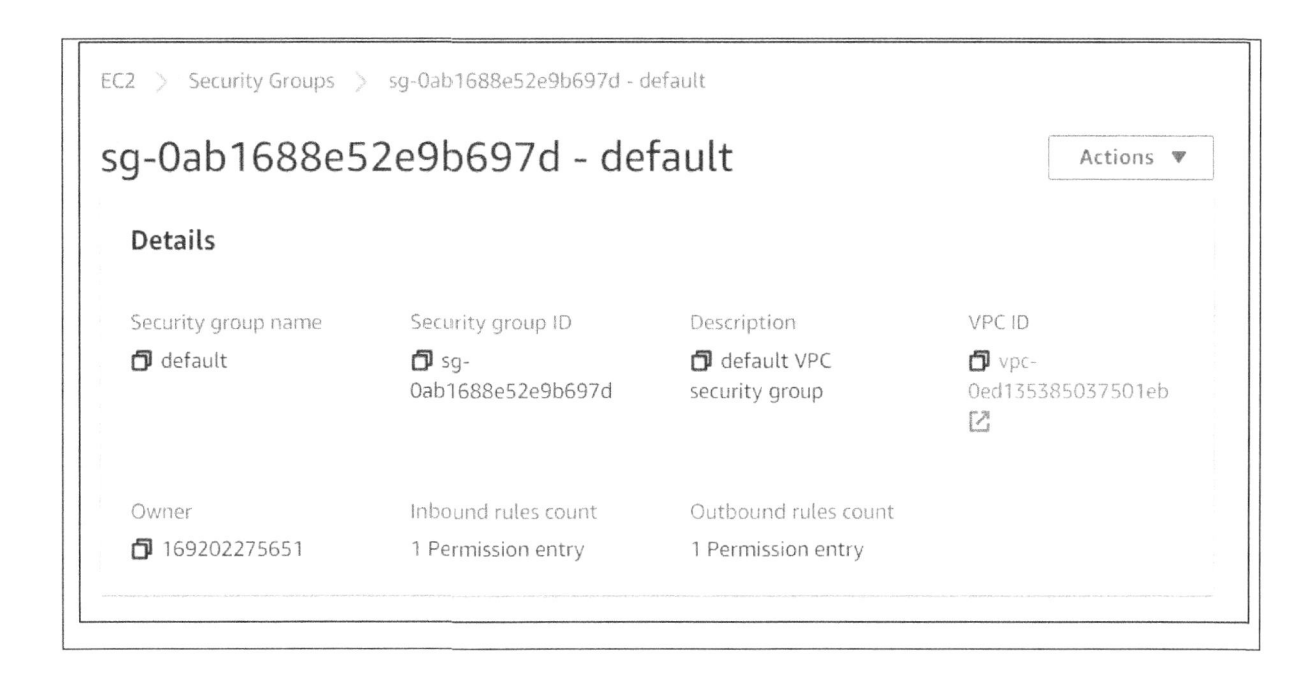

```
EC2  >  Security Groups  >  sg-0ab1688e52e9b697d - default
```

sg-0ab1688e52e9b697d - default   Actions ▼

Details

Security group name	Security group ID	Description	VPC ID
default	sg-0ab1688e52e9b697d	default VPC security group	vpc-0ed135385037501eb

Owner	Inbound rules count	Outbound rules count
169202275651	1 Permission entry	1 Permission entry

Deploy Infrastructure in the Default Workspace and Confirm Deployment via AWS

1. Back in the CLI, verify that you are still within the default workspace:

   terraform state list

   ```
   [cloud_user@ip-10-0-1-13 ~]$ terraform state list
   No state file was found!

   State management commands require a state file. Run this command
   in a directory where Terraform has been run or use the -state flag
   to point the command to a specific state location.
   ```

2. Deploy the code again, this time in the default workspace:

   terraform apply --auto-approve

Chapter 06: Terraform CLI

```
[cloud_user@ip-10-0-1-13 section4-lesson3]$ terraform apply --auto-approve
data.aws_availability_zones.azs: Refreshing state...
data.aws_ssm_parameter.linuxAmi: Refreshing state...
aws_vpc.vpc_master: Creating...
aws_vpc.vpc_master: Creation complete after 1s [id=vpc-098a33acd9c3e0870]
aws_subnet.subnet: Creating...
aws_security_group.sg: Creating...
aws_subnet.subnet: Creation complete after 1s [id=subnet-076860f9e3c48a502]
aws_security_group.sg: Creation complete after 2s [id=sg-0208ca3705e65e019]
aws_instance.ec2-vm: Creating...
aws_instance.ec2-vm: Still creating... [10s elapsed]
aws_instance.ec2-vm: Creation complete after 13s [id=i-0487be339429fbef1]

Apply complete! Resources: 4 added, 0 changed, 0 destroyed.
```

3. Once the code has been executed successfully, confirm that Terraform is now tracking resources in this workspace:

terraform state list

```
[cloud_user@ip-10-0-1-13 section4-lesson3]$ terraform state list
data.aws_availability_zones.azs
data.aws_ssm_parameter.linuxAmi
aws_instance.ec2-vm
aws_security_group.sg
aws_subnet.subnet
aws_vpc.vpc_master
```

Some resources should now be tracked, including the ones that were spun up by the deployed code.

4. Verify that the deployment in the default workspace was successful by viewing the resources that were created in the AWS Management Console:

    o Navigate to the AWS Management Console in your browser

Chapter 06: Terraform CLI

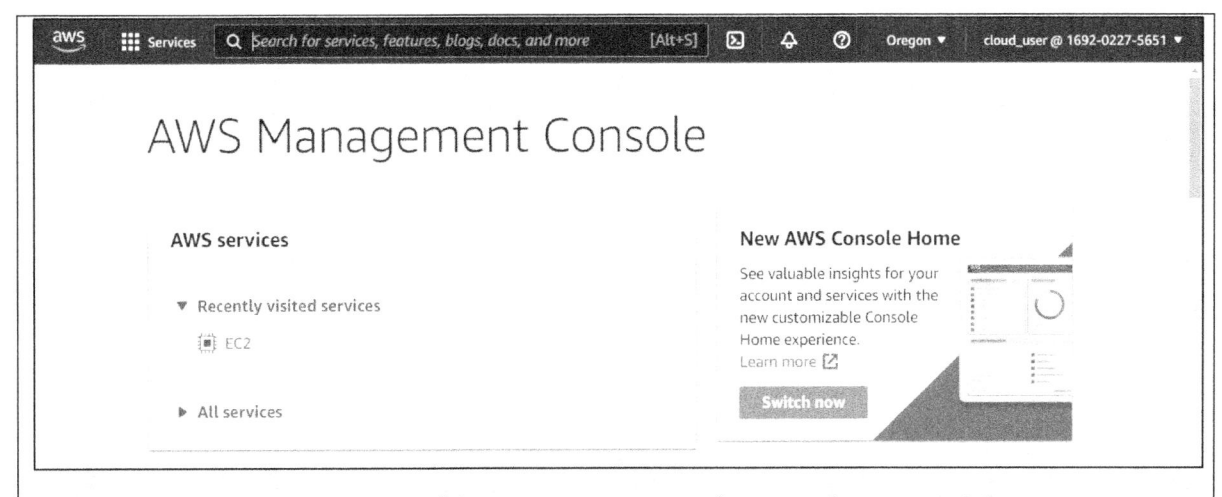

o Click on **Oregon** (the *us-west-2* region) at the top-right to engage the *Region* drop-down, and select **US East (N. Virginia)** or **us-east-1**.

o In the menu on the left, click **Instances**.

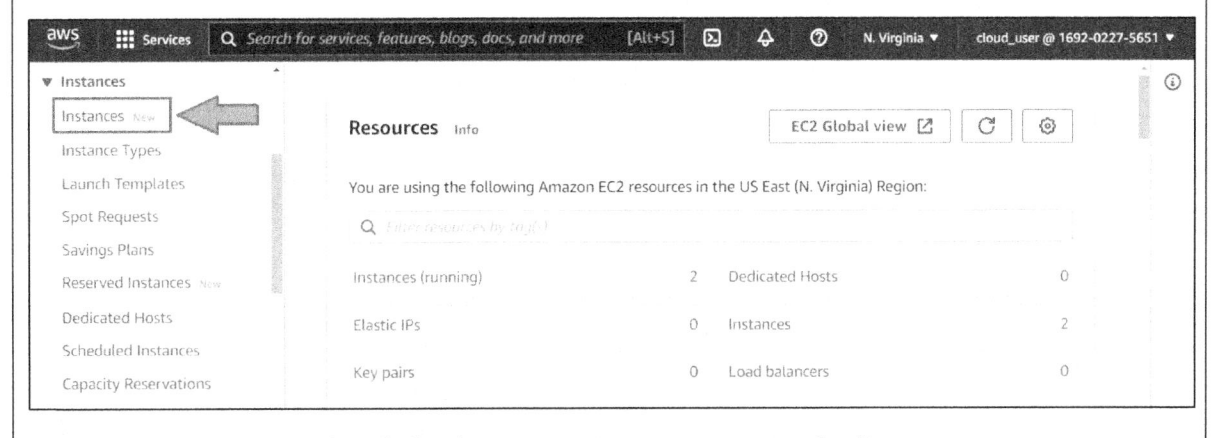

o Verify that the *default-ec2* instance appears in the list.

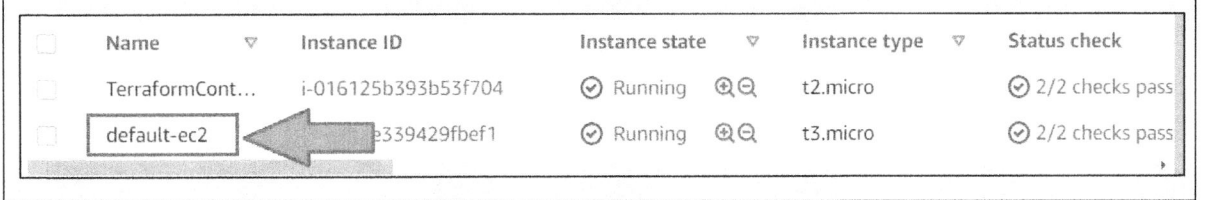

Chapter 06: Terraform CLI

Destroy Resources in the Test Workspace and Delete the Workspace

1. Back in the CLI, switch over to the test workspace:

terraform workspace select test

```
[cloud_user@ip-10-0-1-13 section4-lesson3]$ terraform workspace select test
Switched to workspace "test".
```

2. Tear down the infrastructure you just created in the test workspace:

terraform destroy --auto-approve

```
aws_instance.ec2-vm: Still destroying... [id=i-0cf207490c3ae31db, 20s elapsed]
aws_instance.ec2-vm: Still destroying... [id=i-0cf207490c3ae31db, 30s elapsed]
aws_instance.ec2-vm: Still destroying... [id=i-0cf207490c3ae31db, 40s elapsed]
aws_instance.ec2-vm: Destruction complete after 42s
aws_subnet.subnet: Destroying... [id=subnet-0004729189778317a]
aws_security_group.sg: Destroying... [id=sg-0dd685a076a08bd6a]
aws_security_group.sg: Destruction complete after 0s
aws_subnet.subnet: Destruction complete after 0s
aws_vpc.vpc_master: Destroying... [id=vpc-0ed135385037501eb]
aws_vpc.vpc_master: Destruction complete after 1s

Destroy complete! Resources: 4 destroyed.
```

3. Verify that the resources were terminated in the AWS Management Console:

    o Navigate to the AWS Management Console in your browser

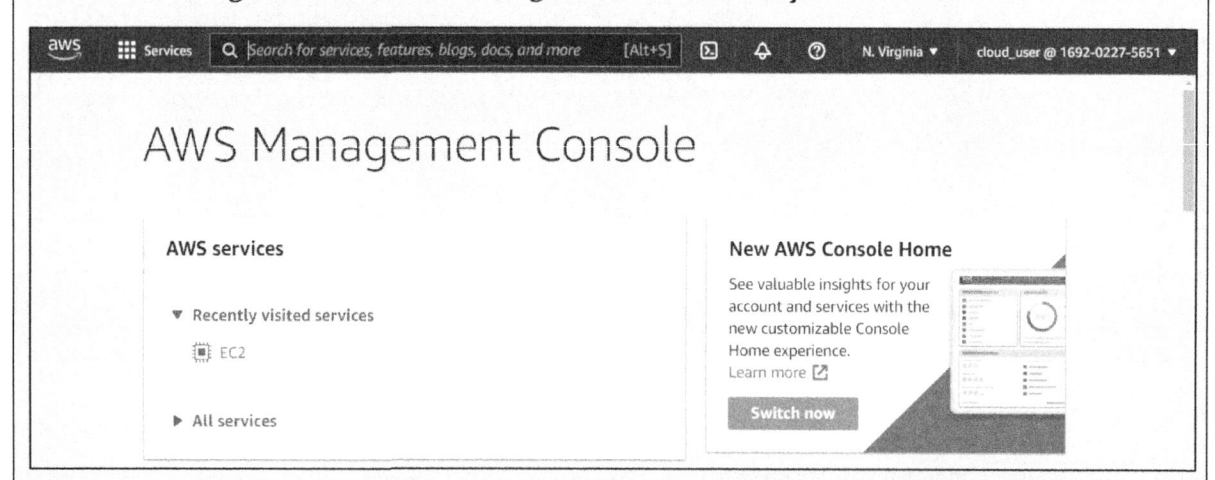

    o Click on **N. Virginia** (the *us-east-1* region) at the top-right to engage the *Region* drop-down, and select **US West (Oregon)** or **us-west-2**.

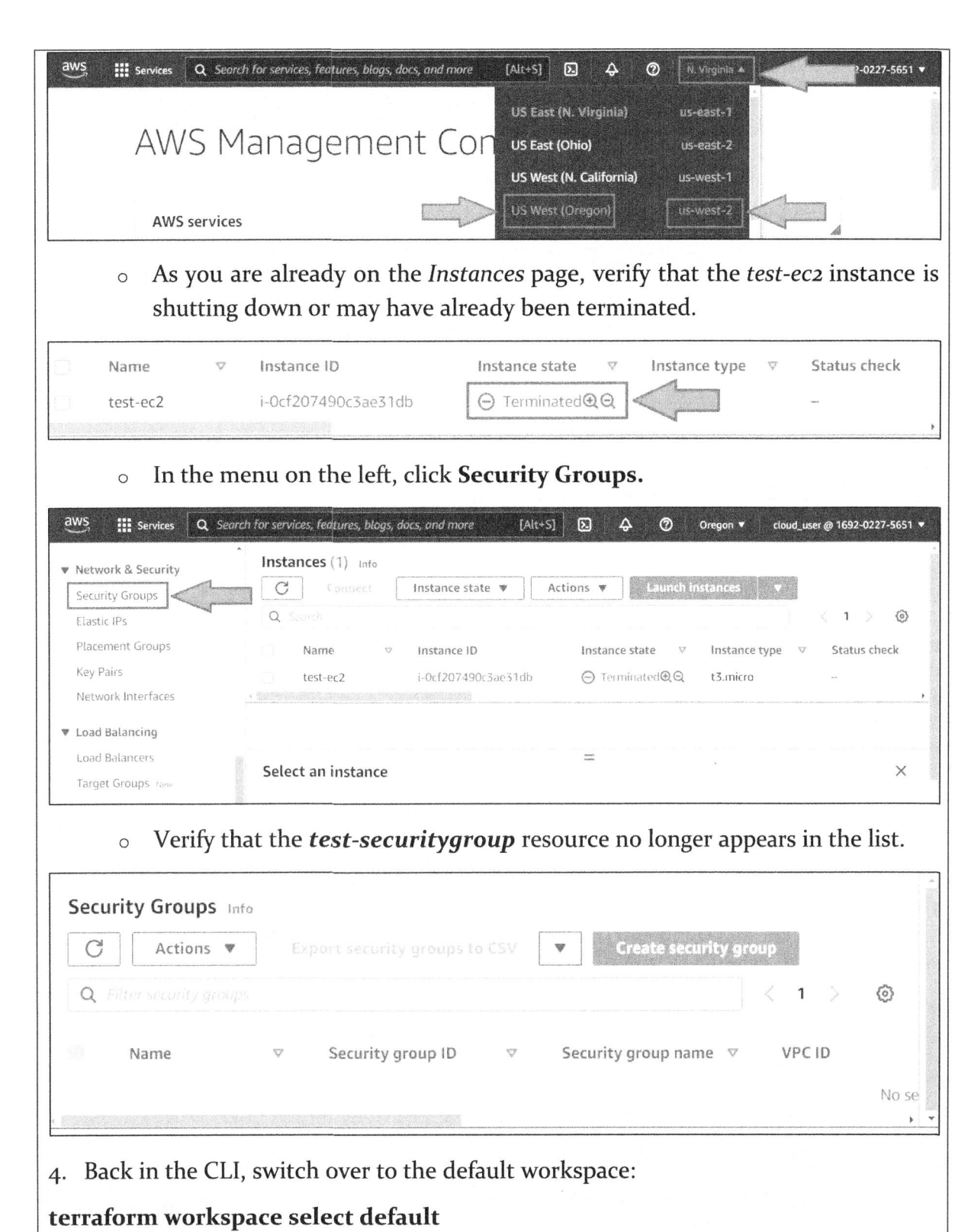

Chapter 06: Terraform CLI

- As you are already on the *Instances* page, verify that the *test-ec2* instance is shutting down or may have already been terminated.

- In the menu on the left, click **Security Groups.**

- Verify that the *test-securitygroup* resource no longer appears in the list.

4. Back in the CLI, switch over to the default workspace:

terraform workspace select default

Chapter 06: Terraform CLI

```
[cloud_user@ip-10-0-1-13 section4-lesson3]$ terraform workspace select default
Switched to workspace "default".
```

5. Delete the test workspace:

terraform workspace delete test

```
[cloud_user@ip-10-0-1-13 section4-lesson3]$ terraform workspace delete test
Deleted workspace "test"!
```

6. Tear down the infrastructure you just created in the default workspace before moving on:

terraform destroy --auto-approve

```
aws_security_group.sg: Refreshing state... [id=sg-0208ca3705e65e019]
aws_subnet.subnet: Refreshing state... [id=subnet-076860f9e3c48a502]
aws_instance.ec2-vm: Refreshing state... [id=i-0487be339429fbef1]
aws_instance.ec2-vm: Destroying... [id=i-0487be339429fbef1]
aws_instance.ec2-vm: Still destroying... [id=i-0487be339429fbef1, 10s elapsed]
aws_instance.ec2-vm: Destruction complete after 20s
aws_subnet.subnet: Destroying... [id=subnet-076860f9e3c48a502]
aws_security_group.sg: Destroying... [id=sg-0208ca3705e65e019]
aws_security_group.sg: Destruction complete after 0s
aws_subnet.subnet: Destruction complete after 0s
aws_vpc.vpc_master: Destroying... [id=vpc-098a33acd9c3e0870]
aws_vpc.vpc_master: Destruction complete after 1s

Destroy complete! Resources: 4 destroyed.
```

Lab 6-03: Build Infrastructure – Terraform Azure Example

Introduction

Hashicorp Terraform is an open-source IaC (Infrastructure-as-Code) cloud infrastructure provisioning and management platform. It stores infrastructure in configuration files that specify your topology's desired state. Terraform providers enable the management of any infrastructure, including public clouds, private clouds, and SaaS services.

Terraform Providers for Azure Infrastructure

There are various Terraform vendors that provide Azure infrastructure management:

AzureRM - Manage Azure resources and functionality including virtual machines, storage accounts, and networking interfaces with AzureRM.

Azure AD - Manage Azure Active Directory resources including groups, users, service principals, and applications with AzureAD.

AzureDevops - Manage Azure DevOps resources including agents, repositories, projects, pipelines, and queries using AzureDevops.

AzAPI - Use the Azure Resource Manager APIs to manage Azure resources and functionality. This provider adds to the AzureRM provider by allowing you to handle Azure resources that have not been released.

Azure Stack - Control virtual machines, DNS, VNets, and storage in Azure Stack.

Benefits of Terraform with Azure

Common IaC software

Terraform Azure providers give you the ability to control all of your Azure infrastructure with the same declarative syntax and tooling. These services allow you to:

- Management groups, policies, users, groups, and policies are all basic platform functions.
- To automate routine infrastructure and application deployments, use Azure DevOps Projects and pipelines.
- Provide Azure resources that your applications demand.

Automate Infrastructure Management

You can configure Azure resources in a repeatable and predictable manner using the Terraform template-based configuration file syntax. Infrastructure automation has the following advantages:

- Reduces the risk of human mistakes in infrastructure deployment and management.
- Creates identical development, test, and production environments by deploying the same template numerous times.
- Creates development and test environments on-demand, which lowers the cost.

Understand Infrastructure Changes before being applied

Understanding the significance and impact of infrastructure changes can be difficult as a resource topology becomes more complicated.

Chapter 06: Terraform CLI

Users can utilize the Terraform CLI to validate and preview infrastructure changes before applying the plan. There are various advantages to safely previewing infrastructure changes:

- Understanding proposed changes and their consequences allow team members to collaborate more successfully.
- Early in the development phase, unintended alterations might be detected.

Problem

A company's on-premises and cloud resources are employed for a variety of purposes. One of the key goals of these resources is to specify configuration files in a human-readable format that you can version, reuse, and share. The infrastructure and management team wants to provide a standardised approach for provisioning and managing all of your infrastructure throughout its lifecycle. How it would be possible?

Solution

You can use Terraform configuration to deploy Azure resources group that hold multiple resources and you can easily use this solution to specify configuration files in a human-readable format that you can version, reuse, and share.

To perform this lab, you must have:

- Terraform 0.14.9 or later installed
- Azure CLI tool installed

Step 01: Install the Azure CLI tool

Note: You can use this CLI tool to authenticate with Azure

1. Run the following command in your terminal.

Invoke-WebRequest -Uri https://aka.ms/installazurecliwindows -OutFile .\AzureCLI.msi; Start-Process msiexec.exe -Wait -ArgumentList '/I AzureCLI.msi /quiet'; rm .\AzureCLI.msi

```
root@workstation:~# Invoke-WebRequest -Uri https://aka.ms/installazurecliwindows -OutFile .\AzureCLI.msi; Start-Process msiexec.exe -Wait -ArgumentList '/I AzureCLI.msi /quiet'; rm .\AzureCLI.msi
```

Note: This command will be given an output showing the successful installation of Azure CLI.

Step 02: Authenticate using the Azure CLI

Chapter 06: Terraform CLI

2. Run the following command to use Azure CLI to setup the account permissions locally.

az login

```
root@workstation:~#
root@workstation:~# az login
```

3. When your browser loads, you will be prompted to provide your Azure login credentials. Your terminal will display your subscription information after successful authentication. An example is shown in the following screenshot.

```
[
  {
    "cloudName": "AzureCloud",
    "homeTenantId": "0envbwi39-home-Tenant-Id",
    "id": "35akss-subscription-id",
    "isDefault": true,
    "managedByTenants": [],
    "name": "Subscription-Name",
    "state": "Enabled",
    "tenantId": "0envbwi39-TenantId",
    "user": {
      "name": "your-username@domain.com",
      "type": "user"
    }
  }
]
```

4. Now, run the following command to set the account with Azure CLI.

az account set --subscription "<subscription-id>"

```
root@workstation:~#
root@workstation:~# az account set --subscription "************************"
```

Step 03: Create a Service Principal

5. A Service Principal is an Azure Active Directory application that provides Terraform with the authentication tokens it needs to perform operations on your behalf. Substitute

Chapter 06: Terraform CLI

the subscription ID you specified in the previous step for <SUBSCRIPTION ID> in the following command.

az ad sp create-for-rbac --role="Contributor" --scopes="/subscriptions/<SUBSCRIPTION_ID>"

```
root@workstation:~#
root@workstation:~# az ad sp create-for-rbac --role="Contributor" --scopes="/subscriptions/<SUBSCRIPT
ION_ID>"
```

6. The following output will appear.

```
Creating 'Contributor' role assignment under scope '/subscriptions/35akss-subscription-id'
The output includes credentials that you must protect. Be sure that you do not include these credentials
{
  "appId": "xxxxxx-xxx-xxxx-xxxx-xxxxxxxxxx",
  "displayName": "azure-cli-2022-xxxx",
  "password": "xxxxxx~xxxxxx~xxxxx",
  "tenant": "xxxxx-xxxx-xxxxx-xxxx-xxxxx"
}
```

Step 04: Set up Environmental Variables

7. Rather than preserving these values in your Terraform setup, HashiCorp recommends setting them as environment variables.

Set the following environment variables in your terminal. Make sure the variable values match the ones supplied by Azure in the preceding command.

$ $Env:ARM_CLIENT_ID = "<APPID_VALUE>"
$ $Env:ARM_CLIENT_SECRET = "<PASSWORD_VALUE>"
$ $Env:ARM_SUBSCRIPTION_ID = "<SUBSCRIPTION_ID>"
$ $Env:ARM_TENANT_ID = "<TENANT_VALUE>"

Step 05: Write Configurations

8. Create a folder called **"learn-terraform-azure"** by using the following command.

New-Item -Path "c:\" -Name "learn-terraform-azure" -ItemType "directory"

```
root@workstation:~#
root@workstation:~# New-Item -Path "c:\" -Name "learn-terraform-azure" -ItemType "directory"
>
```

8. After that, create a new file with named "main.tf" and add the following configurations.

Configure the Azure provider

```
terraform {
  required_providers {
    azurerm = {
      source  = "hashicorp/azurerm"
      version = "~> 3.0.2"
    }
  }

  required_version = ">= 1.1.0"
}

provider "azurerm" {
  features {}
}

resource "azurerm_resource_group" "rg" {
  name     = "myTFResourceGroup"
  location = "westus2"
}
```

Chapter 06: Terraform CLI

```
# Configure the Azure provider
terraform {
  required_providers {
    azurerm = {
      source  = "hashicorp/azurerm"
      version = "~> 3.0.2"
    }
  }

  required_version = ">= 1.1.0"
}

provider "azurerm" {
  features {}
}

resource "azurerm_resource_group" "rg" {
  name     = "myTFResourceGroup"
  location = "westus2"
}
```

Note: In this example, the location of your resource group is hardcoded. If you don't have access to the westus2 resource group location, replace it with your Azure region in the main.tf file.

Step 06: Initialize Terraform Configuration

9. Run the following command to initialize the Terraform directory.

terraform init

```
root@workstation:~#
root@workstation:~# terraform init
```

10. You will observe the following output.

Chapter 06: Terraform CLI

```
Initializing modules...

Initializing the backend...

Initializing provider plugins...
- Reusing previous version of hashicorp/random from the dependency lock file
- Reusing previous version of kreuzwerker/docker from the dependency lock file
- Using previously-installed hashicorp/random v3.1.0
- Using previously-installed kreuzwerker/docker v2.16.0

Terraform has been successfully initialized!

You may now begin working with Terraform. Try running "terraform plan" to see
any changes that are required for your infrastructure. All Terraform commands
should now work.

If you ever set or change modules or backend configuration for Terraform,
rerun this command to reinitialize your working directory. If you forget, other
commands will detect it and remind you to do so if necessary.
```

Step 07: Formate and Validate the Configuration

11. All of your configuration files should have consistent formatting. For readability and consistency, the terraform fmt tool automatically updates configurations in the current directory.

Note: Create a new configuration. If any files were modified by Terraform, the names of those files will be printed. Terraform will not return any file names in this situation because your configuration file was already formatted appropriately.

terraform fmt

12. You may also use the following command to ensure that your configuration is syntactically correct and internally consistent.

terraform validate

```
root@workstation:~# terraform fmt
root@workstation:~# terraform validate
Success! The configuration is valid.

root@workstation:~#
```

Step 08: Apply Terraform Configuration

13. Run the following command to apply your Terraform configurations.

terraform apply

Chapter 06: Terraform CLI

```
root@workstation:~#
root@workstation:~# terraform apply
```

14. The following sample output will appear.

```
An execution plan has been generated and is shown below.
Resource actions are indicated with the following symbols:
  + create

Terraform will perform the following actions:

  # azurerm_resource_group.rg will be created
  + resource "azurerm_resource_group" "rg" {
      + id       = (known after apply)
      + location = "westus2"
      + name     = "myTFResourceGroup"
    }

Plan: 1 to add, 0 to change, 0 to destroy.

Do you want to perform these actions?
  Terraform will perform the actions described above.
  Only 'yes' will be accepted to approve.

  Enter a value: yes
azurerm_resource_group.rg: Creating...
azurerm_resource_group.rg: Creation complete after 1s [id=/subscriptions/c9ed8610-47a3-4107-a2

Apply complete! Resources: 1 added, 0 changed, 0 destroyed.
```

Note: This output displays the execution plan and will ask for your approval before moving further. If anything in the plan appears to be inaccurate or harmful, you can abort now without affecting your infrastructure. To continue, answer yes to the confirmation question.

Step 09: Inspect the current state

15. Terraform uploads data to a file named terraform.tfstate after you apply your configuration. This file holds the IDs and properties of the resources Terraform produced, allowing it to manage and destroy them in the future.

Chapter 06: Terraform CLI

> **Note:** Do not share or check in your state file to source control because it contains all of the data in your configuration and may also contain sensitive information in plaintext.
>
> Use **terraform show** command to inspect the present state.

Mind Map

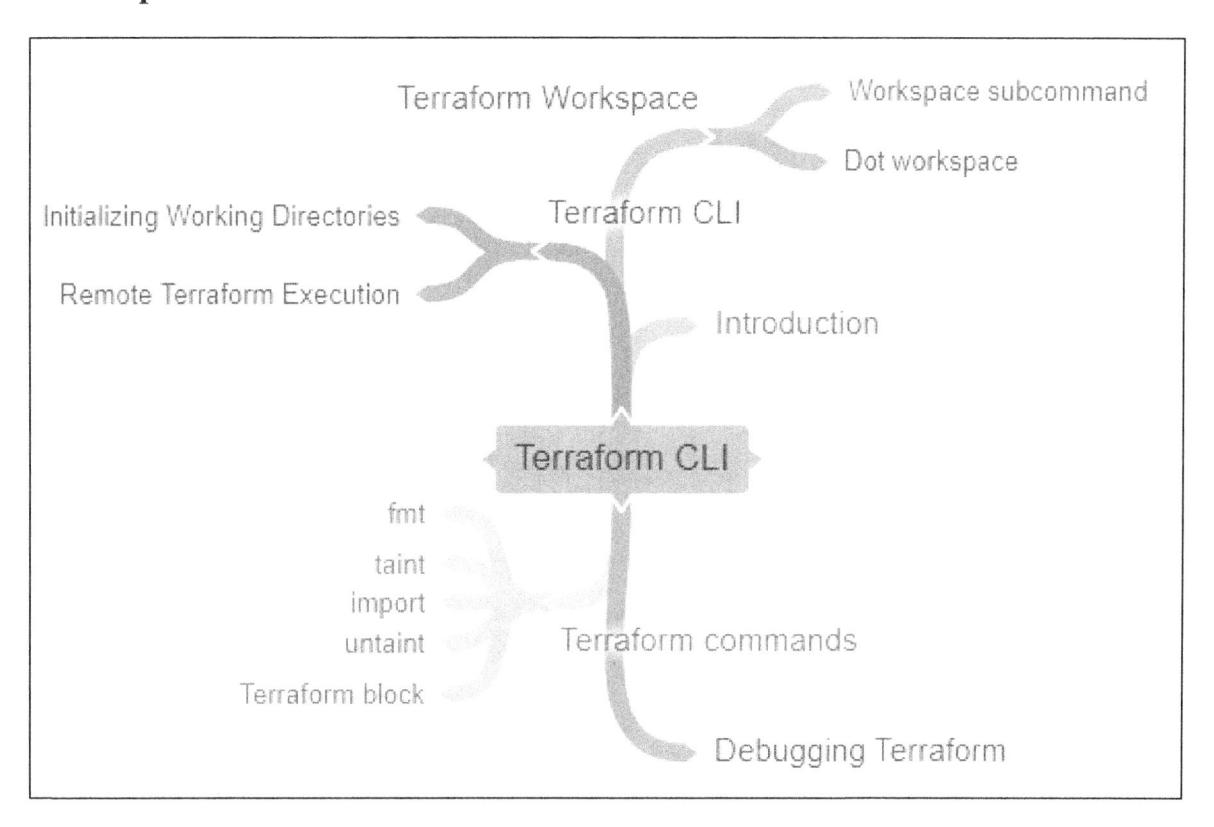

Figure 6-01: Mind Map

Practice Questions

1. _____ command only modifies the look of the code, but it does not change anything else otherwise.

   A. fmt
   B. taint
   C. Import
   D. None of the above

Chapter 06: Terraform CLI

2. The _____ command marks an existing Terraform resource to be deleted and recreated.

A. fmt
B. taint
C. Import
D. None of the above

3. Provisioners only run when a resource is created or destroyed, you can use terraform _____ command to delete and recreate a resource.

A. fmt
B. taint
C. Import
D. None of the above

4. You can use the Terraform _____ command to replace misbehaving resources forcefully.

A. fmt
B. taint
C. Import
D. None of the above

5. _____ command takes an existing resource that Terraform manages and maps it to a resource within Terraform code using an ID.

A. fmt
B. taint
C. Import
D. None of the above

6. The configuration block only allows constant _____, and you cannot use named resources or variables within this block.

A. Values
B. String
C. Both of the above

D. None of the above

7. Terraform only run if the Terraform binary version is greater than version ____.
A. 11
B. 12
C. 13
D. 14

8. Each workspace tracks a separate _____ copy of the state file against Terraform code in that directory.
A. Dependent
B. Independent
C. Both of the above
D. None of the above

9. In the Terraform workspace, select command _____ to the workspace of your choice that already exists.
A. Selects
B. Switches
C. Both of the above
D. None of the above

10. If the terraform dot workspace variable has the value default when the Terraform applies is executed, it will spin up to _____ instances.
A. Three
B. Five
C. Seven
D. Nine

11. If the workspace is not default, then _____ instance will be spun up.
A. One
B. Two

C. Three
D. Four

12. Terraform pulls down the providers when you initialize your different projects using the Terraform _____ command.

A. wget
B. init
C. Both of the above
D. None of the above

13. Terraform state is stored into flat files as _____ data.

A. SQL
B. JSON
C. Both of the above
D. None of the above

14. You can tear down the infrastructure you just created in the test workspace by using _____ command.

A. destroy
B. tear
C. delete
D. None of the above

15. Use the _____ command to view the contents of the webpage.

A. curl
B. view
C. vim
D. None of the above

Chapter 07: Terraform Modules

Introduction

A module is a container for a collection of related resources. Modules can be used to construct lightweight abstractions to describe your infrastructure in terms of its architecture rather than physical things. Every Terraform configuration has at least one root module, which comprises the resources defined in the main working directory .tf files.

A module can call other modules, allowing you to quickly integrate the resources of a child module in the setup. Modules can also be called numerous times in the same or different configurations, allowing resource configurations to be packaged and reused.

Accessing and Using Terraform Module

The Terraform Module is just another folder or collection of Terraform code files. You reference the output of that code in other parts of your Terraform project. It groups together different resources that are used together in a project. The directory which holds the code is called the root module. Once you invoke other modules inside your code, these newly referenced modules are known as child modules, and one can pass inputs and get outputs from these child modules.

> **Note:** The main purpose of these modules is to reuse the code instead of reinventing the wheel.

Accessing Terraform Modules

Modules can be downloaded or referenced from the Terraform Public Registry, which contains a collection of all publicly available modules. On referencing modules from Terraform Public Registry, Terraform downloads them and places them in a directory on a system. You can also host your modules in a private registry hosted by yourself or an organization and reference them in the same way as Public Registry. You can use it when your concern is security and closed source code. In addition, you can have the module code saved in a local folder on your system and reference that folder using its path.

The Module is a reserved keyword, as you can see in the snippet of the figure below. Then, you have the name of the module itself. The source module block mainly defines the source where module code resides. It also defines the version of the module and the number of inputs that can be arbitrary.

```
Reserved          Module
keyword           name
    module "my_vpc_module"{
        source = "./modules/vpc"     Module source
        version = "0.0.5"            Module version
        region = var.region          Input parameters
    }
```

Figure 7-01: Terraform Module

Other parameters allowed inside the module block include count, which allows spawning multiple separate instances of the module's resources; for_each parameter. This permits iterating over a complex variable. Providers parameter allows you to tie specific providers to your module, while the depends_on module allows you to set dependencies.

> **EXAM TIP:** As a best practice, when using third-party modules or modules within an organization, you should always require a specific version to ensure that the updates do not cause unwanted effects on your deployments.

Using Terraform Modules

Modules can take an arbitrary number of inputs and written outputs back into your main code. Once you have invoked a module using the module block in your code, you can use these outputs that it returns and plug them back into your code.

The following figure includes the resources referenced from Figure 06-01. It returns the output as subnet_id, which is the subnet ID where we want to spin up an instance on the AWS network. This example would save us from having to write separate code for creating a VPC and subnets in the VPC where we need to spin up our instance.

```
resource "aws_instance" "my_vpc_module"{
    ......# other arguments
    subnet_id = module.my_vpc_module.subnet_id
}
```

Figure 7-02: Using Terraform Module

Interacting with Terraform Module Inputs and Outputs

Terraform module inputs are arbitrarily named parameters that you pass inside the module block. These inputs can be used as a variable inside the module code. Below is an example of how you will declare a module inside your code. This module code is just like any other module code that you may have come across here. You are passing the server-name input variable. Once the module consumes this server-name input variable, you will be using this variable using the standard variable reference notation interval; var. server-name.

```
module "my_vpc_module"{
    source = "./modules/vpc"
    server-name = 'us-east-1'
}
```

Figure 7-03: Terraform Module Inputs

Terraform Module Outputs

The outputs declared inside Terraform module code can be feedback in the root module or your main code. For example, the output invocation convention when using an output returned by a module back inside your main code is the module.<name-of-module>.<name-of-output>

To use the following output module, which has been declared inside your Terraform module code, the convention to use it back inside your main code is module.my_vpc_module.ip_address. This will give you the IP address of the AWS instance, which was created and calculated inside your module and is feedback to your Terraform code.

```
output = "ip_address"{
    value = aws_instance.private_ip
}
```

Figure 7-04: Terraform Module Outputs

Lab 7-01: Building and Testing a Basic Terraform Module

Introduction

A module is a container for a collection of related resources. Every Terraform configuration has at least one root module, which is made up of the resources defined in the main working directory's .tf files. A module can call other modules, allowing you to quickly integrate the resources of a child module in the setup. Modules can also be called numerous times in the same or different configurations, allowing resource configurations to be packaged and reused. This page explains how to invoke a module from another module. See Module Development for further information on developing reusable child modules.

Problem

Your company wants to use infrastructure as a code phenomenon to deploy certain instances on their AWS cloud. How will they do it?

Solution

They can use Terraform platform to deploy instances by first creating a main Terraform project folder, and within this folder, they must create a sub-folder that will house all modules. The module would have files main.tf, output.tf, and variable.tf. They will then head back to the main project, write the main Terraform code, and reference the module that we have written back into the main Terraform code using the path for that module.

Step:01 Creating Directory Structure for Terraform Project

Chapter 07: Terraform Modules

1. Log into the Terraform server and check the Terraform status using the **terraform version** command.

```
/ $ ssh cloud_user@54.88.36.135
Host '54.88.36.135' is not in the trusted hosts file.
(ssh-ed25519 fingerprint sha1!! 44:00:90:4f:33:d5:c3:1b:54:e1:3f:cb:d7:97:07:17:a1:16:28:11)
Do you want to continue connecting? (y/n) y
cloud_user@54.88.36.135's password:

       __|  __|_  )
       _|  (     /   Amazon Linux 2 AMI
      ___|\___|___|

https://aws.amazon.com/amazon-linux-2/
15 package(s) needed for security, out of 20 available
Run "sudo yum update" to apply all updates.
[cloud_user@ip-10-0-1-12 ~]$ terraform version
Terraform v0.14.4

Your version of Terraform is out of date! The latest version
is 1.1.4. You can update by downloading from https://www.terraform.io/downloads.html
[cloud_user@ip-10-0-1-12 ~]$
```

2. If the Terraform version returns, it means that the Terraform is installed.

```
Your version of Terraform is out of date! The latest version
is 1.1.4. You can update by downloading from https://www.terraform.io/downloads.html
```

3. Create a new main directory using the **mkdir terraform_project** command. Switch to this directory using the **cd terraform_project** command.

```
[cloud_user@ip-10-0-1-12 ~]$ mkdir terraform_project
[cloud_user@ip-10-0-1-12 ~]$ cd terraform_project
[cloud_user@ip-10-0-1-12 terraform_project]$
```

4. Create a custom directory "modules" and a subdirectory "vpc" using **mkdir -p modules/vpc** command. Switch to the "vpc" directory using the following command:

cd /home/cloud_user/terraform_project/modules/vpc/

```
[cloud_user@ip-10-0-1-12 terraform_project]$ mkdir -p modules/vpc
[cloud_user@ip-10-0-1-12 terraform_project]$ cd /home/cloud_user/terraform_project/modules/vpc/
[cloud_user@ip-10-0-1-12 vpc]$
```

Step: 02 Write Terraform VPC Module Code

1. Create a new file in the vpc directory, namely "main.tf" using the following command:

Chapter 07: Terraform Modules

vim main.tf

2. In the file, insert the following code:

```
provider "aws" {
  region = var.region
}

resource "aws_vpc" "this" {
  cidr_block = "10.0.0.0/16"
}

resource "aws_subnet" "this" {
  vpc_id     = aws_vpc.this.id
  cidr_block = "10.0.1.0/24"
}

data "aws_ssm_parameter" "this" {
  name = "/aws/service/ami-amazon-linux-latest/amzn2-ami-hvm-x86_64-gp2"
}
```

3. To save and exit the file, enter **Escape** and enter the following command:

:wq

4. Create a new file, namely **variable.tf**, by using the following command:

vim variable.tf

5. In the file, insert the following code:

```
variable "region" {
  type    = string
  default = "us-east-1"
}
```

6. To save and exit the file, hit **Escape** and enter the following command:

:wq

7. Create a new file, namely outputs.tf, by using the following command:

vim outputs.tf

8. In the file, insert the following code:

Chapter 07: Terraform Modules

```
output "subnet_id" {
  value = aws_subnet.this.id
}

output "ami_id" {
  value = data.aws_ssm_parameter.this.value
}
```

9. To save and exit the file, hit **Escape** and enter the following command:

:wq

Step: 03 Write Main Terraform Project Code

1. Go to the main project directory by entering the **cd ~/terraform_project** command.

```
[cloud_user@ip-10-0-1-12 vpc]$ cd ~/terraform_project
[cloud_user@ip-10-0-1-12 terraform_project]$
```

2. Create a new file main.tf by using the following command:

vim main.tf

3. Insert the following code in the file. The source block tells us where this code resides. Notice our resource is an AWS instance.

Chapter 07: Terraform Modules

```
on"
{ type = string
default = "us-east-1"
}
provider "aws"
{
    region = var.main_region
}
module "vpc"
{
  source = "./modules/vpc"
  region = var.main_region
}
resource "aws_instance" "my-instance"
{
  ami = module.vpc.ami_id
  subnet_id = module.vpc.subnet_id
  instance_type = "t3.micro"
}
```

4. To save and exit the file, hit **Escape** and enter the following command:

:wq

5. Create a new file, outputs.tf, by using the following command:

vim outputs.tf

6. Insert the following code in the file. This output block returns the private IP of the EC2 instance.

```
utput "PrivateIP"
    description = "Private IP of EC2 instance"
    value       = aws_instance.my-instance.private_ip
```

7. To save and exit the file, hit **Escape** and enter the following command.

:wq

Step:04 Deploy Code and Test Module

Chapter 07: Terraform Modules

1. To prepare for deployment, format the code in all your files using **terraform fmt -recursive** command.

```
[cloud_user@ip-10-0-1-6 terraform_project]$ terraform fmt -recursive
```

2. Get the code being referenced in the module block and initialize the Terraform configuration to collect any relevant providers by using the **terraform init** command.

```
[cloud_user@ip-10-0-1-6 terraform_project]$ terraform init
Initializing modules...
- vpc in modules/vpc

Initializing the backend...

Initializing provider plugins...
- Finding latest version of hashicorp/aws...
- Installing hashicorp/aws v3.26.0...
- Installed hashicorp/aws v3.26.0 (signed by HashiCorp)

Terraform has created a lock file .terraform.lock.hcl to record the provider
selections it made above. Include this file in your version control repository
so that Terraform can guarantee to make the same selections by default when
you run "terraform init" in the future.

Terraform has been successfully initialized!

You may now begin working with Terraform. Try running "terraform plan" to see
any changes that are required for your infrastructure. All Terraform commands
should now work.

If you ever set or change modules or backend configuration for Terraform,
rerun this command to reinitialize your working directory. If you forget, other
commands will detect it and remind you to do so if necessary.
[cloud_user@ip-10-0-1-6 terraform_project]$
```

3. Validate the code for any syntax, parameter, or attribute problems in Terraform resources that could prevent it from deploying properly; use the **terraform validate** command in the shell. You should be notified that the configuration is correct.

```
[cloud_user@ip-10-0-1-6 terraform_project]$ terraform validate
Success! The configuration is valid.

[cloud_user@ip-10-0-1-6 terraform_project]$
```

Chapter 07: Terraform Modules

4. Review the steps that will be taken when the Terraform code is deployed by using **terraform plan** command. In this scenario, it will construct three resources: the EC2 instance set up in the root code and any resources set up in the module.

```
# module.vpc.aws_vpc.this will be created
+ resource "aws_vpc" "this" {
    + arn                                = (known after apply)
    + assign_generated_ipv6_cidr_block   = false
    + cidr_block                         = "10.0.0.0/16"
    + default_network_acl_id             = (known after apply)
    + default_route_table_id             = (known after apply)
    + default_security_group_id          = (known after apply)
    + dhcp_options_id                    = (known after apply)
    + enable_classiclink                 = (known after apply)
    + enable_classiclink_dns_support     = (known after apply)
    + enable_dns_hostnames               = (known after apply)
    + enable_dns_support                 = true
    + id                                 = (known after apply)
    + instance_tenancy                   = "default"
    + ipv6_association_id                = (known after apply)
    + ipv6_cidr_block                    = (known after apply)
    + main_route_table_id                = (known after apply)
    + owner_id                           = (known after apply)
  }

lan: 3 to add, 0 to change, 0 to destroy.
```

5. Deploy the code by using **terraform apply --auto-approve** command. Note that three resources have been produced in the output, and the private IP address of the EC2 instance has been returned, as specified in the outputs.tf file in the main project code.

```
module.vpc.aws_vpc.this: Creating...
module.vpc.aws_vpc.this: Creation complete after 1s [id=vpc-0d4c709689a09c508]
module.vpc.aws_subnet.this: Creating...
module.vpc.aws_subnet.this: Creation complete after 0s [id=subnet-071ee7f3005c9baec]
aws_instance.my-instance: Creating...
aws_instance.my-instance: Still creating... [10s elapsed]
aws_instance.my-instance: Creation complete after 12s [id=i-0fefe091e1db50397]

Apply complete! Resources: 3 added, 0 changed, 0 destroyed.

Outputs:

PrivateIP = "10.0.1.221"
[cloud_user@ip-10-0-1-6 terraform_project]$
```

6. In the state file, you can see all the resources that Terraform has built and is presently tracking by using the **terraform state list** command.

```
[cloud_user@ip-10-0-1-6 terraform_project]$ terraform state list
aws_instance.my-instance
module.vpc.data.aws_ssm_parameter.this
module.vpc.aws_subnet.this
module.vpc.aws_vpc.this
[cloud_user@ip-10-0-1-6 terraform_project]$
```

7. Delete the infrastructure by entering terraform destroy command. Enter yes when they ask for confirmation.

```
Do you really want to destroy all resources?
  Terraform will destroy all your managed infrastructure, as shown above.
  There is no undo. Only 'yes' will be accepted to confirm.

  Enter a value: yes
```

Terraform Workflow

A workflow, often known as a work pattern, is a defined method of accomplishing a task.

It is tremendously beneficial while working in a group, and it can also be beneficial when working alone. A good workflow allows you to streamline, organize, and reduce the likelihood of errors in a process.

Terraform workflows are made up of five main steps: Write, Init, Plan, Apply, and Destroy. Nonetheless, the specifics of their activities and details differ amongst procedures.

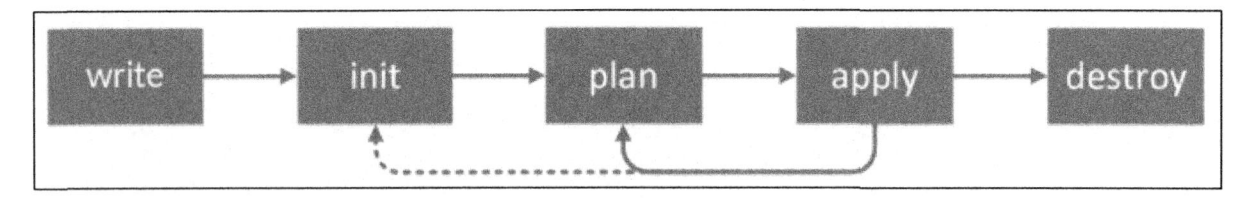

Figure 7-05: Terraform Workflow

Write - This is where you make code modifications.

Init - This is where you set up your code to download the needs you've specified.

Plan - This is where you go over adjustments and decide whether to embrace them or not.

Apply - Accept changes and apply them to real-world infrastructure in this step.

Destroy – Here, you will destroy all of your constructed infrastructures.

Workflow steps

Step # 01

The first step in the Terraform workflow is to write your Terraform configuration in your preferred editor, exactly like you would code. Even if you are working alone, it is normal practice to keep your work in a version-controlled repository.

Step # 02

After writing your code in Terraform, the first thing you should do is initialize it with the command terraform init. The working directory containing Terraform configuration files is initialized using this command. It is safe to use this command more than once.

The init command can be used to do the following:

- Plugin installation
- Child Module Installation
- Backend initialization

Step # 03

We can create an execution plan using the terraform plan command after a successful initialization of the working directory and completion of the plugin download. This is a handy way to check whether the execution plan matches your expectations without making any changes to real resources or the state.

If no changes to resources are discovered by Terraform, the terraform plan implies that no changes to the real infrastructure are necessary.

Step # 04

The terraform apply command is used to build or modify real-world infrastructure. By default, apply looks for configuration changes in the current working directory and makes the necessary adjustments. However, you can additionally provide the location to a previously stored plan file prepared with terraform plan.

Step # 05

The terraform destroy command is used to destroy terraform-controlled infrastructure. We can use the terraform plan -destruct command to check the behavior of the terraform destroy command at any moment.

Lab 7-02: Deploying a VM in AWS Using the Terraform Workflow

Introduction

Infrastructure as code (IaC) manages and supplies computer datacenters using machine-readable definition files rather than physical hardware or interactive setup tools. Terraform is an open-source infrastructure as a code software platform that allows you to manage hundreds of cloud services using a uniform CLI approach. Terraform creates declarative configuration files for cloud APIs. The primary purpose of DevOps is to improve software delivery efficiency and speed. Some tools, such as Terraform, are required to assist businesses with infrastructures such as code and automation. Terraform is transforming the DevOps world by altering how infrastructure is managed and making DevOps execution faster and more efficient.

Problem

Your organization wants you to create AWS instances on their newly deployed Terraform IaC. How will this be done?

Solution

You can utilize the AWS Terraform provider to spin up a VM (EC2 instance) in AWS, following the Terraform workflow of Write > Plan > Apply.

Step 1: Write your Terraform Code

Note: To perform this lab, you need to have your Linux terminal with Terraform Server installed.

1. Log in to the Terraform Cloud Server and save your Terraform code in a new directory called terraform_code, using the command **mkdir terraform_code**

Chapter 07: Terraform Modules

```
[cloud_user@ip-10-0-1-49 ~]$ mkdir terraform_code
```

2. Move to the new directory, using **cd terraform_code**. Create a new file called main.tf in this directory, using **vi main.tf** command.

```
[cloud_user@ip-10-0-1-49 ~]$ mkdir terraform_code
[cloud_user@ip-10-0-1-49 ~]$ cd terraform_code
[cloud_user@ip-10-0-1-49 terraform_code]$ vi main.tf
[cloud_user@ip-10-0-1-49 terraform_code]$
```

3. Enter the code shown in the following snippet into the file to create the VM (EC2 instance) on AWS.

```
" {
  region = "us-east-1"
}
resource "aws_instance" "vm"
  ami           = "DUMMY_VALUE_AMI_ID"
  subnet_id     = "DUMMY_VALUE_SUBNET_ID"
  instance_type = "t3.micro"
  tags = {
    Name = "my-first-tf-node"
  }
}
```

4. Press Escape and enter **:wq** to save and quit the file.

Step 2: Enter AMI and Subnet ID in the Code

1. We have saved AMI and Subnet ID, in the resource ids.txt file on the terminal. To see and copy AMI and Subnet ID, enter **cat /home/cloud_user/resource-ids.txt** in the shell. The values saved in this file for AMI and subnet id will be displayed.

```
[cloud_user@ip-10-0-1-49 terraform_code]$ cat /home/cloud_user/resource_ids.txt
ami: ami-01893222c83843146
subnet_id: subnet-0d397363da72d1a7a
[cloud_user@ip-10-0-1-49 terraform_code]$
```

2. Make a copy of the AMI and Subnet ID values.

Chapter 07: Terraform Modules

3. Open the main.tf file in which your code is stored, using vi main.tf command. Replace the DUMMY_VALUE_AMI_ID with the AMI and add the subnet id value at the DUMMY_VALUE_SUBNET_ID.

```
{
  region = "us-east-1"
}
resource "aws_instance" "vm" {
  ami           = "ami-01893222c83843146"
  subnet_id     = "DUMMY_VALUE_SUBNET_ID"
  instance_type = "t3.micro"
  tags = {
    Name = "my-first-tf-node"
  }
}
```

4. Press Escape and enter **:wq** to save and leave the file.

Step 3: Initialize and Review Your Terraform Code

1. Initialize a Terraform setup and download the providers you will need using **terraform init** command.

Chapter 07: Terraform Modules

```
[cloud_user@ip-10-0-1-49 terraform_code]$ terraform init

Initializing the backend...

Initializing provider plugins...
- Finding latest version of hashicorp/aws...
- Installing hashicorp/aws v3.74.0...
- Installed hashicorp/aws v3.74.0 (self-signed, key ID 34365D9472D7468F)

Partner and community providers are signed by their developers.
If you'd like to know more about provider signing, you can read about it here:
https://www.terraform.io/docs/plugins/signing.html

Terraform has created a lock file .terraform.lock.hcl to record the provider
selections it made above. Include this file in your version control repository
so that Terraform can guarantee to make the same selections by default when
you run "terraform init" in the future.

Terraform has been successfully initialized!

You may now begin working with Terraform. Try running "terraform plan" to see
any changes that are required for your infrastructure. All Terraform commands
should now work.

If you ever set or change modules or backend configuration for Terraform,
rerun this command to reinitialize your working directory. If you forget, other
commands will detect it and remind you to do so if necessary.
[cloud_user@ip-10-0-1-49 terraform_code]$
```

2. Examine the steps taken when your code is deployed using the **terraform plan** command. It will construct the EC2 instance you specified in your code. Notice that only the AMI, instance type, subnet id, and tags properties are there. This is because only they were included in your code.

Chapter 07: Terraform Modules

```
[cloud_user@ip-10-0-1-49 terraform_code]$ terraform plan
An execution plan has been generated and is shown below.
Resource actions are indicated with the following symbols:
  + create

Terraform will perform the following actions:

  # aws_instance.vm will be created
  + resource "aws_instance" "vm" {
      + ami                                  = "ami-01893222c83843146"
      + arn                                  = (known after apply)
      + associate_public_ip_address          = (known after apply)
      + availability_zone                    = (known after apply)
      + cpu_core_count                       = (known after apply)
      + cpu_threads_per_core                 = (known after apply)
      + disable_api_termination              = (known after apply)
      + ebs_optimized                        = (known after apply)
      + get_password_data                    = false
      + host_id                              = (known after apply)
      + id                                   = (known after apply)
      + instance_initiated_shutdown_behavior = (known after apply)
      + instance_state                       = (known after apply)
      + instance_type                        = "t3.micro"
      + ipv6_address_count                   = (known after apply)
      + ipv6_addresses                       = (known after apply)
      + key_name                             = (known after apply)
      + monitoring                           = (known after apply)
```

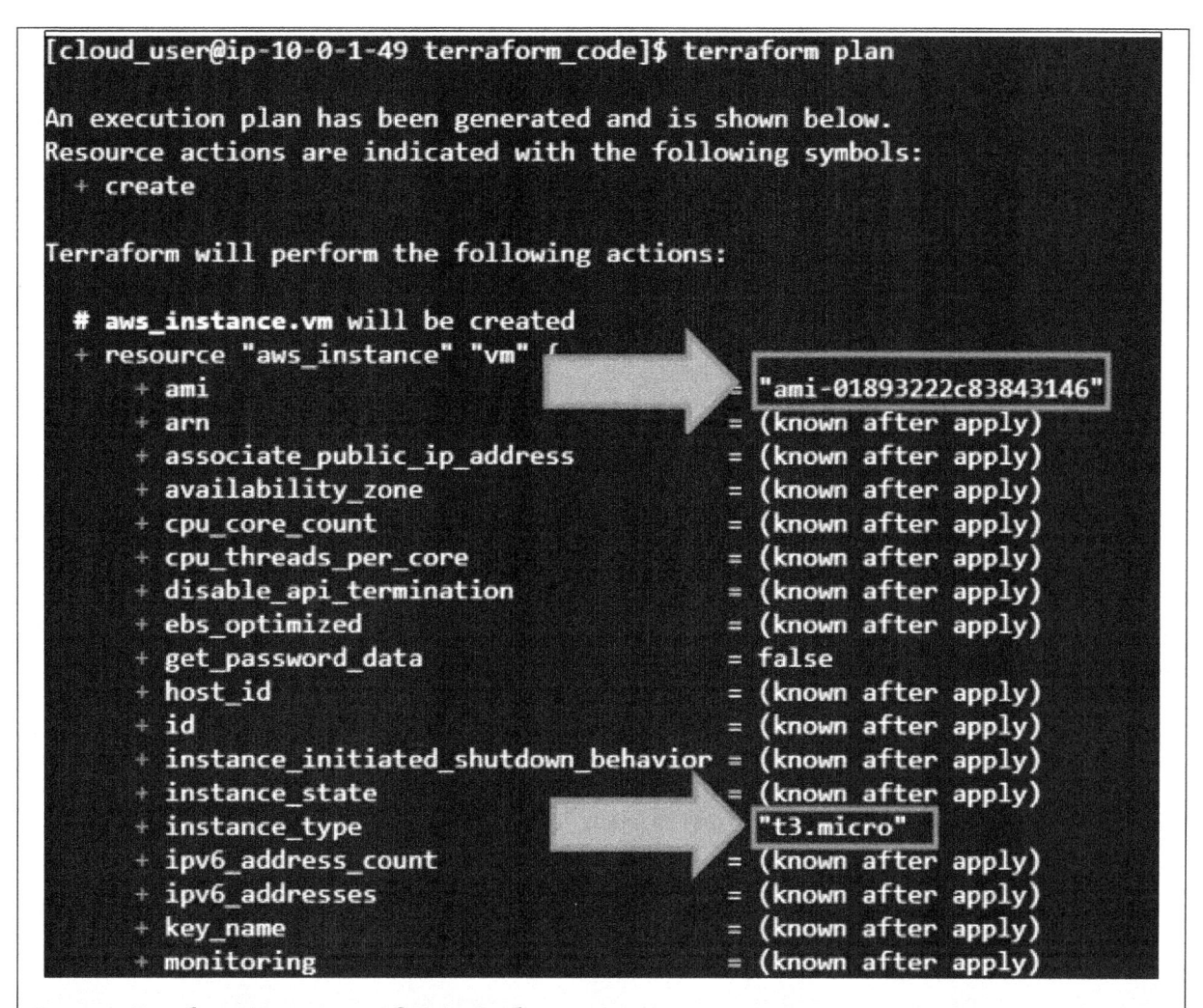

Step 4: Deploy Your Terraform Code

1. Deploy the code using the **terraform apply** command. Type 'yes' and hit Enter when prompted. When the code has been completed successfully, note that one resource has been produced in the output.

Chapter 07: Terraform Modules

```
          + http_put_response_hop_limit = (known after apply)
          + http_tokens                 = (known after apply)
          + instance_metadata_tags      = (known after apply)
        }

      + network_interface {
          + delete_on_termination = (known after apply)
          + device_index          = (known after apply)
          + network_interface_id  = (known after apply)
        }

      + root_block_device {
          + delete_on_termination = (known after apply)
          + device_name           = (known after apply)
          + encrypted             = (known after apply)
          + iops                  = (known after apply)
          + kms_key_id            = (known after apply)
          + tags                  = (known after apply)
          + throughput            = (known after apply)
          + volume_id             = (known after apply)
          + volume_size           = (known after apply)
          + volume_type           = (known after apply)
        }
    }

Plan: 1 to add, 0 to change, 0 to destroy.

Do you want to perform these actions?
  Terraform will perform the actions described above.
  Only 'yes' will be accepted to approve.

  Enter a value: yes
```

2. Log in to AWS Management Console double-check that the resource was created correctly. In your browser, go to the AWS Management Console. Search EC2 in the search bar and select EC2.

Chapter 07: Terraform Modules

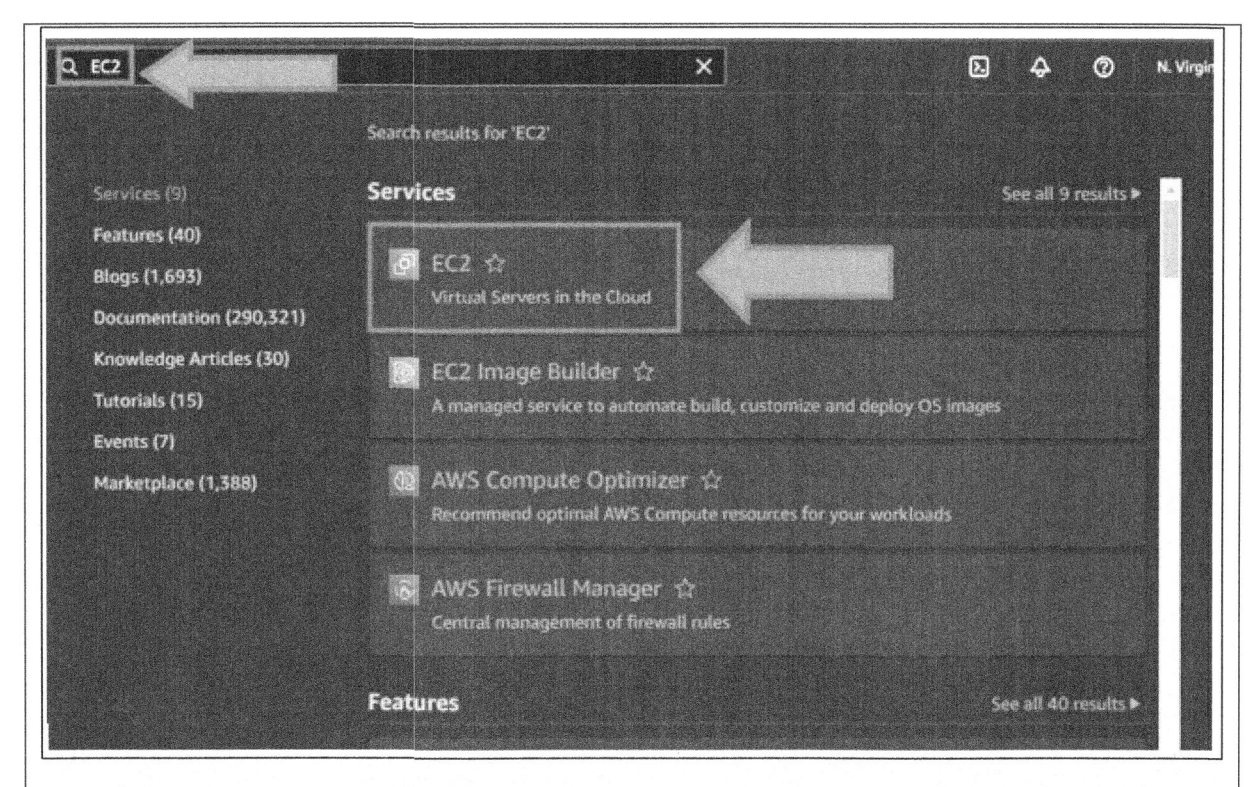

![EC2 search screenshot]

3. Click on **Instances** inside the **Resources** page. Check that the instance named my-first-tf-node is up and running.

![my-first-tf-node running screenshot]

4. Remove the infrastructure you just generated using the **terraform destroy** command. Enter 'yes' when asked.

Chapter 07: Terraform Modules

```
        }

    - root_block_device {
        - delete_on_termination = true -> null
        - device_name           = "/dev/xvda" -> null
        - encrypted             = false -> null
        - iops                  = 100 -> null
        - tags                  = {} -> null
        - throughput            = 0 -> null
        - volume_id             = "vol-0629b2995a18bf72d" -> null
        - volume_size           = 8 -> null
        - volume_type           = "gp2" -> null
      }
  }

Plan: 0 to add, 0 to change, 1 to destroy.

Do you really want to destroy all resources?
  Terraform will destroy all your managed infrastructure, as shown above.
  There is no undo. Only 'yes' will be accepted to confirm.

  Enter a value: yes
```

5. Notice that the EC2 instance you just created has been destroyed.

```
Plan: 0 to add, 0 to change, 1 to destroy.

Do you really want to destroy all resources?
  Terraform will destroy all your managed infrastructure, as shown above.
  There is no undo. Only 'yes' will be accepted to confirm.

  Enter a value: yes

aws_instance.vm: Destroying... [id=i-0c21261fedc643d14]
aws_instance.vm: Still destroying... [id=i-0c21261fedc643d14, 10s elapsed]
aws_instance.vm: Still destroying... [id=i-0c21261fedc643d14, 20s elapsed]
```

6. Verify whether the my-first-tf-node instance is no longer listed in the AWS Management Console by clicking the refresh button on the Instances page.

Name ▽	Instance ID	Instance state ▽	Instance type ▽
TerraformCont...	i-00bf817763611b955	⊘ Running ⊕⊖	t3.micro
my-first-tf-node	i-0c21261fedc643d14	⊖ Terminated ⊕⊖	

Lab 7-03: Automate Infrastructure Deployment with Terraform and Azure Pipeline

Introduction

Terraform is a tool that allows you to build, change, and version infrastructure in a secure and efficient manner. Terraform can manage both mainstream cloud service providers and unique in-house solutions.

Terraform uses configuration files to specify the components required to run a single application or an entire datacenter. Terraform creates an execution plan that explains how it will get to the target state and then executes it to build the infrastructure indicated. Terraform can determine what changed as the configuration changes and provide incremental execution plans that can be applied.

Azure DevOps Generator

Based on the template you select during configuration, Azure DevOps Demo Generator helps you generate team projects on your Azure DevOps Organization with sample material that includes source code, work items, iterations, service endpoints, and build and release specifications.

Problem

The Hard-specialist is an organization that implements an eCommerce website. The development and operation team wants to use an infrastructure management platform to configure the environment with less cost and be applicable for repetitive deployments. How would it be possible?

Solution

Using the Terraform platform and Azure provider, the organization can easily automate the required deployment.

To perform this lab, you will need to have a Microsoft account and Azure DevOps generator.

Chapter 07: Terraform Modules

Step 01: Examine the Terraform File.

Note: You will look at the terraform file that helps you supply the Azure resources you'll need to run the eCommerce website.

1. Navigate to Azure DevOps Generator using your credentials.

2. Select your created organization or create a new organization.

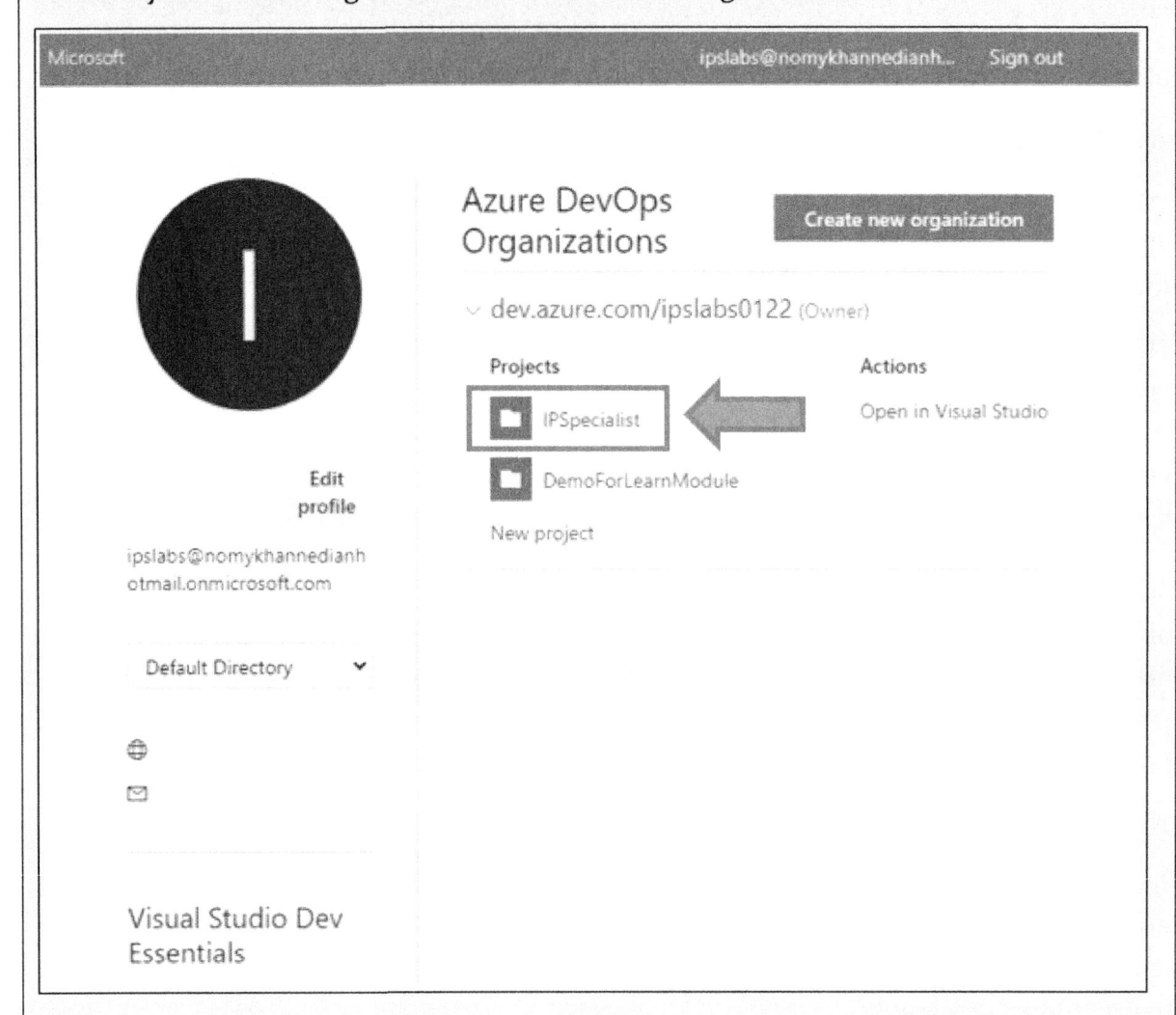

3. If you do not have any project in your organization, then, create a new project.

Chapter 07: Terraform Modules

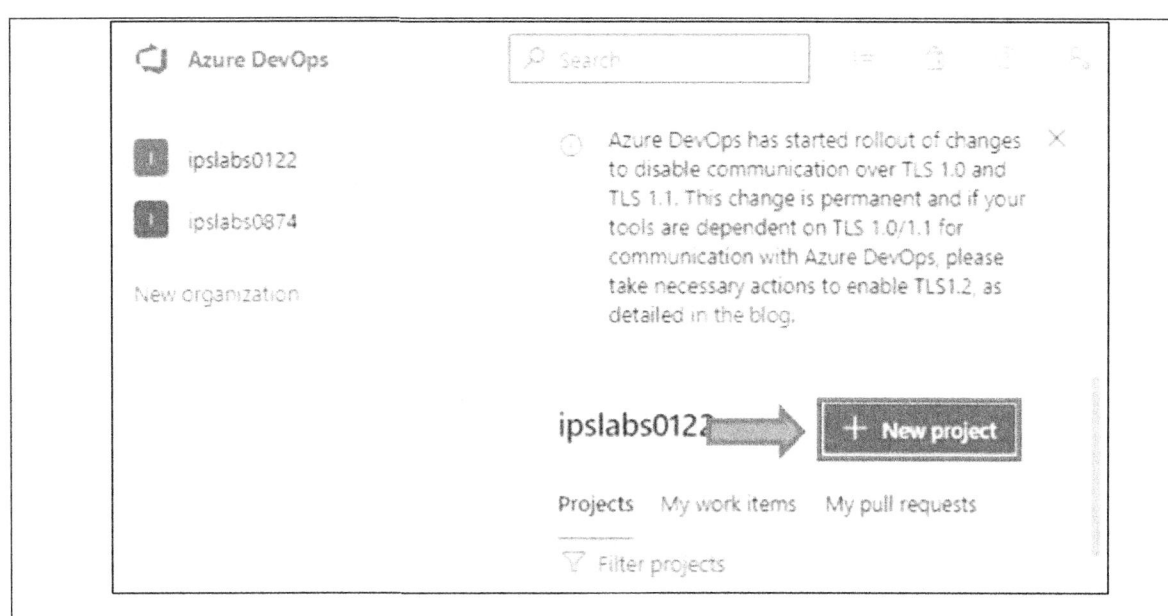

4. Write your project name, select private access, and click on **Create**.

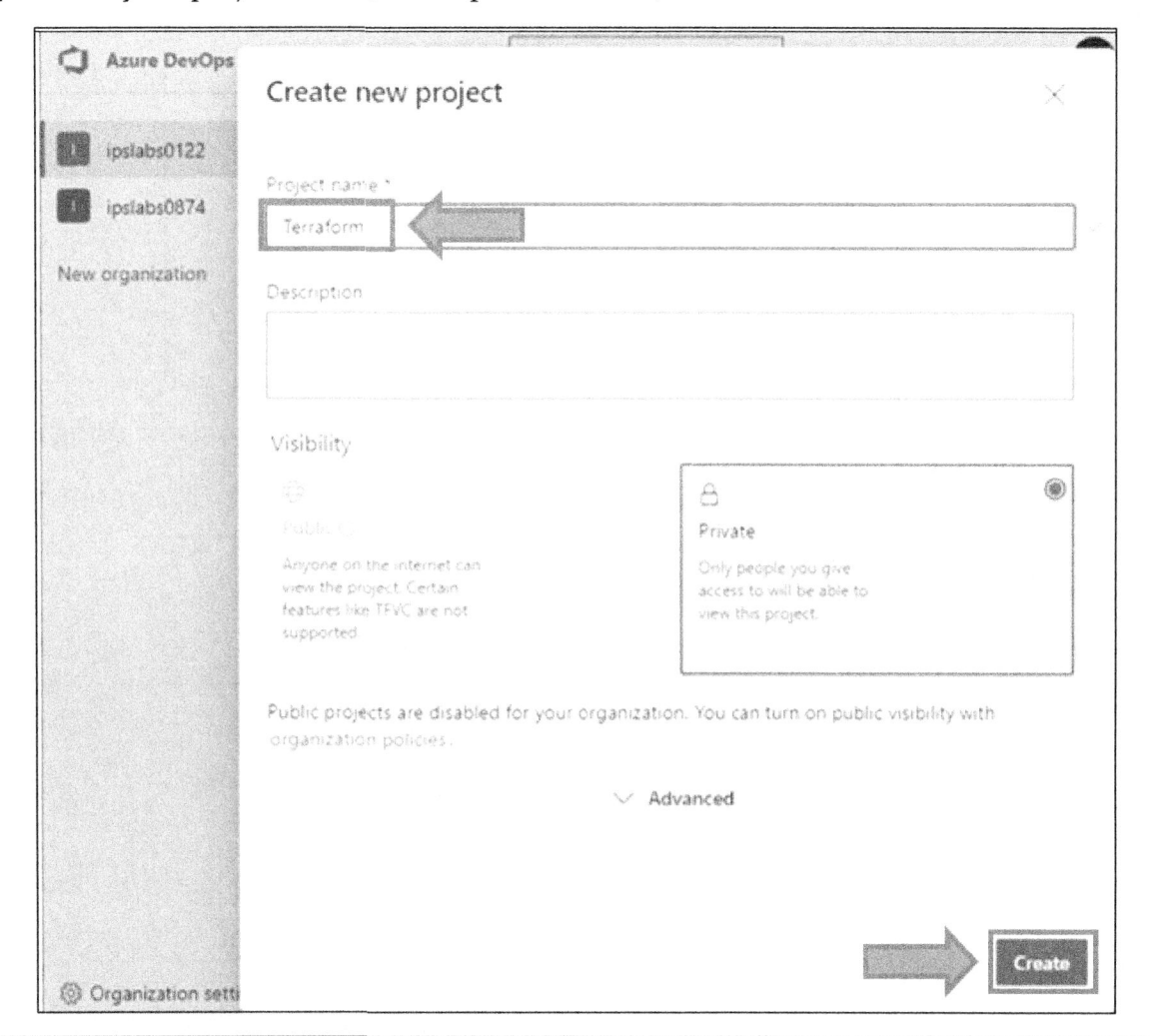

5. Open the **Repos** section and add the Terrform template file under **master** using the following github link.

https://github.com/microsoft/AzureDevOpsDemoGenerator/blob/master/src/VstsDemoBuilder/Templates/TemplateSetting.json

6. Go to the **Terraform** folder through branch.

Chapter 07: Terraform Modules

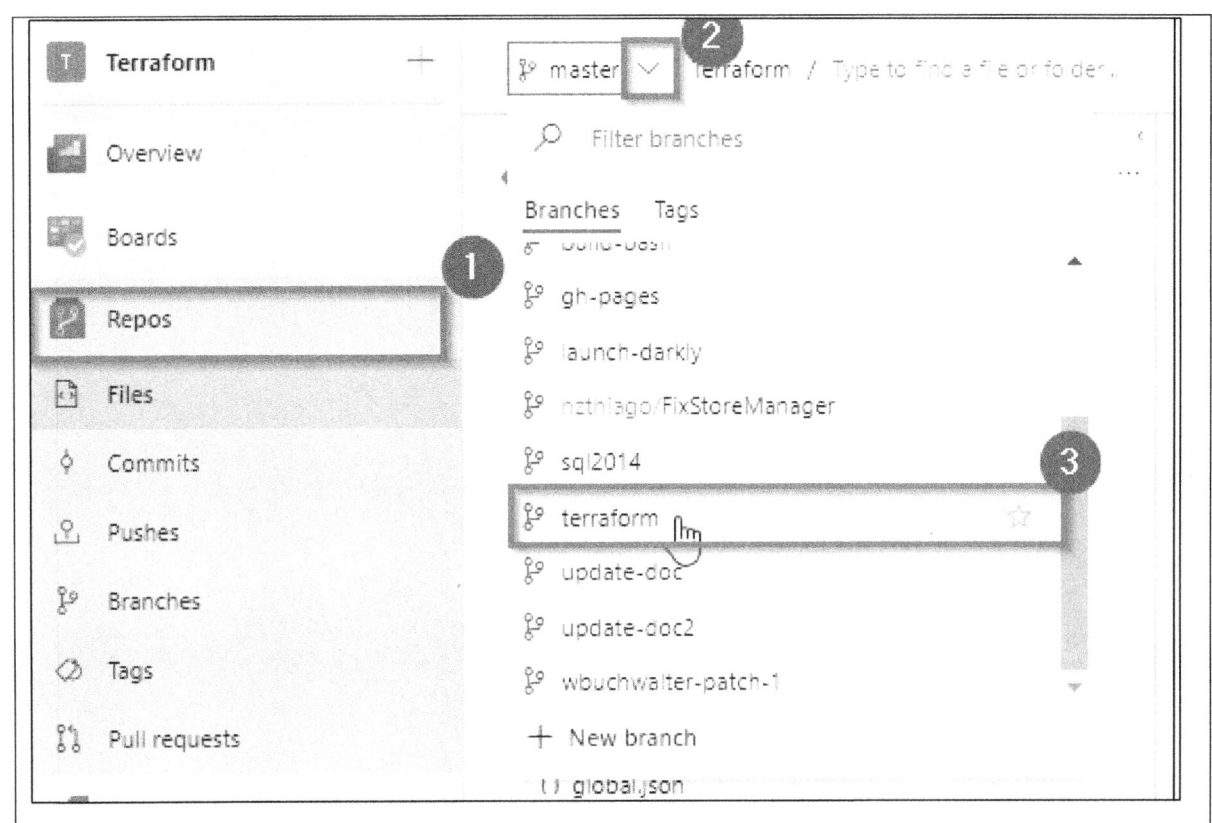

7. Select the webapp.tf file under the Terraform folder. The webapp.tf is the configuration file.

Step 02: Build Application using Azure CI Pipeline

8. To build application, navigate to **Pipelines → Pipelines** and select **Terraform-CI** and click **Edit.**

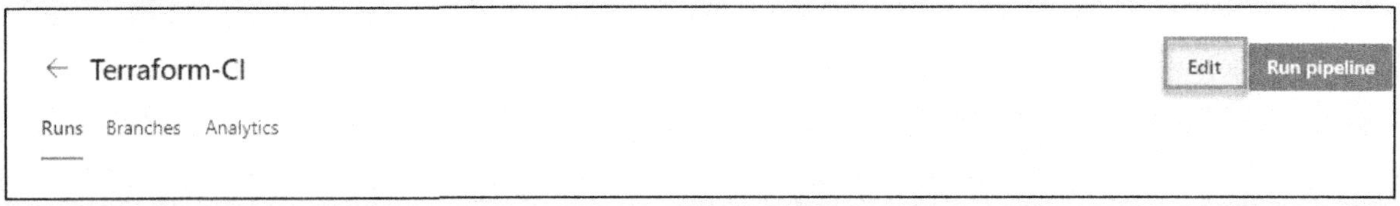

9. The following is an example of your build pipeline. There are tasks to compile in this CI pipeline. Net Core is an open-source project. The pipeline's dotnet jobs will rebuild dependencies, build, test, and publish the build output as a zip file (package) that can be deployed to a web application.

![Terraform-CI pipeline screenshot showing Tasks tab with Get sources, Agent job 1 containing Restore, Build, Test, Publish, Copy Terraform files to artifacts, and Publish Artifact steps]

10. You must also publish terraform files to build artifacts in order for them to be available in the CD pipeline, in addition to the application build. As a result, the Copy files job has been added to copy the Terraform file to the Artifacts directory.

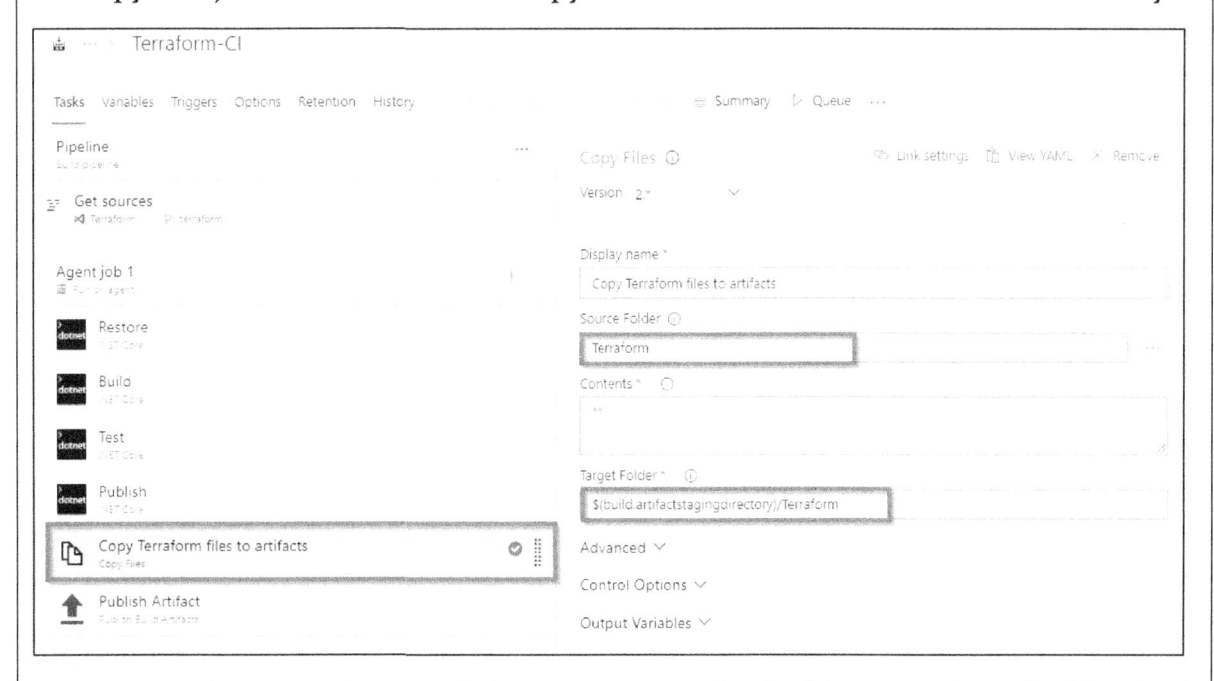

![Terraform-CI pipeline screenshot showing Copy Files task configuration with Source Folder "Terraform", Contents, and Target Folder "$(build.artifactstagingdirectory)/Terraform"]

11. To start the construction, click Queue. Once the build is complete, double-check that the artifacts contain the Terraform folder and the PartsUnlimitedwebsite.zip file.

193

Chapter 07: Terraform Modules

Name	Size
⌄ 🗁 drop	22 MB
📄 PartsUnlimitedWebsite.zip	22 MB
⌄ 🗁 Terraform	913 B
📄 webapp.tf	913 B

12. Open the file and run the **Agent job 1.**

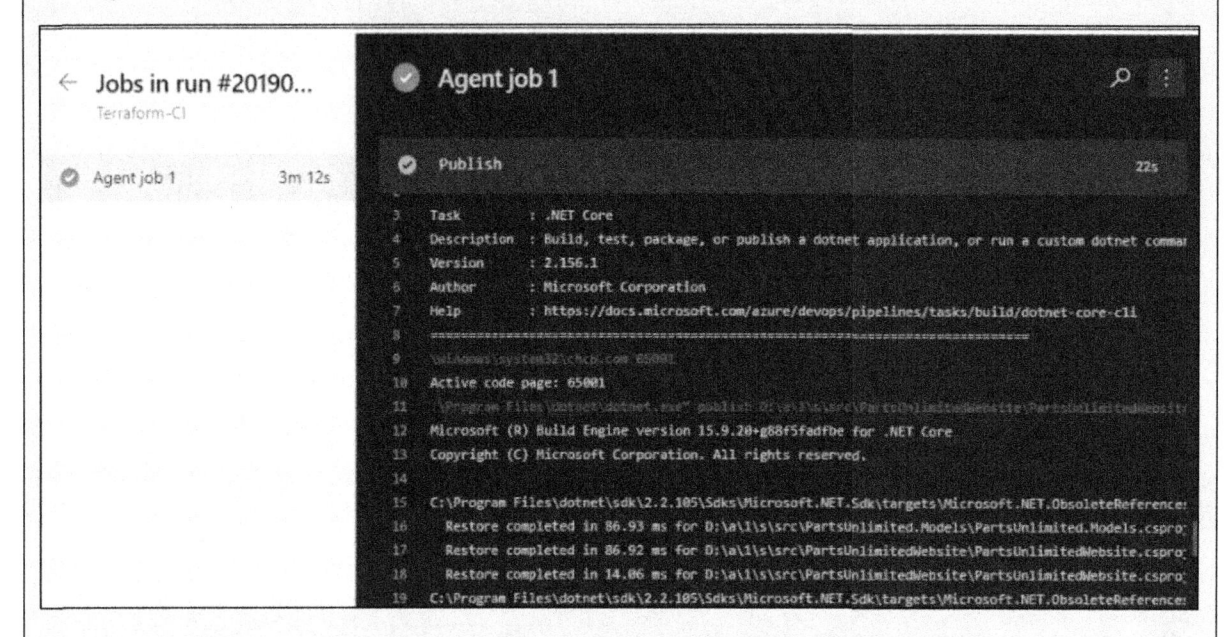

Step 03: Deploy resources using Terraform in Azure CI Pipeline

13. Navigate to **Pipelines → Releases**. Select **Terraform-CD**.

Chapter 07: Terraform Modules

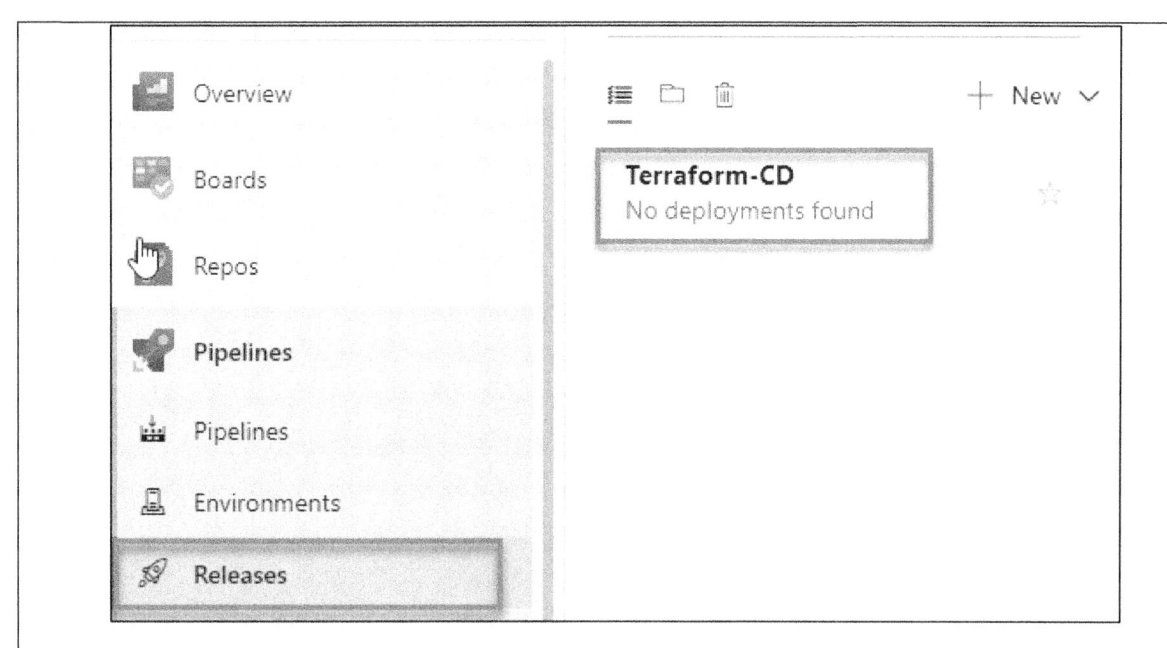

14. To this release, click on **Edit**.

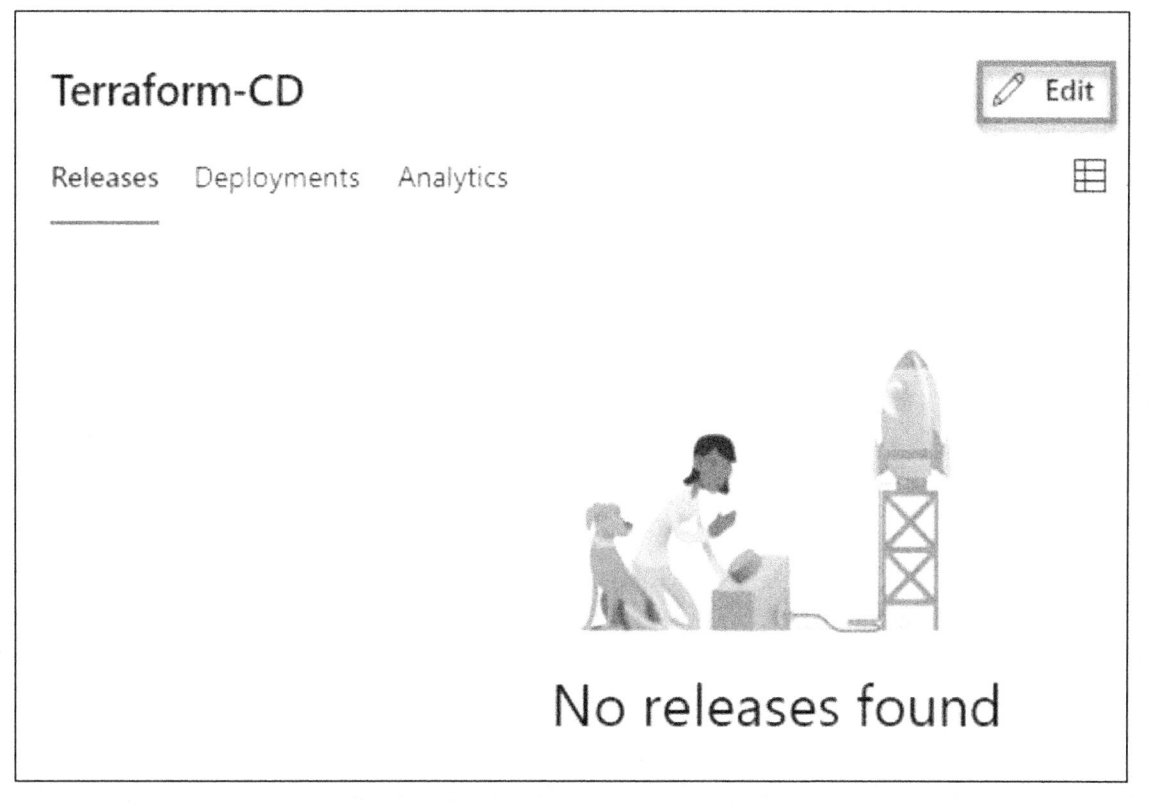

15. Select **Dev** stage and click on **View stage tasks** to view the pipelines.

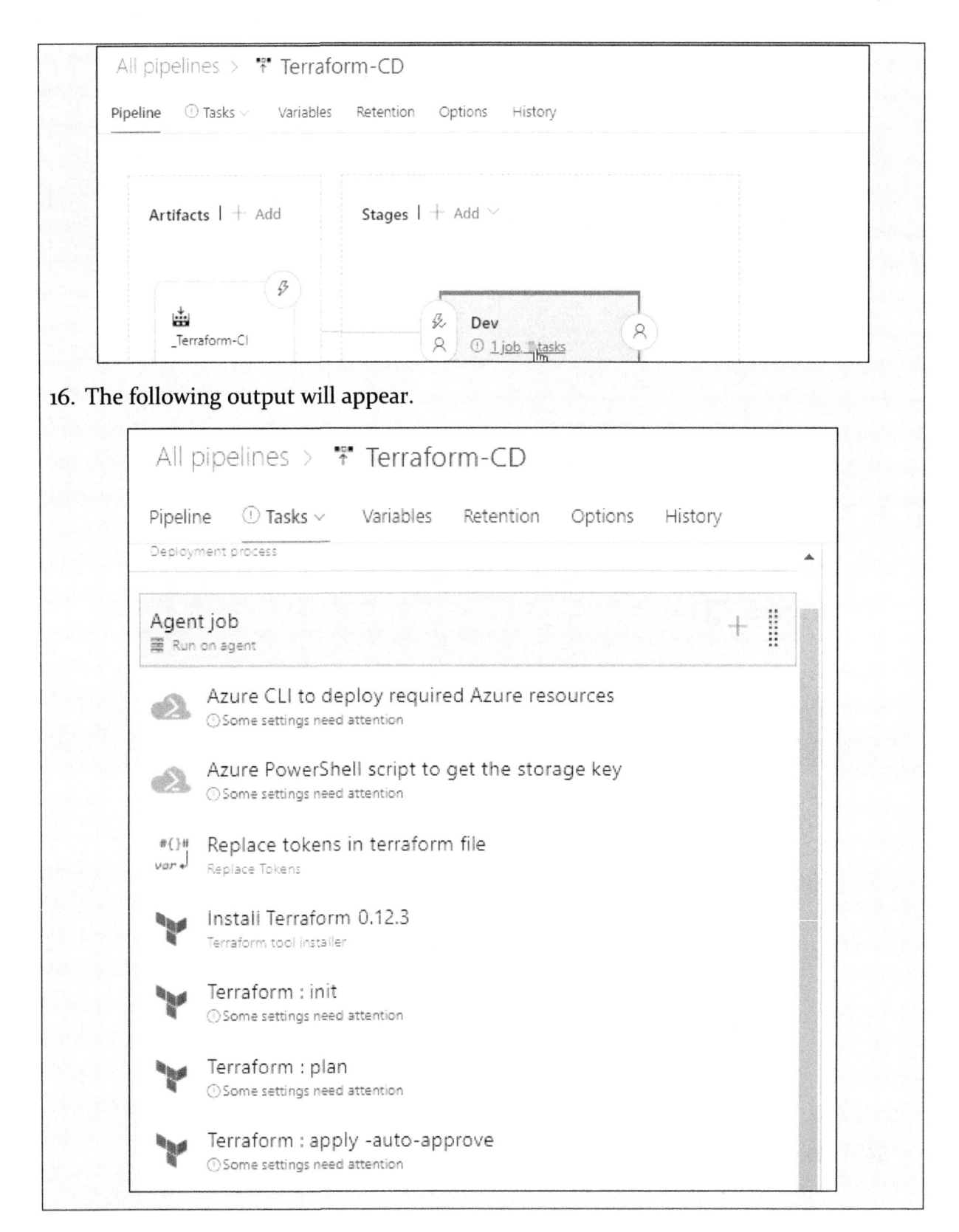

Chapter 07: Terraform Modules

16. The following output will appear.

Chapter 07: Terraform Modules

17. Select **Azure CLI** task. Then, select your subscription and click on **Authorize** for te configuration of Azure Service connection.

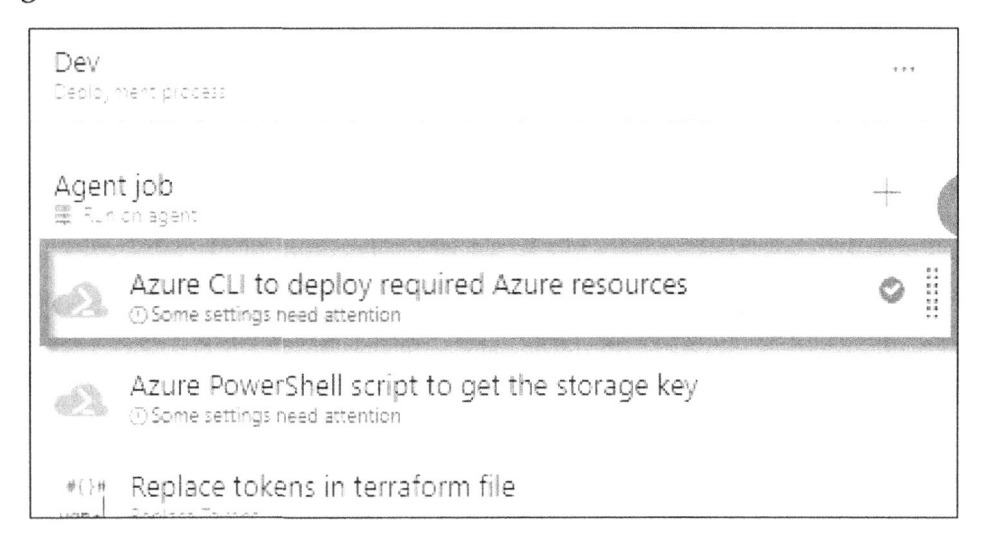

Note: Terraform saves state in a file called terraform.tfstate by default. When working with Terraform in a group, using a local file complicates the process. Terraform writes state data to a remote data store when using remote state. To save Terraform state, we're using the Azure CLI command to create an Azure storage account and a storage container.

18. Select Azure PowerShell and choose ARM for Azure Service connection.

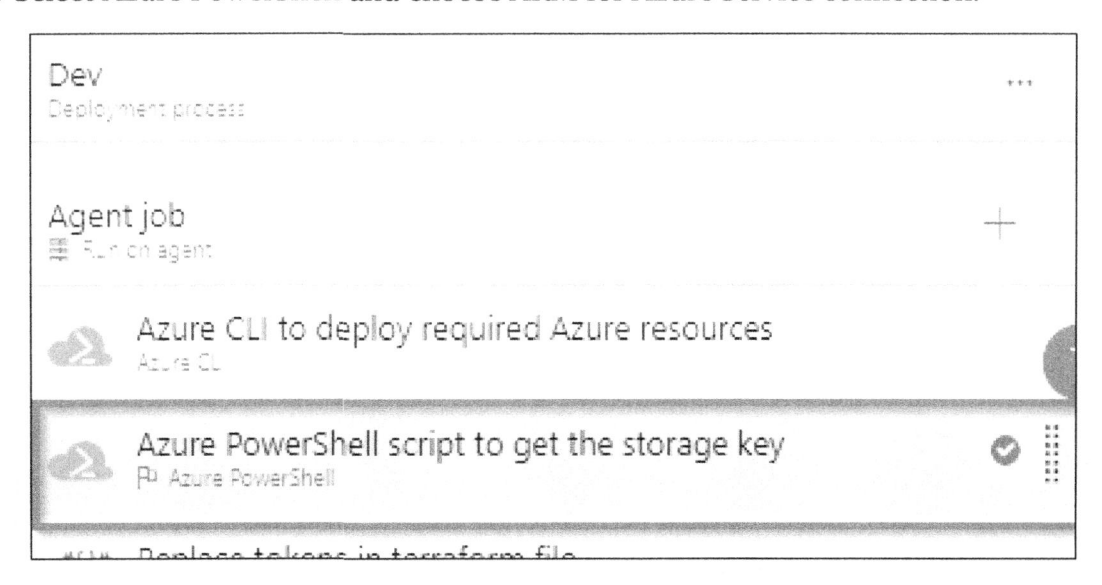

Note: Storage account access key is required to configure the Terraform backend. The Access key of the storage account provisioned in the previous stage is obtained using an Azure PowerShell operation.

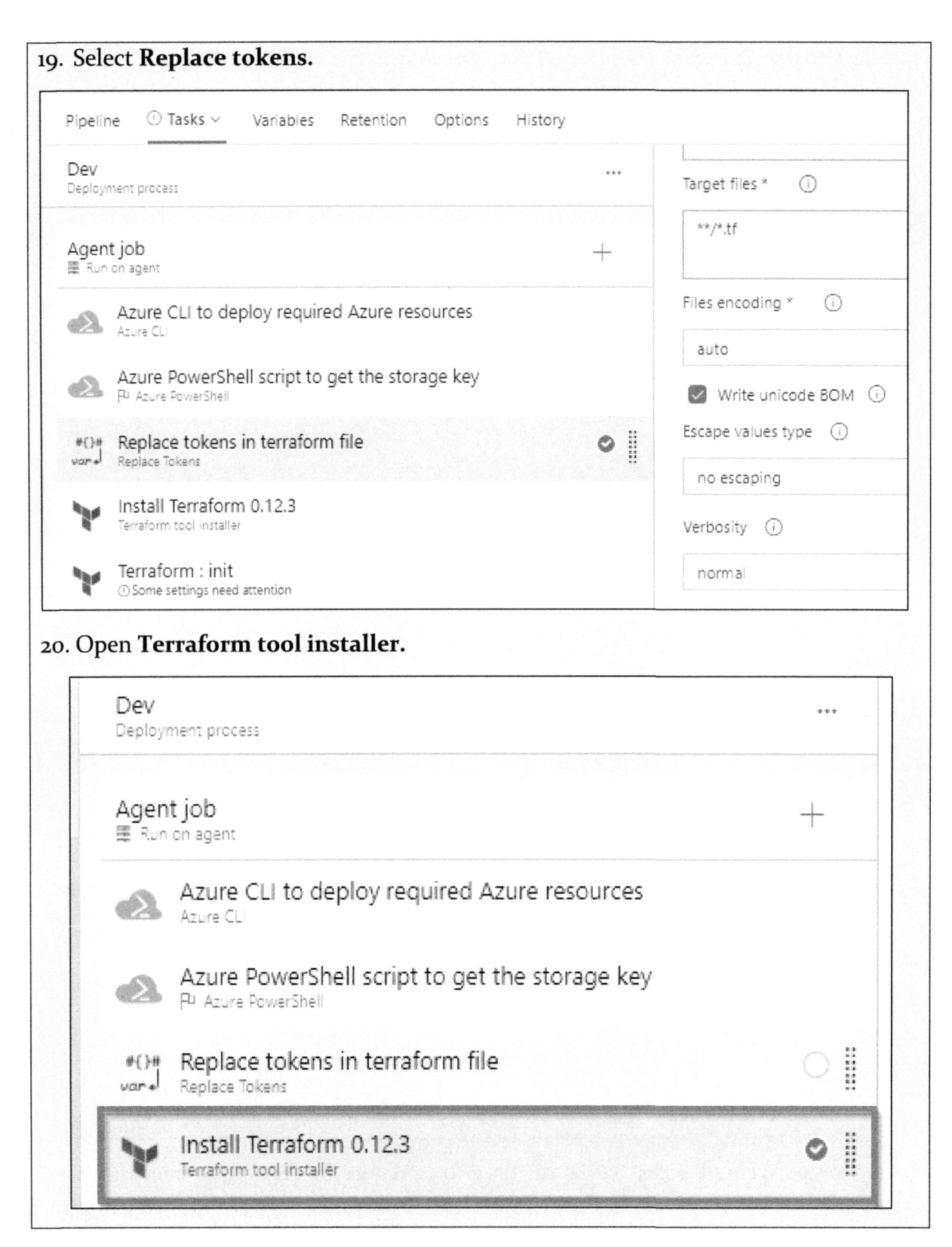

Chapter 07: Terraform Modules

19. Select **Replace tokens**.

20. Open **Terraform tool installer**.

Chapter 07: Terraform Modules

21. Select the Terraform init task from the drop-down menu. From the drop-down menu, choose Azure service connection. Also, make sure the container's name is terraform.

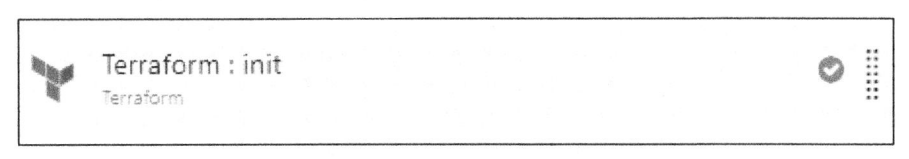

> Terraform : init
> Terraform

Chapter 07: Terraform Modules

Terraform ⓘ	View YAML Remove

Task version 0.*

Display name *

Terraform : init

Provider * ⓘ

azurerm

Command * ⓘ

init

Configuration directory ⓘ

$(System.DefaultWorkingDirectory)/_Terraform-CI/drop/Terraform

AzureRM backend configuration ∧

Azure subscription * ⓘ | Manage

Visual Studio Enterprise

○ Scoped to subscription 'Visual Studio Enterprise'

Resource group * ⓘ

$(terraformstoragerg)

Storage account * ⓘ

$(terraformstorageaccount)

Container * ⓘ

terraform

Key * ⓘ

terraform.tfstate

Note: The terraform init command is run by this task. The terraform init command searches the current working directory for all *.tf files and automatically downloads any providers that are required. It will download the Azure provider in this case because we are going to install Azure resources.

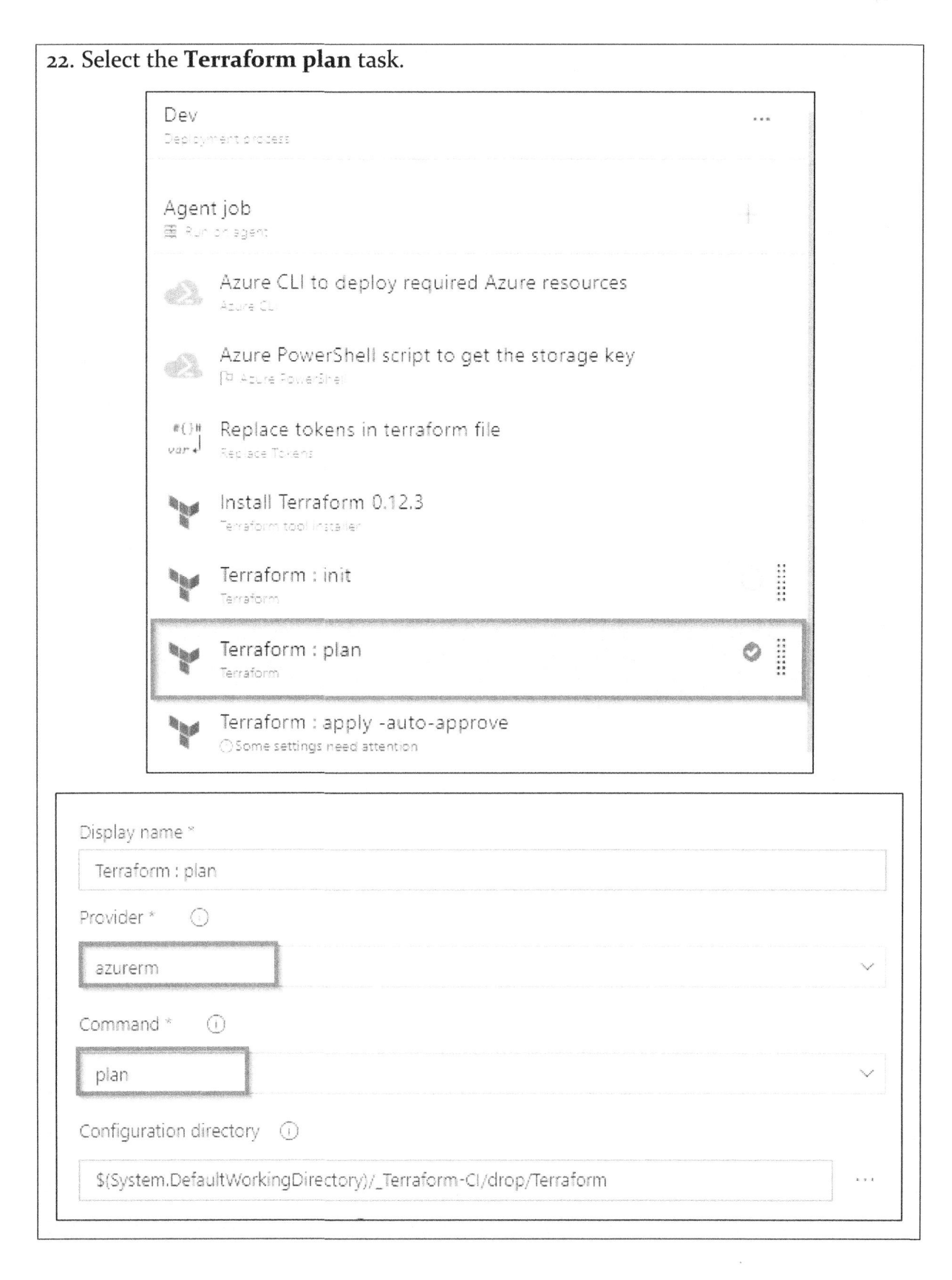

Chapter 07: Terraform Modules

22. Select the **Terraform plan** task.

    Dev
    Deployment process

    Agent job
    Run on agent

    - Azure CLI to deploy required Azure resources
      Azure CLI
    - Azure PowerShell script to get the storage key
      Azure PowerShell
    - Replace tokens in terraform file
      Replace Tokens
    - Install Terraform 0.12.3
      Terraform tool installer
    - Terraform : init
      Terraform
    - **Terraform : plan**
      Terraform
    - Terraform : apply -auto-approve
      Some settings need attention

    Display name *
    `Terraform : plan`

    Provider *
    `azurerm`

    Command *
    `plan`

    Configuration directory
    `$(System.DefaultWorkingDirectory)/_Terraform-CI/drop/Terraform`

201

Chapter 07: Terraform Modules

Note: To establish an execution plan, use the terraform plan command. Terraform works out what steps are required to get to the target state indicated in the configuration files. This is a practice run that demonstrates the activities that will be taken.

23. Select the **Terraform Apply** task.

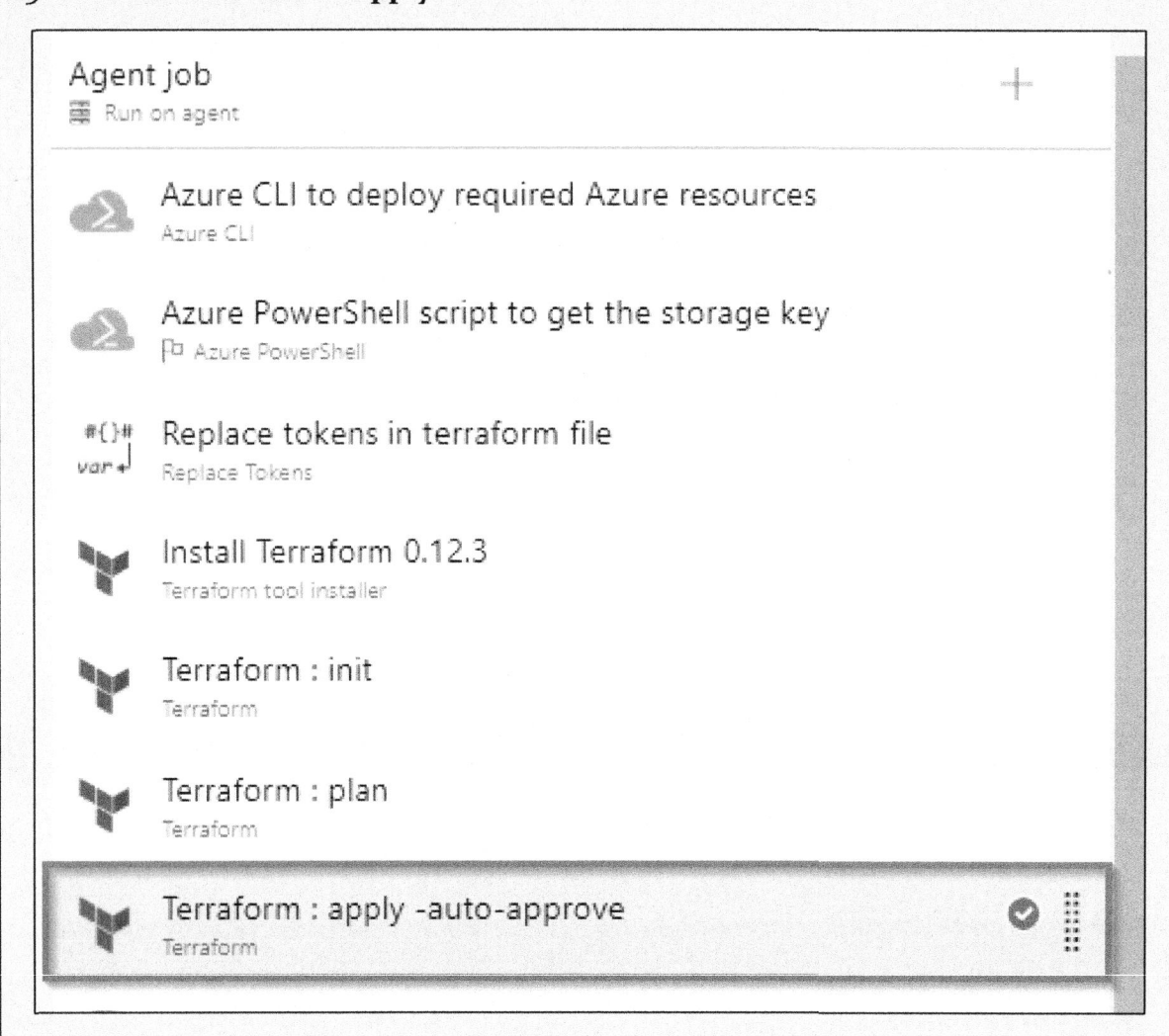

Chapter 07: Terraform Modules

```
Display name *
  Terraform : apply -auto-approve
Provider *
  azurerm
Command *
  validate and apply
Configuration directory
  $(System.DefaultWorkingDirectory)/_Terraform-CI/drop/Terraform
Additional command arguments
  -auto-approve
Azure subscription *    |  Manage
```

24. Select **Azure App Service Deploy** task.

Chapter 07: Terraform Modules

Agent job
Run on agent

- **Azure CLI to deploy required Azure resources**
  Azure CLI

- **Azure PowerShell script to get the storage key**
  Azure PowerShell

- **Replace tokens in terraform file**
  Replace Tokens

- **Install Terraform 0.12.3**
  Terraform tool installer

- **Terraform : init**
  Terraform

- **Terraform : plan**
  Terraform

- **Terraform : apply -auto-approve**
  Terraform

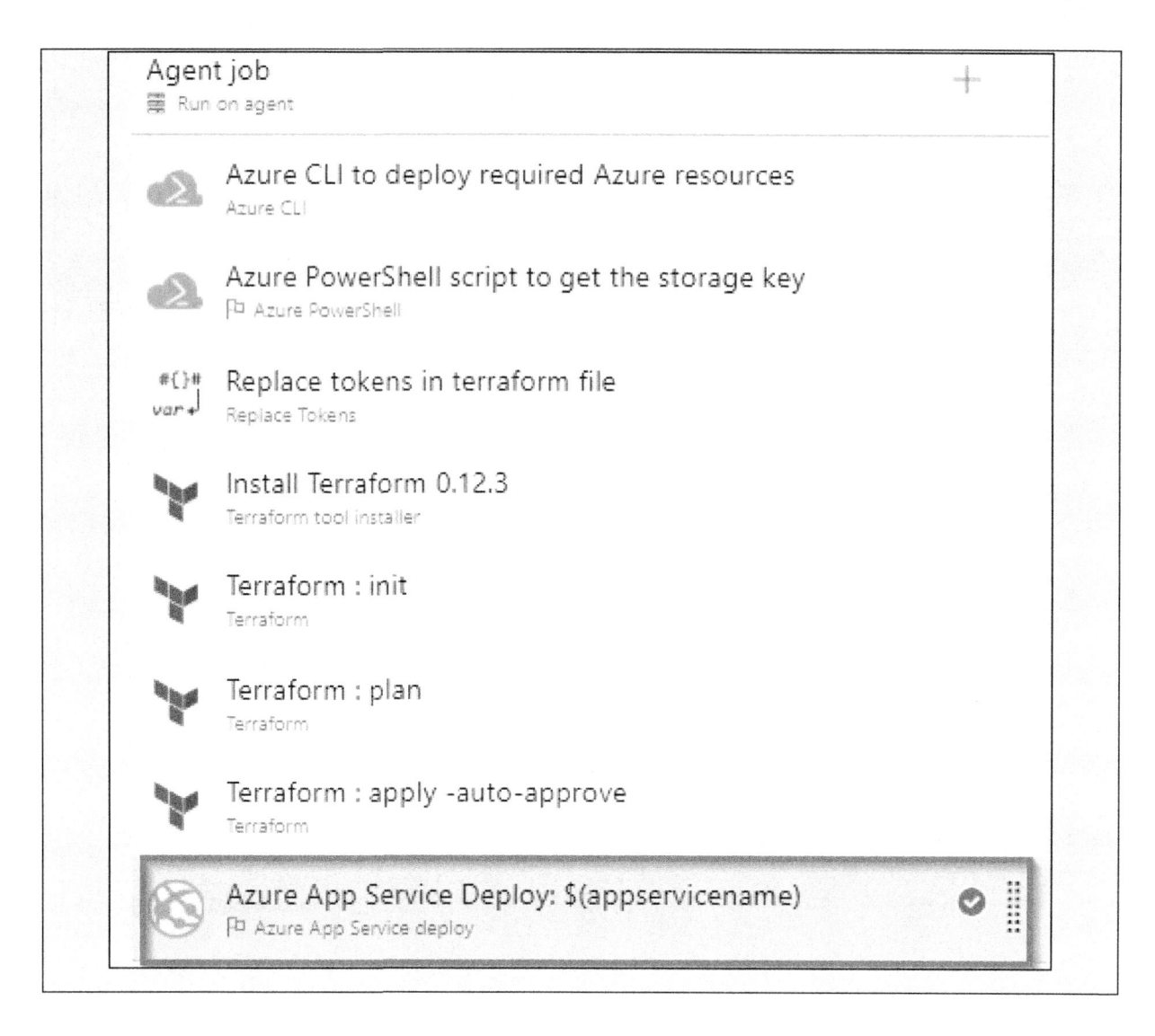

- **Azure App Service Deploy: $(appservicename)**
  Azure App Service deploy

Chapter 07: Terraform Modules

![Azure App Service deploy configuration screen showing Task version 3, Display name "Azure App Service Deploy: $(appservicename)", Azure subscription dropdown, App type "Web App", App Service name "$(appservicename)", Deploy to slot and Virtual application options]

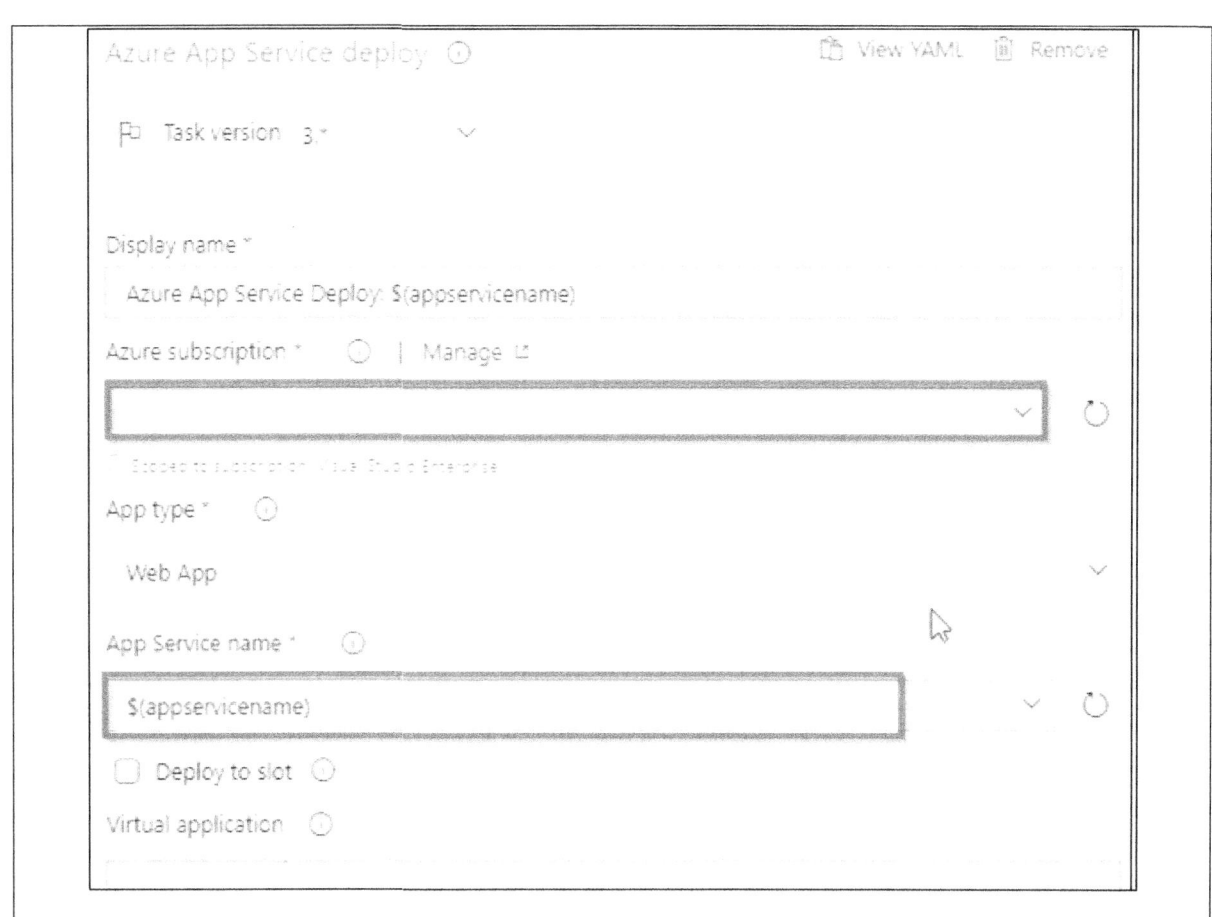

Note: To deploy the resources, this operation will use the terraform apply command. It will also ask for confirmation that you want to apply the modifications by default. You have added the auto-approve argument to avoid prompting for confirmation because you are automating the deployment.

25. Once you are done, **Save** the changes and **Create a release.**

Chapter 07: Terraform Modules

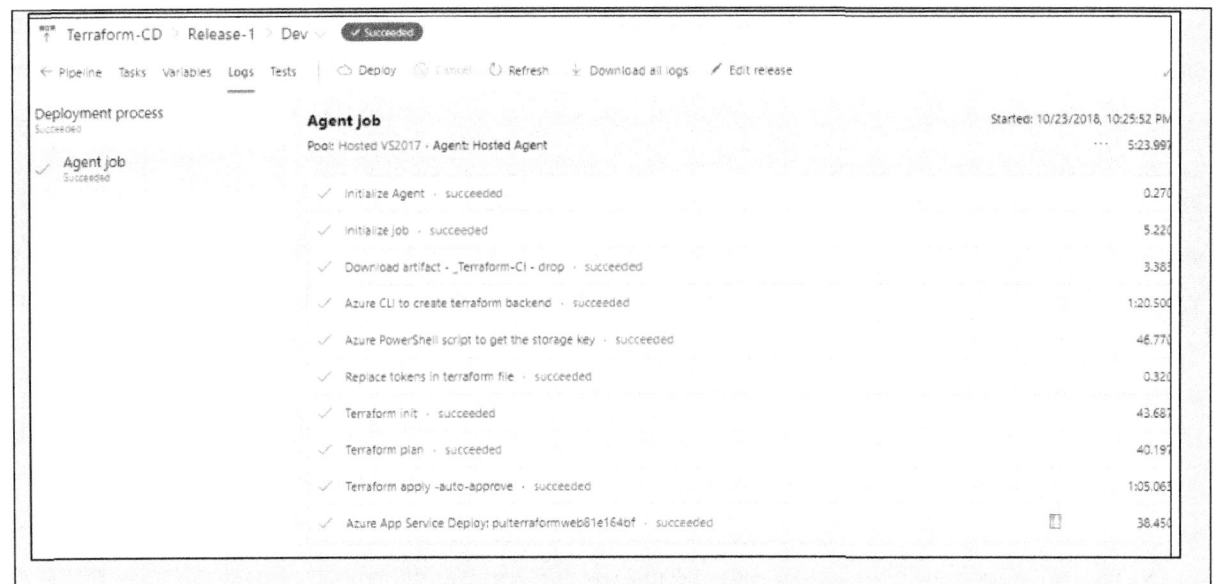

26. Navigate to your Azure portal once the release is complete. In App services, look for eCommerce website and navigate it for verification.

Mind Map

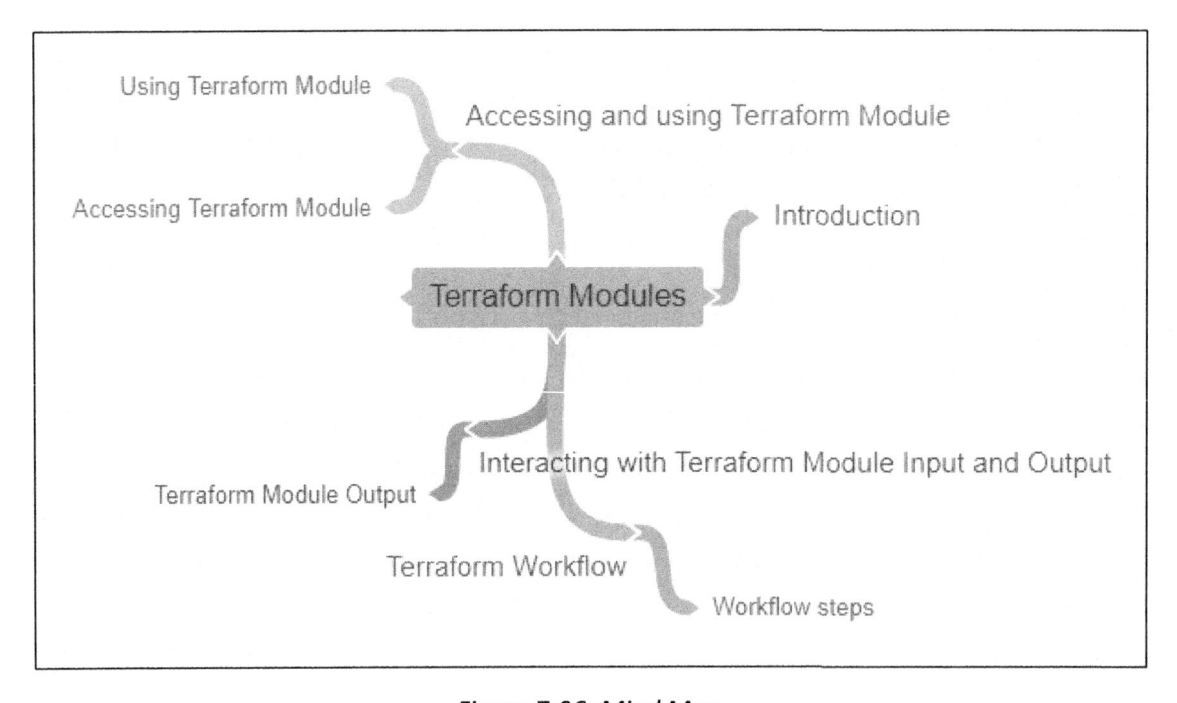

Figure 7-06: Mind Map

Chapter 07: Terraform Modules

Practice Questions

1. Which of the following is the latest version of Terraform?

A. 0.14.6
B. 0.14.7
C. 0.14.8
D. 0.14.10

2. The directory holding the main code in Terraform is called the _____.

A. Root Module
B. Child Module
C. Public Module
D. None of the above

3. Modules can be referenced from _____ resources.

A. Terraform Public Registry
B. Private Registry
C. Local folder
D. All of the above

4. Word modules can be used as a variable in a code. True or false?

A. True
B. False

5. Which of the following is the correct purpose of the for_each parameter?

A. Module blocks include count
B. Iterating over a complex variable
C. Set dependencies
D. None of the above

6. Modules can take a/an _____ inputs.

A. 5
B. Hundreds

Chapter 07: Terraform Modules

C. Arbitrary number of
D. None of the above

7. Terraform module inputs can be used as a _____ inside the module code.

A. Function
B. Variable
C. Dataset
D. All of the above

8. Which of the following is the standard variable reference notation interval; var. server-name?

A. ./module/<variable-name>
B. var.<variable-name>
C. /module/<variable-name>
D. <variable-name>.var

9. The outputs declared inside Terraform module code can be _____ in the root module or your main code.

A. Used as variable
B. Used as a function
C. Feedback
D. None of the above

10. Which of the following are the uses of output values?

A. Child modules
B. Root modules
C. Both A and B
D. None of the above

11. Which of the following are the key uses of Terraform modules?

A. Reliable retrieval and resolution of dependencies
B. To enable enterprises to swiftly upgrade their Terraform version
C. To make Terraform's multi-threaded deployment option available

D. To avoid reinventing the wheel by making code reusable elsewhere

12. Following is the Terraform code, namely prod-module. How will you use output values inside this code?

A. outputs.returned-variable
B. cannot share variables back
C. module.prod-module.returned-variable
D. var.returned-variable

13. How may Terraform module code return outputs that the main Terraform code activating it can use?

A. By running the module code and saving the outputs to GitHub, then referencing them in the main code
B. There is no method to integrate module outputs into the main Terraform code
C. By including them as environment variables in the main code
D. In the Terraform module code, **output** block resources are used

14. Given the following code:

```
module "my-test-module" {
    source = "./testm"
    version = "0.0.5"
    region = var.datacenter
}
```

Which of the attributes in the preceding sample is being passed to the module as an input?

A. region
B. source
C. version
D. This snippet of Terraform code contains no inputs

15. Terraform code is saved as plain text files with the _____ file extension.

A. .py
B. .docx
C. .hcl
D. .tf

Chapter 08: Built-in Functions and Dynamic Blocks

Introduction

In this chapter, we will learn about Terraform's built-in functions and dynamic blocks. Terraform's built-in functions are one of the features of Terraform that will help you open up about the ways and possibilities with Terraform. We will also learn where and when we need to use dynamic blocks in Terraform.

Terraform Built-in Functions

By default, Terraform comes bundled with all the built-in functions. You do not need to use any additional providers or modules to use these functions. In Terraform, you cannot create your user-defined functions like in a programming language because the Terraform language does not support user-defined functions; only the built-in functions are available for use.

You can use these functions inside various places in your Terraform code, for example, resource and data resource blocks, provisioners, variables, etc.

General Syntax

The general syntax of the function is just like how you would invoke functions anywhere else in a programming language. You pass the function with some arguments and get values in return.

The general syntax for function calls is a function name followed by parenthesized comma-separated arguments.

Example:

```
Max (6, 14, 8)
```

Functions

The built-in functions allow you to write flexible and dynamic Terraform code. Let us consider an example of Terraform code showing a variable and an AWS resource. We are giving the AWS resource a tag, and for that, we are using the join built-in function. This function takes two arguments: the separator, which you want to join strings with, and the list of strings to join together. For example, the result of the join function execution will join the string terraform with the value of the variable project-name, which by default, and in this case, is prod. So we will get the **terraform-prod** as the result of the execution of the join function.

```
variable "project-name" {
type = string
default= "prod"
}
```
⬅ variable

```
resource "aws_vpc" "my-vpc" {
cidr_block = "10.0.0.0/16"
tags = {
Name = join ("-", ["terraform", var.project-name])
}
```
⬅ AWS resource

Separator   list of strings
Output: terraform-prod

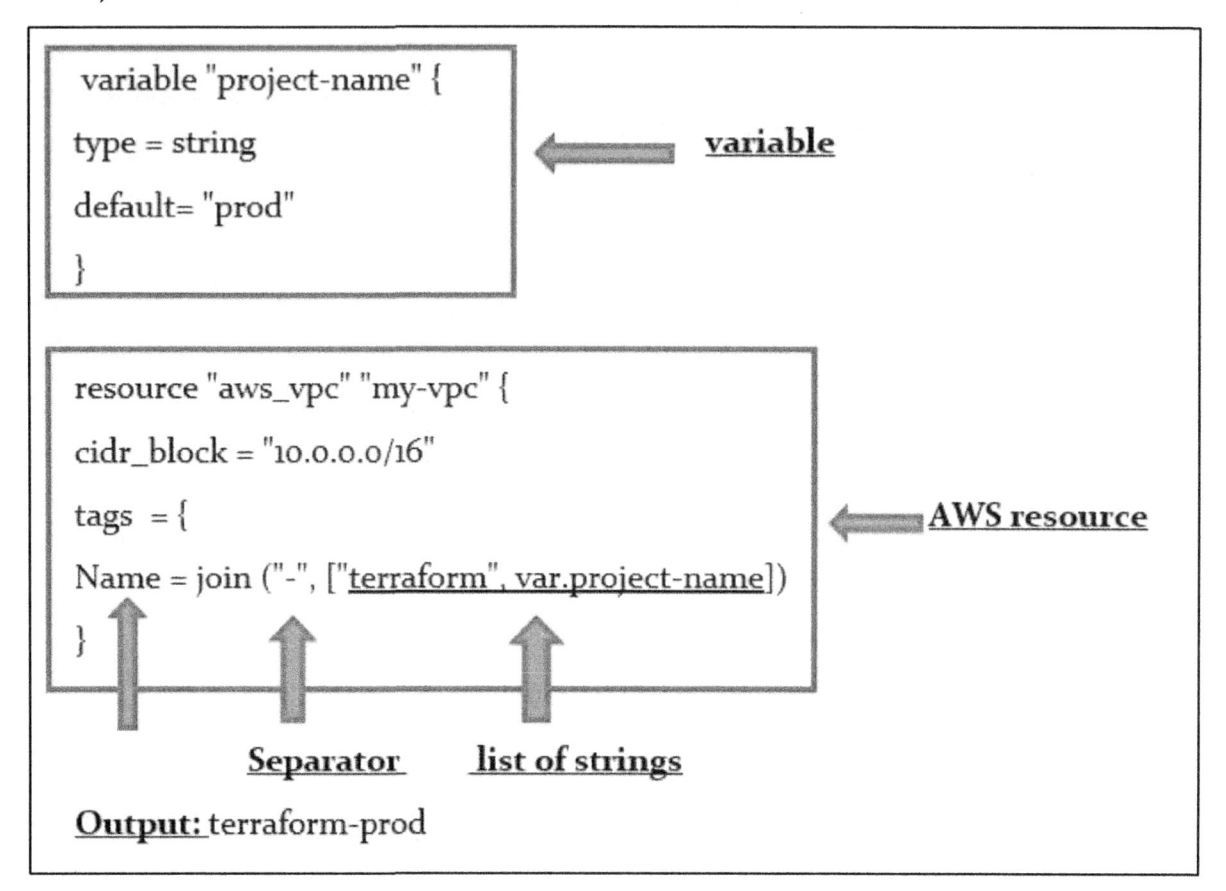

Figure 8-01: Terraform Code Showing a Variable and an AWS Resource

Some Useful Functions

There is a huge array of useful functions. A few examples of such functions are:

- **file function**, for inserting files into your resources where applicable
- **max function**, for determining the max integer value from a provided list
- **flatten function**, for creating a singular list out of a provided set of lists

Note: Log into a CentOS 7 Linux virtual machine and get Terraform install on it.

Function Testing

By running the terraform console command, you can experiment with the behavior of Terraform's built-in functions from the Terraform expression console. The Terraform console command provides an interactive console for evaluating expressions. If the current state of your deployment is empty or has not yet been created, the console can be used to experiment with expression syntax and built-in functions.

First, we need to execute the command **terraform console**. Once we execute this command, it will drop us down into the interactive console CLI and then you can test out the built-in functions.

max Function

The max function will return us the greatest value from the list of values entered.

Figure 8-02: max Function

timestamp Function

The timestamp function returns an RFC 3339 timestamp string in UTC format.

Figure 8-03: timestamp Function

join Function

The join function generates a string by concatenating all elements of a given list of strings with the specified delimiter. The join function expects a separator as the first argument, so we will be giving it the separator comma and then a list of strings that we want to concatenate using that separator.

Chapter 08: Built-in Functions and Dynamic Blocks

```
> join(", ", ["foo", "bar", "baz"])
foo, bar, baz
> join(", ", ["foo"])
foo
```

Figure 8-04: join Function

contains Function

The contains function takes in a list of elements and searches it for the value that you want to provide to it.

```
> contains(["a", "b", "c"], "a")
true
> contains(["a", "b", "c"], "d")
false
```

Figure 8-05: contains Function

> **EXAM TIP:** The *contains* function is very useful, especially when you are trying to weave flexibility into your Terraform code.

Type Constraints

Type constraints control the type of variable values that you can pass to your Terraform code.

There are two types of constraints:

1. **Primitive:**

It allows for a single type of value to be assigned to a variable, such as a number type, string type, or boolean (or bool) type.

Examples

- replicas = 3 (number type)

- name = "cluster2" (enclosed between double quotes and is a string type)
- backup = true (a bool type)

2. **Complex types:**

It includes multiple value types in a single variable. Such value types can be constructed using list, tuple, map, or object data structures.

Example:

An example of Complex type could be a variable that has multiple values assigned within it.

The complex types can be broken into two further types:

1. **Collection Types**

Collection types allow multiple values of a single or one primitive type to be grouped against a variable. For example, you can have a list of type strings, or you can have a map of type numbers, or you can have a set of type strings, but you cannot mix more than one type against a single variable.

Example:

You have a variable declared inside your Terraform code of the type list of strings, and in the default value, you are assigning two separate strings inside the list to that variable as a default value.

```
variable "training" {
                      the variable will be a list
                        several strings
    type= list (string)
    default = ["IPS", "LA"]
              two separate
              strings in one
                variable
}
```

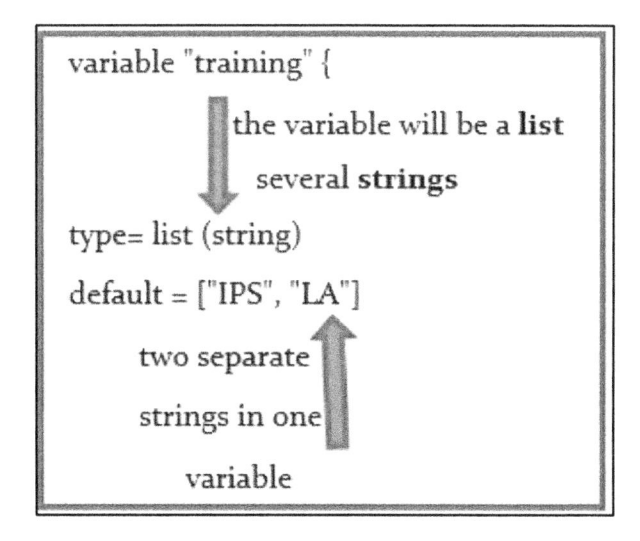

Figure 8-06: Example of Collection Types

2. Structural Types

Structural types allow multiple values of different primitive types to be grouped. So, as opposed to the type of the collection, which only allows a single type of value within a variable, the structural type allows more than one type of value assigned within a variable.

Example:

You can have an object with values of type strings, bool, or even numbers, and you can group similar variables using the tuple or set variable types. An example of this could be a variable type that allows items of type string, number, and bool against it.

Let us look at an example of a structural complex type in Figure 7-07. So here, we have got a variable defined in Terraform code and defined it using the object constructor. Now within that object constructor, we are passing in two primitive types, which are different; the first one is **name = string,** and the other one is **age = number.** Both of these primitive types within this object are combined to form a complex structural constraint.

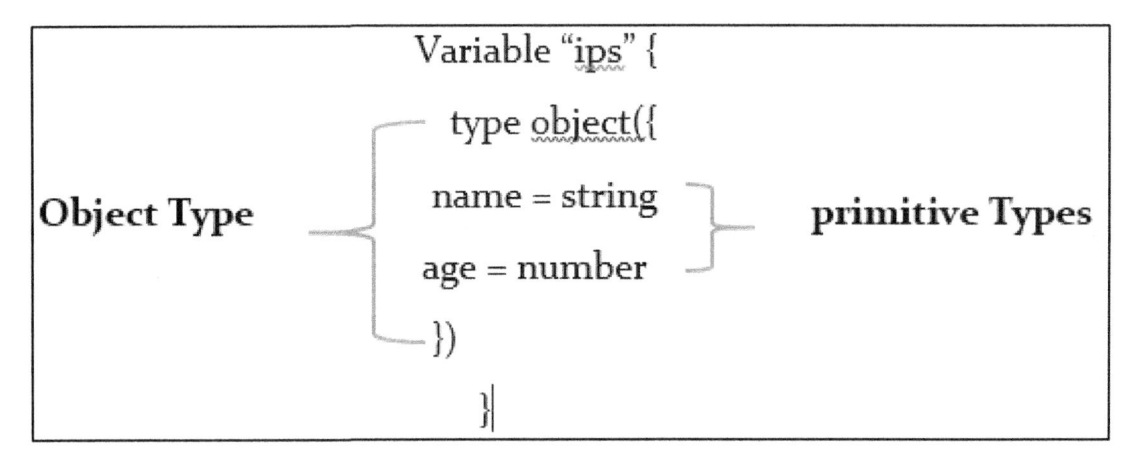

Figure 8-07: Variable Defined in Terraform Code

any constraint

any is a placeholder for a primitive type that is yet to be decided. Terraform allows you to leave out the type of a variable when you are defining it because it is an optional field. Furthermore, Terraform makes a best-effort attempt to figure out what kind of variable you have passed and assign it a proper primitive type. The actual type of a variable that has been assigned, and **any constraint** will be determined at runtime by Terraform.

Example:

An example of any constraint is shown below. You have a code where you are defining a variable in Terraform, and within the type value, you have passed to the constructor list the type any. Now, Terraform will recognize all values passed inside the default value of this variable as numbers and therefore assign the type of the list as numbers.

```
variable "data" {

    type = list (any)

    default = [1, 42, 7]
```

Figure 8-08: Example of Any Constraint

Dynamic Block - The Complex Variable Example

In this complex variable, we are creating a list of objects which contain key-value pairs. The default value contains two items: the first and the second.

```
variable "rules" {
default = [
port =80
proto= "tcp"                    ── 1st item within the complex variable type
cidr_blocks = ["0.0.0.0/0"]
},
{
port = 22
proto "tcp"                     ── 2nd item within the complex variable type
cidr_blocks = ["1.2.3.4/32"]

}
}
```

Figure 8-09: Dynamic Block - The Complex Variable Example

Take another example of the dynamic block it is used in. We are passing in our complex variable to the **for_each** loop. The for_each loop is plugging in the value of each item iterated over in the variable to the ingress variable within the content block, using the attribute via an **ingress.value.**

```
resourse "aws_security_group" "my-sg" {
name = 'my-aws-security-group'
vpc_id = aws_vpc.my-vpc.id
dynamic "ingress" {
for_each = var.rules
content {
from_port = ingress.value["port"]
to_port = ingress.value["port"]
protocol = ingress.value["proto"]
cidr_blocks = ingress.value ["cidrs"]
}
}
```

Figure 8-10: Example of dynamic block

Note: Dynamic blocks expect complex variable types to iterate over.

EXAM TIP: Though dynamic blocks are good at cutting down the lines of code, they can make your code hard to read and maintain.

Dynamic Blocks in Terraform

Dynamic blocks help construct repeatable nested configuration blocks inside Terraform resources. They can be used inside resources, such as resource blocks, data blocks, provider blocks, and provisional blocks inside a Terraform resource.

Take an example of Terraform code, which creates an AWS security group with several rules. Each of those rules takes in several inputs and is represented by the ingress block in the case of this resource. This means that we will need to write a separate ingress block for every security group rule in this resource, which can get very tedious, difficult to maintain, and bloat your code.

```
resource "aws_security_group" "my-sg" {
name = 'my-aws-security-group'
vpc_id = aws_vpc.my-vpc.id
ingress {
from_port = 22
to_port = 22
a normal snippet of protocol = "top"
terraform code with
cidr_block ["1.2.3.4/32"]
dynamic block
}
Ingress {
# more ingress rules
}
}
```

Figure 8-11: Example of Terraform Code, which Creates an AWS Security Group with Several Rules

Now, take the example of how the same code can be streamlined using dynamic blocks. So you have got the dynamic block keyword, and then you pass it the name of whatever block inside the resource you are trying to replicate. In this case, it is the nested ingress block inside the AWS security group resource. Now inside the dynamic block, we have a for_each loop statement, which provides complex values to iterate over. The variable passed to the loop is provided by you, the user. The content block defines the body of each generated block and is part of the syntax of a dynamic block. The ingress variable inside the content block is the iterator argument. You can provide it with a custom name; however, by default, this variable takes the name of the actual nested block being worked on, which is the ingress block.

```
resource "aws_security_group" "my-sg" {
'my-aws-security-group' vpc_id = aws_vpc.my-vpc.id
name
dynamic "ingress" {
for_each = var.rules content {
from_port = ingress.value["port"]
to_port = ingress.value["port"]
protocol = ingress.value["proto"]
cidr_blocks = ingress.value ["cidr"]
}
}
}
```

Figure 8-12: Example of Terraform Code, which Creates an AWS Security Group with Dynamic Block

Lab 8-01: Using Terraform Dynamic Blocks and Built-in Functions to Deploy to AWS

Introduction

Terraform provides a robust set of features to assist you in optimizing your Terraform code. Dynamic blocks allow you to generate static repeated blocks within Terraform resources.

While the built-in functions allow you to manipulate variables and data to suit your needs and help make your Terraform deployments automated and fault resilient, they are two extremely useful features.

Problem

Terraform takes a Push method, meaning that it starts the provisioning process by communicating the necessary infrastructure directly with AWS. It accomplishes this by utilizing the Terraform AWS Provider Plugin and the provided AWS credentials.

Chapter 08: Built-in Functions and Dynamic Blocks

Terraform dynamic blocks are used to generate nested blocks that can be repeated within an argument. These dynamic blocks represent independent items that are linked to or embedded in the contained entity. Dynamic blocks are similar to expressions, but they iterate over-complicated values.

The excessive use of dynamic blocks can make configuration difficult to read and maintain. A dynamic block can generate only arguments belonging to the resource type, data source, provider, or provisioner being configured. Meta-argument blocks, such as lifecycle and provisioner blocks, cannot be generated.

Solution

We can solve the problem by using Terraform Dynamic Blocks and Built-in Functions to deploy to AWS. Follow the steps below to resolve the problem:

1. Log in to the terminal.

ssh <username>@<PublicIP>

2. Log in to the AWS Management Console using the credentials provided in a web browser.

Step 01: Clone Terraform Code and Switch to Proper Directory

3. The Terraform code required for this lab has already been cloned onto the provided VM:

cd lab_code

```
[cloud_user@ip-10-0-1-121 ~]$ cd lab_code
[cloud_user@ip-10-0-1-121 lab_code]$
```

4. Switch to the directory where the code is located:

cd section7-HoL-TF-DynBlocks-Funcs

```
[cloud_user@ip-10-0-1-121 lab_code]$ cd section7-HoL-TF-DynBlocks-Funcs
[cloud_user@ip-10-0-1-121 section7-HoL-TF-DynBlocks-Funcs]$
```

5. List the files in the directory:

ls

The files in the directory should include the main.tf, outputs.tf, script.sh, and variables.tf.

```
[cloud_user@ip-10-0-1-121 section7-HoL-TF-DynBlocks-Funcs]$ ls
main.tf  outputs.tf  script.sh  variables.tf
[cloud_user@ip-10-0-1-121 section7-HoL-TF-DynBlocks-Funcs]$
```

Step 02: Examine the Code in the Files

6. View the contents of the main.tf file using the less command:

less main.tf

The **main.tf** file spins up AWS networking components such as a virtual private cloud (VPC), security group, internet gateway, route tables, and an EC2 instance bootstrapped with an Apache web server that is publicly accessible.

7. Closely examine the code and note the following:
   - We have selected **AWS** as our provider, and our resources will be deployed in the us-east-1 region
   - We are using the **ssm_parameter** public endpoint resource to get the AMI ID of the Amazon Linux 2 image that will spin up the EC2 webserver
   - We are using the **vpc** module (provided by the Terraform Public Registry) to create our network components like subnets, internet gateway, and route tables
   - For the **security_group** resource, we are using a dynamic block on the ingress attribute to dynamically generate as many ingress blocks as we need. The dynamic block includes the **var.rules** complex variable configured in the variables.tf file
   - We are also using a couple of built-in functions and some logical expressions in the code to get it to work the way we want, including the join function for the name attribute in the security group resource, and the **fileexists** and file functions for the **user_data** parameter in the **EC2** instance resource

Chapter 08: Built-in Functions and Dynamic Blocks

```
provider "aws" {
  region = "us-east-1"
}

data "aws_ssm_parameter" "ami_id" {
  name = "/aws/service/ami-amazon-linux-latest/amzn2-ami-hvm-x86_64-gp2"
}

module "vpc" {
  source = "terraform-aws-modules/vpc/aws"

  name = "my-vpc"
  cidr = "10.0.0.0/16"

  azs            = ["us-east-1a"]
  public_subnets = ["10.0.1.0/24"]
}

resource "aws_security_group" "my-sg" {
  vpc_id = module.vpc.vpc_id
  name   = join("_", ["sg", module.vpc.vpc_id])
  dynamic "ingress" {
    for_each = var.rules
    content {
      from_port = ingress.value["port"]
      to_port   = ingress.value["port"]
main.tf
```

8. Press **Escape** and enter **:q!** to exit the file.
9. View the contents of the **variables.tf** file:

less variables.tf

The **variables.tf:** file contains the complex variable type that we will be iterating over with the dynamic block in the **main.tf file**.

Chapter 08: Built-in Functions and Dynamic Blocks

```
variable "rules" {
  type = list(object({
    port        = number
    proto       = string
    cidr_blocks = list(string)
  }))
  default = [
    {
      port        = 80
      proto       = "tcp"
      cidr_blocks = ["0.0.0.0/0"]
    },
    {
      port        = 22
      proto       = "tcp"
      cidr_blocks = ["0.0.0.0/0"]
    },
    {
      port        = 3689
      proto       = "tcp"
      cidr_blocks = ["6.7.8.9/32"]
    }
  ]
}
variables.tf (END)
```

10. **Press Escape** and enter **:q!** to exit the file.
11. View the contents of the script.sh file using the cat command:

cat script.sh

The **script.sh** file is passed into the EC2 instance using its **user_data** attribute and the **"fileexists"** and **"file functions"** (as you saw in the main.tf file), which then installs the Apache webserver and starts up the service.

Chapter 08: Built-in Functions and Dynamic Blocks

```
[cloud_user@ip-10-0-1-235 section7-HoL-TF-DynBlocks-Funcs]$ cat script.sh
#!/bin/bash
sudo yum -y install httpd
sudo systemctl start httpd && sudo systemctl enable httpd
[cloud_user@ip-10-0-1-235 section7-HoL-TF-DynBlocks-Funcs]$
```

12. View the contents of the **outputs.tf file**:

cat outputs.tf

The **outputs.tf file** returns the values we have requested upon deployment of our Terraform code.

- The Web-Server-URL output is the publicly accessible URL for our webserver. Notice here that we are using the **join** function for the **value** parameter to generate the URL for the webserver
- The **Time-Date** output was the timestamp when we executed our Terraform code

```
[cloud_user@ip-10-0-1-235 section7-HoL-TF-DynBlocks-Funcs]$ cat outputs.tf
output "Web-Server-URL" {
  description = "Web-Server-URL"
  value       = join("", ["http://", aws_instance.my-instance.public_ip])
}
```

```
output "Time-Date" {
  description = "Date/Time of Execution"
  value       = timestamp()
}
[cloud_user@ip-10-0-1-235 section7-HoL-TF-DynBlocks-Funcs]$
```

Step03: Review and Deploy the Terraform Code

13. As a best practice, format the code in preparation for deployment:

   terraform fmt

14. Initialize the working directory and download the required providers:

terraform init

Chapter 08: Built-in Functions and Dynamic Blocks

```
[cloud_user@ip-10-0-1-109 section7-HoL-TF-DynBlocks-Funcs]$ terraform fmt
[cloud_user@ip-10-0-1-109 section7-HoL-TF-DynBlocks-Funcs]$ terraform init
Initializing modules...
Downloading terraform-aws-modules/vpc/aws 3.11.4 for vpc...
- vpc in .terraform/modules/vpc

Initializing the backend...

Initializing provider plugins...
- Finding hashicorp/aws versions matching ">= 3.63.0"...
- Installing hashicorp/aws v3.73.0...
- Installed hashicorp/aws v3.73.0 (self-signed, key ID 34365D9472D7468F)

Partner and community providers are signed by their developers.
If you'd like to know more about provider signing, you can read about it here:
https://www.terraform.io/docs/plugins/signing.html

Terraform has created a lock file .terraform.lock.hcl to record the provider
selections it made above. Include this file in your version control repository
so that Terraform can guarantee to make the same selections by default when
you run "terraform init" in the future.

Terraform has been successfully initialized!

You may now begin working with Terraform. Try running "terraform plan" to see
any changes that are required for your infrastructure. All Terraform commands
should now work.

If you ever set or change modules or backend configuration for Terraform,
rerun this command to reinitialize your working directory. If you forget, other
commands will detect it and remind you to do so if necessary.
[cloud_user@ip-10-0-1-109 section7-HoL-TF-DynBlocks-Funcs]$
```

15. Validate the code to look for any errors in syntax, parameters, or attributes within Terraform resources that may prevent it from deploying correctly:

terraform plan

You should receive a notification stating that the configuration is valid.

```
[cloud_user@ip-10-0-1-109 section7-HoL-TF-DynBlocks-Funcs]$ terraform validate
Success! The configuration is valid.

[cloud_user@ip-10-0-1-109 section7-HoL-TF-DynBlocks-Funcs]$
```

16. Review the actions that will be performed when you deploy the Terraform code.

terraform plan

Chapter 08: Built-in Functions and Dynamic Blocks

Note the **Change to Outputs**, where you can see the **Time-Date** and **Web-Server-URL** outputs configured in the **outputs.tf** file earlier.

17. Deploy the code:

    terraform apply --auto-approve

Note: The --auto-approve flag prevents Terraform from explicitly prompting you to enter yes before deploying the code

```
[cloud_user@ip-10-0-1-109 section7-HoL-TF-DynBlocks-Funcs]$ terraform apply --auto-approve
module.vpc.aws_vpc.this[0]: Creating...
module.vpc.aws_vpc.this[0]: Creation complete after 2s [id=vpc-0d5c8af1731a02ed5]
module.vpc.aws_route_table.public[0]: Creating...
module.vpc.aws_subnet.public[0]: Creating...
aws_security_group.my-sg: Creating...
module.vpc.aws_internet_gateway.this[0]: Creating...
module.vpc.aws_route_table.public[0]: Creation complete after 0s [id=rtb-0040ef059c7e3890a]
module.vpc.aws_internet_gateway.this[0]: Creation complete after 0s [id=igw-092f2dd977c80324d]
module.vpc.aws_route.public_internet_gateway[0]: Creating...
module.vpc.aws_route.public_internet_gateway[0]: Creation complete after 1s [id=r-rtb-0040ef059c7e3890a1080289494]
aws_security_group.my-sg: Creation complete after 2s [id=sg-0ac90e909c5e1a8b3]
module.vpc.aws_subnet.public[0]: Still creating... [10s elapsed]
module.vpc.aws_subnet.public[0]: Creation complete after 10s [id=subnet-0422c2947d0710975]
module.vpc.aws_route_table_association.public[0]: Creating...
aws_instance.my-instance: Creating...
module.vpc.aws_route_table_association.public[0]: Creation complete after 2s [id=rtbassoc-0c488f1cf16de6c04]
aws_instance.my-instance: Still creating... [10s elapsed]
aws_instance.my-instance: Creation complete after 13s [id=i-04bbff96f050a5a3e]

Apply complete! Resources: 8 added, 0 changed, 0 destroyed.

Outputs:

Time-Date = "2022-01-27T12:26:57Z"
Web-Server-URL = "http://54.162.121.52"
[cloud_user@ip-10-0-1-109 section7-HoL-TF-DynBlocks-Funcs]$
```

Step 04: Test Out the Deployment and Clean Up

18. Once the code has been executed successfully, view the outputs at the end of the completion message:
    - The **Time-Date** output displayed the **timestamp** when the code was executed.
    - The **Web-Server-URL** output displays the web address for the Apache webserver we created during deployment

Note: You could also use the **Terraform Output** command at any time in the CLI to view these outputs on demand.

Chapter 08: Built-in Functions and Dynamic Blocks

Step 05: Verify that the Resources were Created Correctly in the AWS Management Console:

19. Navigate to the **AWS Management Console** in your browser.
20. Type VPC in the search bar and select VPC from the contextual menu.

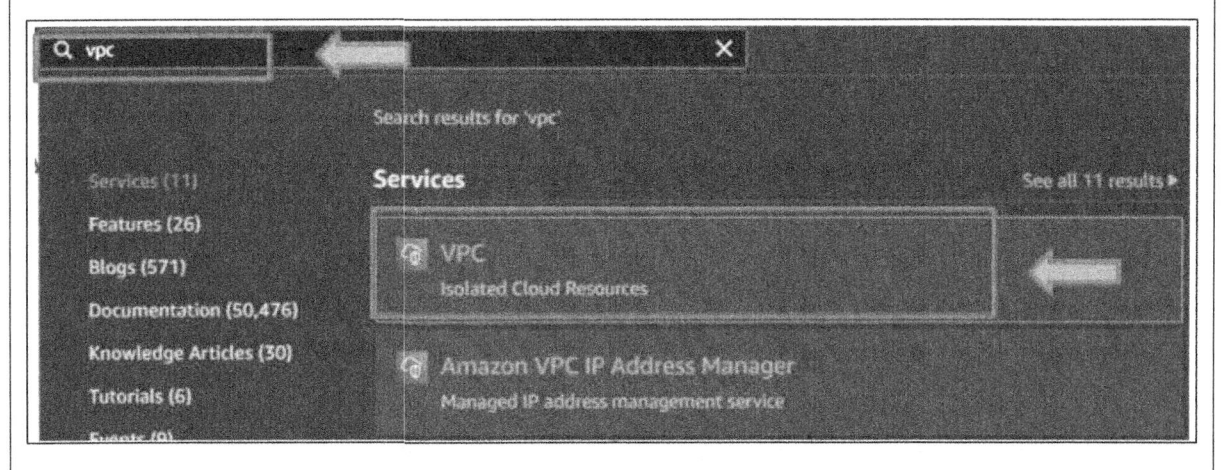

21. On the Resources by Region page, click **VPCs**.

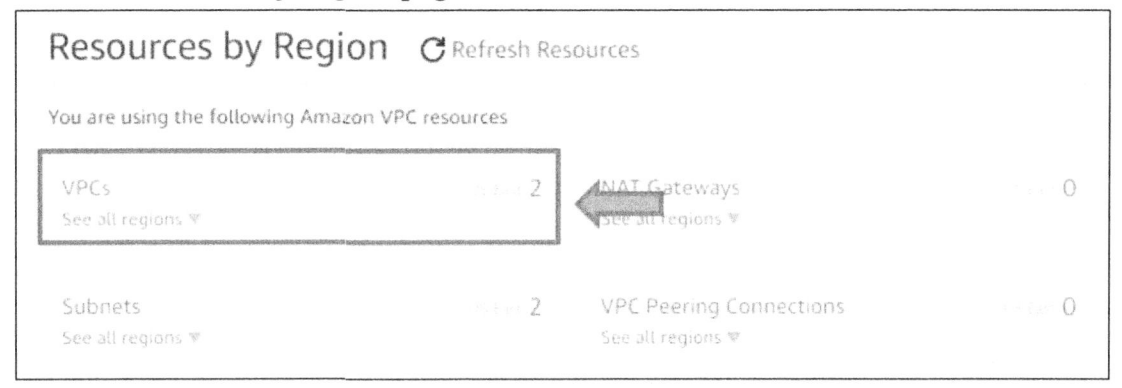

22. Verify that the **my-vpc** resource appears in the list.

23. Type **EC2** in the search bar and select **EC2** from the contextual menu.

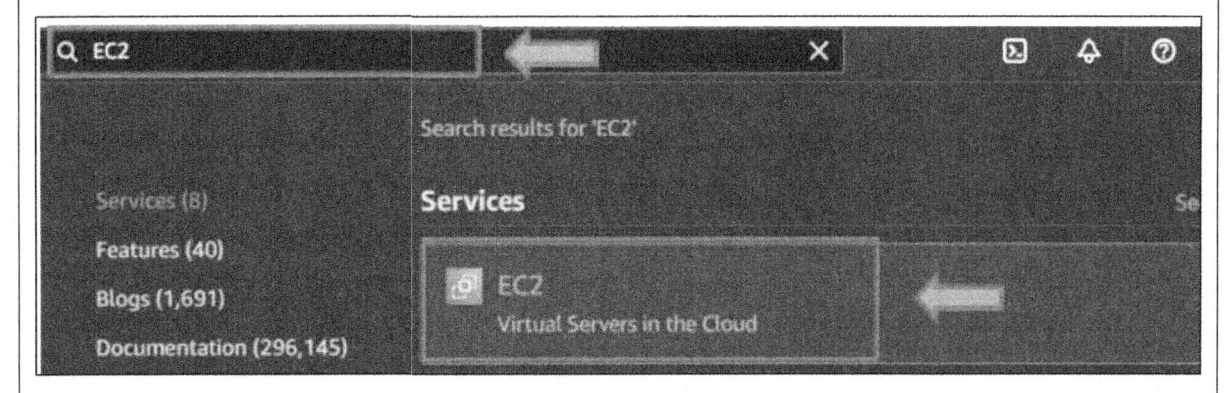

24. On the Resources page, click **Instances (running)**.

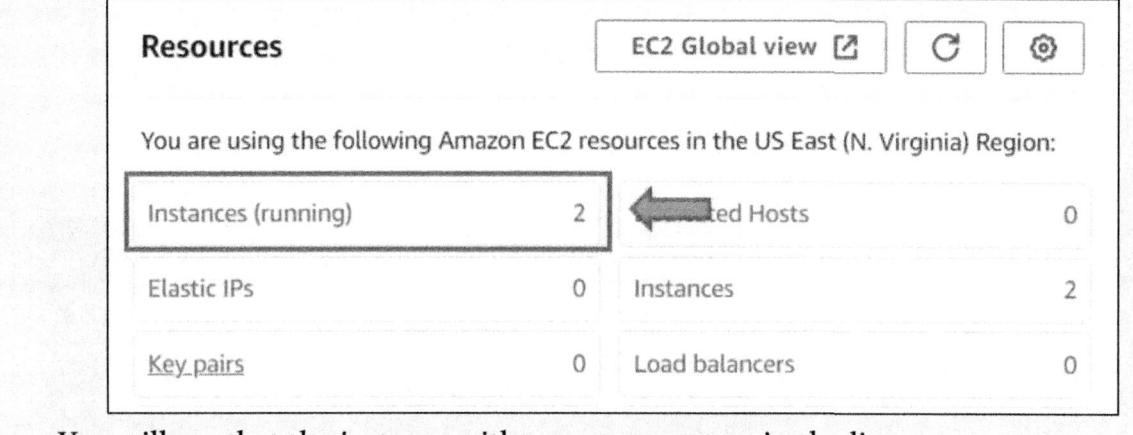

Chapter 08: Built-in Functions and Dynamic Blocks

![Resources panel showing Instances (running) 2, Elastic IPs 0, Key pairs 0, Dedicated Hosts 0, Instances 2, Load balancers 0]

25. You will see that the instance with no name appears in the list.

![Instances list showing TerraformCont... i-0cf27f1d90451c690 Running t3.micro, and a second instance i-04bbff96f050a5a3e Running t3.micro]

26. In the menu on the left, click **Security Groups**.

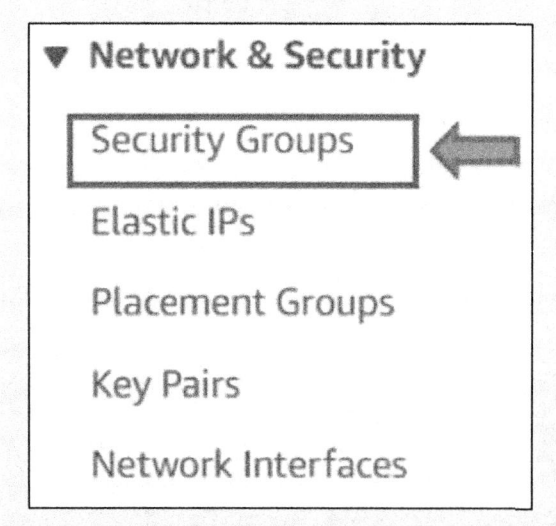

![Network & Security menu with Security Groups, Elastic IPs, Placement Groups, Key Pairs, Network Interfaces]

27. You will see that the **Terraform-Dynamic-SG** security group appears in the list.
28. Select the **Security Group** to see further details.
29. Click on the **Inbound Rules** tab, and note that three separate rules were created from the single dynamic block used on the ingress parameter in the code.

Chapter 08: Built-in Functions and Dynamic Blocks

30. In the **CLI**, copy the URL displayed as the Web-Server_URL output value.
31. In a new browser window or tab, paste the URL and press Enter.
32. Verify that the Apache Test Page loads, validating that the code is executed correctly and the logic within the AWS instance in Terraform has worked correctly, as it was able to locate the **script.sh, file** in the folder, and bootstrap the **EC2** instance accordingly.

Chapter 08: Built-in Functions and Dynamic Blocks

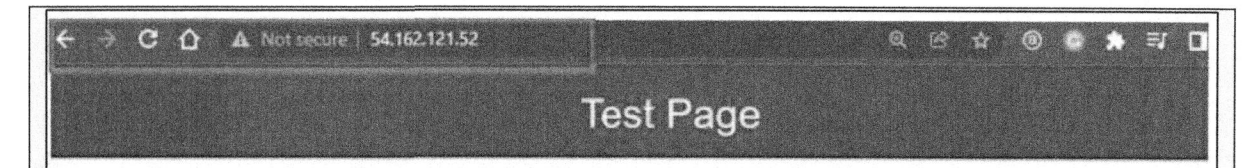

Test Page

This page is used to test the proper operation of the Apache HTTP server after it has been installed. If you can read this page, it means that the Apache HTTP server installed at this site is working properly.

If you are a member of the general public:

The fact that you are seeing this page indicates that the website you just visited is either experiencing problems, or is undergoing routine maintenance.

If you would like to let the administrators of this website know that you've seen this page instead of the page you expected, you should send them e-mail. In general, mail sent to the name "webmaster" and directed to the website's domain should reach the appropriate person.

For example, if you experienced problems while visiting www.example.com, you should send e-mail to "webmaster@example.com".

If you are the website administrator:

You may now add content to the directory /var/www/html/. Note that until you do so, people visiting your website will see this page, and not your content. To prevent this page from ever being used, follow the instructions in the file /etc/httpd/conf.d/welcome.conf.

You are free to use the image below on web sites powered by the Apache HTTP Server:

Powered by APACHE 2.4

33. In the CLI, tear down the infrastructure you just created before moving on:

    terraform destroy --auto-approve

```
[cloud_user@ip-10-0-1-180 section7-HoL-TF-DynBlocks-Funcs]$ terraform destroy --auto-approve
module.vpc.aws_route_table_association.public[0]: Destroying... [id=rtbassoc-0aeb52820bf13a546]
module.vpc.aws_route.public_internet_gateway[0]: Destroying... [id=r-rtb-08b11b53cefd729cf1080289494]
aws_instance.my-instance: Destroying... [id=i-060270584871385e6]
module.vpc.aws_route.public_internet_gateway[0]: Destruction complete after 0s
module.vpc.aws_internet_gateway.this[0]: Destroying... [id=igw-049b0b05521414a70]
module.vpc.aws_route_table_association.public[0]: Destruction complete after 0s
module.vpc.aws_route_table.public[0]: Destroying... [id=rtb-08b11b53cefd729cf]
module.vpc.aws_route_table.public[0]: Destruction complete after 0s
aws_instance.my-instance: Still destroying... [id=i-060270584871385e6, 10s elapsed]
module.vpc.aws_internet_gateway.this[0]: Still destroying... [id=igw-049b0b05521414a70, 10s elapsed]
```

Conclusion

Congratulations — you have completed this hands-on lab!

Chapter 08: Built-in Functions and Dynamic Blocks

Mind Map

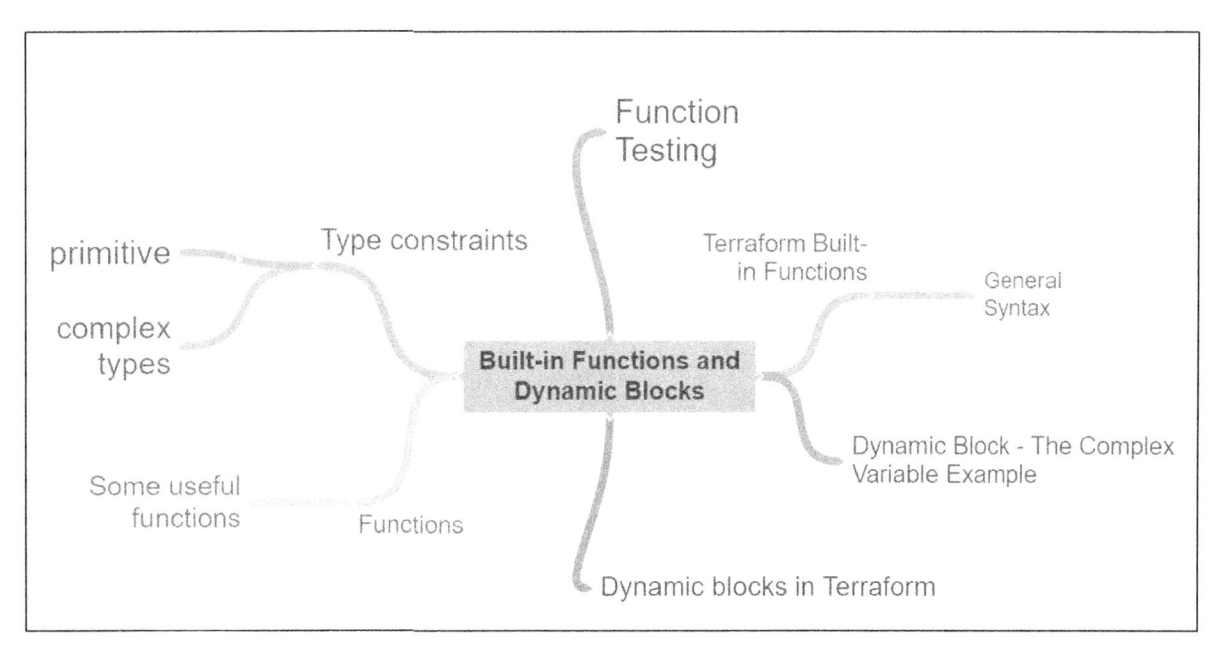

Figure 8-13: Mind Map

Chapter 08: Built-in Functions and Dynamic Blocks

Practice Questions

1. By default, Terraform comes bundled with _____
   A. All the built-in functions
   B. No built-in functions
   C. User-defined functions
   D. All of the above

2. In Terraform, you can create your user-defined functions. True or false?
   A. True
   B. False

3. The general syntax for function calls is a function name followed by _____
   A. Parenthesized underscore-separated arguments
   B. Parenthesized comma-separated arguments
   C. Parenthesized hyphen-separated arguments
   D. None of the above

4. Which function is used for inserting files into your resources where applicable?
   A. file function
   B. max function
   C. flatten function
   D. All of the above

5. Which function is used to create a singular list out of a provided set of lists?
   A. file function
   B. max function
   C. flatten function
   D. None of the above

6. Which function is used for determining the max integer value from a provided list?
   A. file function
   B. max function
   C. flatten function
   D. All of the above

Chapter 08: Built-in Functions and Dynamic Blocks

7. The Terraform console command provides an interactive console for evaluating _____.
A. Expressions
B. Equations
C. Boolean
D. All of the above

8. How many type constraints are there?
A. One
B. Two
C. Three
D. Four

9. Which type constraints allows for a single type of value to be assigned to a variable, such as a number type, string type, or boolean (or bool) type?
A. Primitive
B. Complex
C. Any Constraint
D. None of the above

10. Which type of constraint includes multiple value types in a single variable?

Note: Such value types can be constructed using list, tuple, map, or object data structures.

A. Primitive
B. Complex
C. Any Constraint
D. All of the above

11. The complex types can be broken into _____ further types.
A. One
B. Two
C. Three
D. All of the above

12. Structural type is a type of primitive. True or false?
A. True

B. False

13. Which of the following allows multiple values of a single or one primitive type to be grouped against a variable?
A. Collection type
B. Structural Type
C. Complex Type
D. All of the above

14. Which of the following allows multiple values of different primitive types to be grouped?
A. Collection type
B. Structural Type
C. Complex Type
D. None of the above

15. Which of the following helps to construct repeatable nested configuration blocks inside Terraform resources?
A. Terraform Functions
B. Type Constraints
C. Dynamic Block
D. All of the above

Chapter 09: Terraform State

Introduction

Terraform needs to keep track of the condition of your controlled infrastructure and settings. Terraform uses this state to map real-world resources to your configuration, keep track of information, and optimize large-scale infrastructure performance. By default, this state is saved in a local file called "terraform."

Terraform State Command

Terraform State maps real-world resources to resources defined in your Terraform code or configuration. By default, Terraform state is stored locally in a file called terraform.tfstate, but it can be stored remotely in services such as AWS S3. Before performing any modification, Terraform refreshes the state file. Terraform also tracks the dependency between the resources deployed. For example, Terraform must know that it must configure a subnet before deploying a virtual machine in AWS. State file also helps boost deployment performance by acting as a cache for resource attributes. Terraform state command is a utility for reading Terraform state files and advanced state management.

- **Scenarios**

We usually do not need to mess with the Terraform state file outside the core workflow of Terraform. There are some scenarios in which you might want to tweak the state outside the workflow to remove or change resources tracked by Terraform. You can use it for advanced state management. You can remove the resource so that Terraform does not track them. You can use Terraform state commands list subcommand to drag the details of resources and names of resources managed by Terraform.

Terraform State Subcommand	Use
terraform state list	List out all resources tracked by the Terraform state file
terraform state rm	Delete a resource from the Terraform state file
terraform state show	Show details of a resource tracked in the Terraform state file

Table 9-01: Terraform State Subcommand

> **EXAM TIP:** Terraform state's primary purpose is to store bindings between external system objects and resource instances described in your configuration. When Terraform creates a remote object in reaction to a configuration change, it records the remote object's identification against a specific resource instance, which it can then update or delete in response to future configuration changes.

Demo 9-01: Terraform command

1. Enter the following code to spin up a Docker image with linked Terraform to pull down the centos seven images. We spun up a container using the image that was pulled down and ran the command inside the container to live it immediately. It simply pulls down an image and starts the container on the local system.

```
# Configure the Docker provider
provider "docker" {}

#Image to be used by container
resource "docker_image" "terraform-centos" {
    name         = "centos:7"
    keep_locally = true
}

# Create a container
resource "docker_container" "centos" {
    image   = docker_image.terraform-centos.latest
    name    = "terraform-centos"
    start   = true
    command = ["/bin/sleep", "500"]
}
```

2. Run the **terraform apply** command to add two resources: a Docker image and a Docker container. Enter yes when prompted.

Chapter 09: Terraform State

```
      + id                   = (known after apply)
      + image                = (known after apply)
      + ip_address           = (known after apply)
      + ip_prefix_length     = (known after apply)
      + ipc_mode             = (known after apply)
      + log_driver           = (known after apply)
      + log_opts             = (known after apply)
      + logs                 = false
      + must_run             = true
      + name                 = "terraform-centos"
      + network_data         = (known after apply)
      + read_only            = false
      + restart              = "no"
      + rm                   = false
      + shm_size             = (known after apply)
      + start                = true
      + user                 = (known after apply)
      + working_dir          = (known after apply)
    }

  # docker_image.terraform-centos will be created
  + resource "docker_image" "terraform-centos" {
      + id           = (known after apply)
      + keep_locally = true
      + latest       = (known after apply)
      + name         = "centos:7"
    }

Plan: 2 to add, 0 to change, 0 to destroy.

Do you want to perform these actions?
  Terraform will perform the actions described above.
  Only 'yes' will be accepted to approve.

  Enter a value:
```

3. Run the **terraform state list** command to see that Terraform is recently tracking resources.

```
→ state_command terraform state list
docker_container.centos
docker_image.terraform-centos
```

4. Run the **Docker ps** command to ensure the container that we spun up using Terraform is available from the Docker command.

```
→ state_command docker ps
CONTAINER ID   IMAGE         COMMAND           CREATED          STATUS              PORTS   NAMES
439919009e1c   7e6257c9f8d8  "/bin/sleep 500"  38 seconds ago   Up 37 seconds               terraform-centos
93d66ca02de9   centos:7      "/bin/bash"       2 weeks ago      Up About an hour            mk
→ state_command
```

5. Run the **terraform state show <name-of-resource>** command to see details of the resources. Details are the same as details in terraform.tfstate file has in it.

```
→ state_command terraform state show docker_container.centos
# docker_container.centos:
resource "docker_container" "centos" {
    attach              = false
    command             = [
        "/bin/sleep",
        "500",
    ]
    cpu_shares          = 0
    dns                 = []
    dns_opts            = []
    entrypoint          = []
    gateway             = "172.17.0.1"
    hostname            = "439919009e1c"
    id                  = "439919009e1c32a8efdad8c3cd53bcf98f22644203f7a80ddf44a89b05b4ae57"
    image               = "sha256:7e6257c9f8d8d4cdff5e155f196d67150b871bbe8c02761026f803a704acb3e9"
    ip_address          = "172.17.0.3"
    ip_prefix_length    = 16
    ipc_mode            = "private"
    log_driver          = "json-file"
    log_opts            = {}
    logs                = false
    max_retry_count     = 0
    memory              = 0
    memory_swap         = 0
    must_run            = true
    name                = "terraform-centos"
    network_data        = [
        {
            gateway          = "172.17.0.1"
            ip_address       = "172.17.0.3"
            ip_prefix_length = 16
            network_name     = "bridge"
        },
```

6. To retain the resources you deployed through Terraform, run **terraform state rm <name-of-resource>** command to help you un-manage a resource from within Terraform. Now the resource is removed and not managed by Terraform anymore.

Chapter 09: Terraform State

```
→ state_command terraform state rm docker_container.centos
Removed docker_container.centos
Successfully removed 1 resource instance(s).
→ state_command
```

7. Issue the **terraform destroy** command, and you will see only one resource was destroyed when we created two originally.

```
→ state_command terraform destroy
docker_image.terraform-centos: Refreshing state... [id=sha256:7e6257c9f8d8d4cdff5e155f196d67150b871bbe8c02761026f803a704acb3e9centos:7]

An execution plan has been generated and is shown below.
Resource actions are indicated with the following symbols:
  - destroy

Terraform will perform the following actions:

  # docker_image.terraform-centos will be destroyed
  - resource "docker_image" "terraform-centos" {
      - id           = "sha256:7e6257c9f8d8d4cdff5e155f196d67150b871bbe8c02761026f803a704acb3e9centos:7" -> null
      - keep_locally = true -> null
      - latest       = "sha256:7e6257c9f8d8d4cdff5e155f196d67150b871bbe8c02761026f803a704acb3e9" -> null
      - name         = "centos:7" -> null
    }

Plan: 0 to add, 0 to change, 1 to destroy.

Do you really want to destroy all resources?
  Terraform will destroy all your managed infrastructure, as shown above.
  There is no undo. Only 'yes' will be accepted to confirm.

  Enter a value: yes

docker_image.terraform-centos: Destroying... [id=sha256:7e6257c9f8d8d4cdff5e155f196d67150b871bbe8c02761026f803a704acb3e9centos:7]
docker_image.terraform-centos: Destruction complete after 0s

Destroy complete! Resources: 1 destroyed.
```

8. Run the **Docker ps** command to see if the container is still running. You can see it is still running because Terraform no longer manages it.

```
→ state_command docker ps
CONTAINER ID   IMAGE          COMMAND          CREATED         STATUS         PORTS   NAMES
5347291469c5   7e6257c9f8d8   "/bin/sleep 500"  3 minutes ago   Up 3 minutes           terraform-centos
93d66ca02de9   centos:7       "/bin/bash"       2 weeks ago     Up 2 hours             mk
→ state_command
```

Local and Remote State Storage

We know that the state file is essential to Terraform. It is the reason why we need to pay attention to its availability, safety, and integrity.

Local State Storage

Terraform saves state files locally on the same system that generates these commands by default. This method is usually used for individual projects or testing purposes. Depending on the criticality of the state file, you can also store it in a version control system.

Terraform back up your last known Terraform state file recorded after a successful Terraform applies locally.

Remote State Storage

Unlike local state storage, which does not offer flexibility in collaboration and availability, Terraform offers remote state storage. The advantages of storing files remotely are reading files across the distributed teams and better security and availability in the Cloud, which ensure solid backups. Several Terraform platforms store state remotely, including AWS S3 storage and GCP Storage.

Imagine a team in the US was working on deployment and making changes to it. They would configure Terraform to save the state file in remote state storage if another team in Europe wants to look at the state file for review or work on the shared Terraform code base from the remotely saved state file. Since different cloud vendors offer different security policies for files, you can get granular control of who can read and write to the files. It is how a remote state enables collaboration between distributed teams securely.

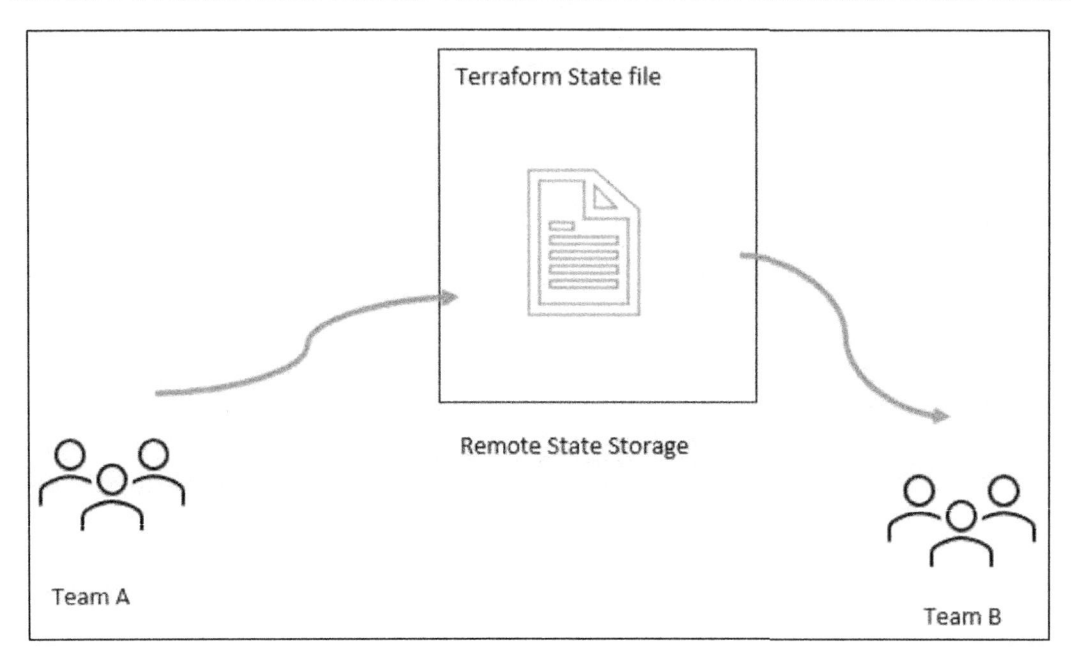

Figure 9-01: Remote State Storage

State locking is a feature common to both local and remote state storage. It locks the state file, so another operator who has access to your system or code repository does not end up executing a parallel run of Terraform deployment by mistake. Not all-remote state storage backends support State locking. Some backend that supports state locking includes AWS S3, GCP storage, and HashiCorp's console.

> **EXAM TIP:** For local state storage, state locking is enabled by default when you issue a terraform apply.

Output Values

Output values provide information about your infrastructure to other Terraform setups and make it available on the command line. In computer languages, output values are equivalent to return values.

There are various applications for output values:

- A parent module can access a portion of a child module's resource properties via outputs.
- After running terraform apply, a root module can use outputs to print specific values in the CLI output.
- Root module outputs can be accessed by other configurations using a terraform_remote_state data source when using a remote state.

Each Terraform resource instance exports characteristics whose values can be utilized elsewhere in configuration. Output values are a way to give your module's user access to some of that data.

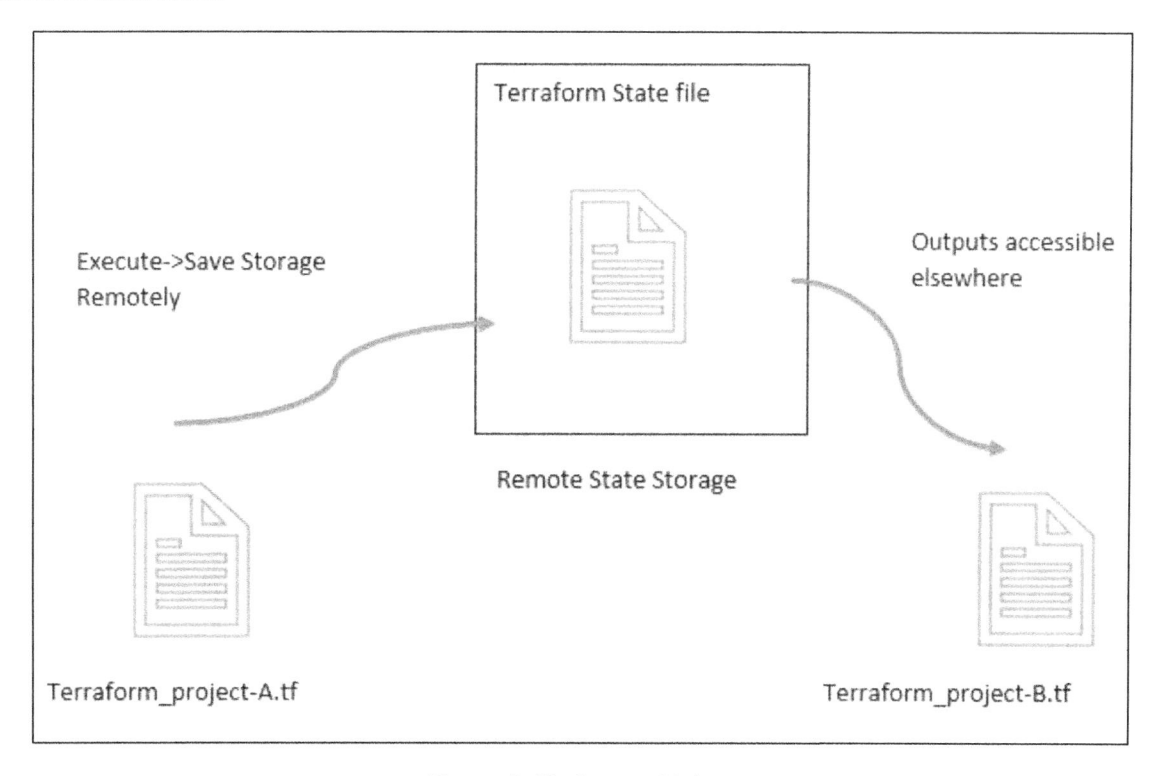

Figure 9-02: Output Values

Chapter 09: Terraform State

Demo 9-02: Persisting Terraform State in AWS S3

1. Clone the Terraform code using the following command.

   git clone https://github.com/12920/IPSpecialist01/blob/main/content-hashicorp-certified-terraform-associate-foundations-master%20(2).zip

   Note: Open the file "section5-demo-aws-s3-remote-storage".

2. The code is split into three files.

   ```
   → demo ls
   backend.tf    main.tf    variables.tf
   ```

3. See backend.tf file by using **cat backend.tf.** This block helps set different configuration options for Terraform. See that we have configured the code for Terraform version used greater than or equal to 0.13.

   ```
   → demo ls
   backend.tf    main.tf    variables.tf
   → demo cat backend.tf
   terraform {
     required_providers {
       docker = {
         source = "kreuzwerker/docker"
       }
     }
     required_version = ">= 0.13"
     backend "s3" {
       profile = "demo"
       region  = "us-east-1"
       key     = "terraform.tfstate"
       bucket  = "myawesomes3bucket3344"
     }
   }
   → demo
   ```

4. Set up AWS CLI for authentication using **AWS –profile <name-of-profile> configure.**

Chapter 09: Terraform State

```
→ demo aws --profile demo configure
AWS Access Key ID [None]: AKIAUYGQPAJ5IH74P4CR
AWS Secret Access Key [None]: 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
Default region name [us-east-1]: us-east-1
Default output format [json]:
→ demo
```

5. Enter AWS –profile <name-of-profile> s3api create-bucket –bucket <name-of-bucket>. Make sure the bucket name is unique, or you must change the name of the bucket both in the backend and in AWS CLI.

```
→ demo aws --profile demo s3api create-bucket --bucket myawesomes3bucket33444
{
    "Location": "/myawesomes3bucket33444"
}
→ demo
```

6. View main.tf using the **cat main.tf** command. In this main.tf file, we declare the Docker provider, define the Docker image, and pass the image name. We passed the internal and external ports to access the container once it was up and running.

```
→ demo cat main.tf
provider "docker" {}

resource "docker_image" "nginx-image" {
  name = "nginx"
}

resource "docker_container" "nginx" {
  image = docker_image.nginx-image.latest
  name  = "nginx"
  ports {
    internal = 80
    external = var.external_port
    protocol = "tcp"
  }
}

output "url" {
  description = "Browser URL for container site"
  value       = join(":", ["http://localhost", tostring(var.external_port)])
}
→ demo
```

7. View variable.tf using the **cat variable.tf** command. This file declares the variable of type number, and this file uses a validation block with a condition.

245

Chapter 09: Terraform State

```
→ demo cat variables.tf
variable "external_port" {
  type    = number
  default = 8080
  validation {
    condition     = can(regex("8080|80", var.external_port))
    error_message = "Port values can only be 8080 or 80."
  }
}
→ demo
```

8. Enter the **terraform init** command to make sure that the right provider is pulled from the public registry of Terraform.

```
→ demo terraform init

Initializing the backend...

Successfully configured the backend "s3"! Terraform will automatically
use this backend unless the backend configuration changes.

Initializing provider plugins...
- Finding latest version of kreuzwerker/docker...
- Installing kreuzwerker/docker v2.10.0...
- Installed kreuzwerker/docker v2.10.0 (self-signed, key ID 24E54F214569A8A5)

Partner and community providers are signed by their developers.
If you'd like to know more about provider signing, you can read about it here:
https://www.terraform.io/docs/plugins/signing.html

The following providers do not have any version constraints in configuration,
so the latest version was installed.

To prevent automatic upgrades to new major versions that may contain breaking
changes, we recommend adding version constraints in a required_providers block
in your configuration, with the constraint strings suggested below.

* kreuzwerker/docker: version = "~> 2.10.0"

Terraform has been successfully initialized!

You may now begin working with Terraform. Try running "terraform plan" to see
any changes that are required for your infrastructure. All Terraform commands
should now work.

If you ever set or change modules or backend configuration for Terraform,
rerun this command to reinitialize your working directory. If you forget, other
commands will detect it and remind you to do so if necessary.
→ demo
```

9. Issue the **terraform plan** command to review the code to be deployed.

```
        + start_period = (known after apply)
        + test         = (known after apply)
        + timeout      = (known after apply)
      }

    + labels {
        + label = (known after apply)
        + value = (known after apply)
      }

    + ports {
        + external = 8080
        + internal = 80
        + ip       = "0.0.0.0"
        + protocol = "tcp"
      }
    }

  # docker_image.nginx-image will be created
  + resource "docker_image" "nginx-image" {
      + id     = (known after apply)
      + latest = (known after apply)
      + name   = "nginx"
      + output = (known after apply)
    }

Plan: 2 to add, 0 to change, 0 to destroy.
```

10. Use **terraform apply** to deploy the code, enter yes when prompted.
11. Enter **terraform apply -var external port=8181**. The validation has picked the wrong port, so we got an error message set in the validation process.

```
→ demo terraform apply -var external_port=8181

Error: Invalid value for variable

  on variables.tf line 1:
   1: variable "external_port" {

Port values can only be 8080 or 80.

This was checked by the validation rule at variables.tf:4,3-13.

→ demo
```

12. We will use the AWS command for retrieving the file that was stored remotely on your system by using **aws --profile <name-of-profile> cp s3://<name-of-bucket><name-of-state-file>**

```
→ demo aws --profile demo s3 cp s3://myawesomes3bucket33444/terraform.tfstate .
download: s3://myawesomes3bucket33444/terraform.tfstate to ./terraform.tfstate
→ demo
```

13. Takedown the infrastructure you have just built via the **terraform destroy** command. Type yes and hit **Enter** when prompted.

```
Plan: 0 to add, 0 to change, 2 to destroy.

Do you really want to destroy all resources?
  Terraform will destroy all your managed infrastructure, as shown above.
  There is no undo. Only 'yes' will be accepted to confirm.

  Enter a value:
```

Lab 9-01: Exploring Terraform State Functionality

Introduction

Terraform needs to keep track of the condition of your controlled infrastructure and settings. Terraform state's primary purpose is to store bindings between external system objects and resource instances described in your configuration. Terraform uses this state to map real-world resources to your configuration, keep track of information, and optimize large-scale infrastructure performance. Terraform makes plans and adjustments to your infrastructure using this local state. It performs a refresh before any operation to keep the state up to current with the actual infrastructure.

Problem

Your organization wants you to deploy infrastructure using Terraform and keep track of all resources created. How will you do it?

Solution

We will have Terraform's main code to deploy resources into a Kubernetes cluster. The code will first create objects or resources and tag them in the Terraform state file. Create real-world resources in the Kubernetes cluster. The gel that connects both the Terraform objects and real-world resources in Kubernetes is the Terraform state file. Terraform state file will track changes made to code and apply all those changes to real-world resources

Step 01: Check Terraform and Minikube Status

Chapter 09: Terraform State

1. Log into Terraform server using **ssh <username>@<PublicIP>** and check the terraform status using the **terraform version** command.

   ```
   [cloud_user@ip-10-0-1-124 ~]$ terraform version
   Terraform v0.13.3
   ```

2. If you get a message that a newer version of Terraform is available, disregard it; the experiment will run well with the version currently installed on the VM.

   ```
   Your version of Terraform is out of date! The latest version
   is 1.1.4. You can update by downloading from https://www.terraform.io/downloads.html
   [cloud_user@ip-10-0-1-124 ~]$
   ```

3. Check the state of the minikube using the **minikube status** command.

   ```
   [cloud_user@ip-10-0-1-124 ~]$ minikube status
   minikube
   type: Control Plane
   host: Running
   kubelet: Running
   apiserver: Running
   kubeconfig: Configured

   [cloud_user@ip-10-0-1-124 ~]$
   ```

Step 02: Clone Terraform Code

1. Clone the Terraform code using the following command.

git clone https://github.com/12920/IPSpecialist01/blob/main/content-hashicorp-certified-terraform-associate-foundations-master%20(2).zip

2. Go to the directory where the code is present. Using the **cd lab code/ cd section2-hol1/** command.

   ```
   [cloud_user@ip-10-0-1-124 ~]$ cd lab_code/
   [cloud_user@ip-10-0-1-124 lab_code]$ cd section2-hol1/
   [cloud_user@ip-10-0-1-124 section2-hol1]$
   ```

3. View the code in the main.tf file, using **vim main. tf.** The code is configured with Kubernetes as the provider, allowing Terraform to interact with the Kubernetes API to create and destroy resources. Within the Kubernetes deployment resource, the

replicas attribute controls the number of deployments, which controls the deployed number of pods.

```
provider "kubernetes" {
  config_path = "~/.kube/config"
}

resource "kubernetes_deployment" "tf-k8s-deployment" {
  metadata {
    name = "tf-k8s-deploy"
    labels = {
      name = "terraform-k8s-deployment"
    }
  }

  spec {
    replicas = 2

    selector {
      match_labels = {
        name = "terraform-k8s-deployment"
      }
    }

    template {
      metadata {
        labels = {
          name = "terraform-k8s-deployment"
        }
      }

      spec {
        container {
          image = "nginx"
```

4. Press **Escape** and enter:**q!** to exit the file.

Step 03: Deploy the Cloned Terraform Code

1. Initialize operating directory and download required providers using the **terraform init** command.

Chapter 09: Terraform State

```
[cloud_user@ip-10-0-1-124 section2-hol1]$ terraform init
Initializing the backend...

Initializing provider plugins...
- Finding latest version of hashicorp/kubernetes...
- Installing hashicorp/kubernetes v2.7.1...
- Installed hashicorp/kubernetes v2.7.1 (self-signed, key ID 34365D9472D7468F)

Partner and community providers are signed by their developers.
If you'd like to know more about provider signing, you can read about it here:
https://www.terraform.io/docs/plugins/signing.html

The following providers do not have any version constraints in configuration,
so the latest version was installed.

To prevent automatic upgrades to new major versions that may contain breaking
changes, we recommend adding version constraints in a required_providers block
in your configuration, with the constraint strings suggested below.

* hashicorp/kubernetes: version = "~> 2.7.1"

Terraform has been successfully initialized!

You may now begin working with Terraform. Try running "terraform plan" to see
any changes that are required for your infrastructure. All Terraform commands
should now work.

If you ever set or change modules or backend configuration for Terraform,
rerun this command to reinitialize your working directory. If you forget, other
commands will detect it and remind you to do so if necessary.
[cloud_user@ip-10-0-1-124 section2-hol1]$
```

2. Review the activities performed when you send the Terraform code using the **terraform plan** command. Notice that it will make two assets as arranged in the Terraform code.

Chapter 09: Terraform State

```
        + name                          = "terraform-k8s-service"
        + namespace                     = "default"
        + resource_version              = (known after apply)
        + uid                           = (known after apply)
      }

      + spec {
          + cluster_ip                  = (known after apply)
          + external_traffic_policy     = (known after apply)
          + health_check_node_port      = (known after apply)
          + publish_not_ready_addresses = false
          + session_affinity            = "None"
          + type                        = "NodePort"

          + port {
              + node_port   = 30080
              + port        = 80
              + protocol    = "TCP"
              + target_port = "80"
            }
        }
    }

Plan: 2 to add, 0 to change, 0 to destroy.

------------------------------------------------------------------------

Note: You didn't specify an "-out" parameter to save this plan, so Terraform
can't guarantee that exactly these actions will be performed if
"terraform apply" is subsequently run.

[cloud_user@ip-10-0-1-124 section2-hol1]$
```

3. List the records in the index using the **ls** command. Notice that the records do exclude the terraform. tfstate right now. You should convey the Terraform code for the state document to be made.

```
[cloud_user@ip-10-0-1-124 section2-hol1]$ ls
main.tf  README.md  service.tf
[cloud_user@ip-10-0-1-124 section2-hol1]$
```

4. Convey the code using the **terraform apply** command. When asked, type yes and press **Enter**.

Chapter 09: Terraform State

```
          }
        + name                 = "terraform-k8s-service"
        + namespace            = "default"
        + resource_version     = (known after apply)
        + uid                  = (known after apply)
      }

      + spec {
          + cluster_ip                = (known after apply)
          + external_traffic_policy   = (known after apply)
          + health_check_node_port    = (known after apply)
          + publish_not_ready_addresses = false
          + session_affinity          = "None"
          + type                      = "NodePort"

          + port {
              + node_port   = 30080
              + port        = 80
              + protocol    = "TCP"
              + target_port = "80"
            }
        }
    }

Plan: 2 to add, 0 to change, 0 to destroy.

Do you want to perform these actions?
  Terraform will perform the actions described above.
  Only 'yes' will be accepted to approve.

  Enter a value: yes

Apply complete! Resources: 2 added, 0 changed, 0 destroyed.
```

Step 04: Observe How Terraform State File Track Resources

1. List the files in the directory after the code has been completed successfully, using **ls**. The terraform. tfstate file has now been added to the list. This state file keeps track of all Terraform's resources.

```
Apply complete! Resources: 2 added, 0 changed, 0 destroyed.
[cloud_user@ip-10-0-1-124 section2-hol1]$ ls
main.tf   README.md   service.tf   terraform.tfstate
[cloud_user@ip-10-0-1-124 section2-hol1]$
```

2. Use **kubectl get pods** to verify that the code generated the required pods. Notice two pods are running.

Chapter 09: Terraform State

```
[cloud_user@ip-10-0-1-124 section2-hol1]$ kubectl get pods
NAME                              READY   STATUS    RESTARTS   AGE
tf-k8s-deploy-9c7b8d989-j7ngj     1/1     Running   0          76s
tf-k8s-deploy-9c7b8d989-mf7qr     1/1     Running   0          76s
[cloud_user@ip-10-0-1-124 section2-hol1]$
```

3. Use the **terraform state** command to list all the resources that the Terraform state file is tracking.
4. Using **terraform state, show kubernetes_deployment.tf-k8s-deployment | egrep replicas** view replicas tracked by Terraform state file. The state file should keep track of two replicas.

```
[cloud_user@ip-10-0-1-124 section2-hol1]$ terraform state show kubernetes_deployment.tf-k8s-deployment | egrep replicas
    replicas            = "2"
[cloud_user@ip-10-0-1-124 section2-hol1]$
```

5. To edit the main.tf file, open main.tf file by typing the **vim main.tf** command. Change the replicas attribute's integer value from 2 to 4.

```
provider "kubernetes" {
  config_path = "~/.kube/config"
}

resource "kubernetes_deployment" "tf-k8s-deployment" {
  metadata {
    name = "tf-k8s-deploy"
    labels = {
      name = "terraform-k8s-deployment"
    }
  }

  spec {
    replicas = 4        ⬅

    selector {
      match_labels = {
        name = "terraform-k8s-deployment"
      }
    }

    template {
      metadata {
        labels = {
          name = "terraform-k8s-deployment"
```

Chapter 09: Terraform State

6. To save and leave the file, press Escape and enter: **wq**.
7. Review the steps taken when the Terraform code is deployed using **terraform plan** command. Only one resource will change in this case, for which the replicas property in our Terraform code has been modified.

```
                    termination_message_policy   = "File"
                    tty                          = false

                    resources {}
                }
              }
            }
          }
        }

Plan: 0 to add, 1 to change, 0 to destroy.

------------------------------------------------------------------

Note: You didn't specify an "-out" parameter to save this plan, so Terraform
can't guarantee that exactly these actions will be performed if
"terraform apply" is subsequently run.

[cloud_user@ip-10-0-1-124 section2-hol1]$
```

8. Re-deploy the code, run **terraform apply** command. Type yes and hit **Enter** when prompted.

```
                    tty                          = false

                    resources {}
                }
              }
            }
          }
        }

Plan: 0 to add, 1 to change, 0 to destroy.

Do you want to perform these actions?
  Terraform will perform the actions described above.
  Only 'yes' will be accepted to approve.

  Enter a value: yes
```

Chapter 09: Terraform State

9. Double-check that the code produces the required pods as expected, using the **kubectl get pods** command. The deployment currently consists of four pods.

```
[cloud_user@ip-10-0-1-124 section2-hol1]$ kubectl get pods
NAME                              READY   STATUS    RESTARTS   AGE
tf-k8s-deploy-9c7b8d989-httmx     1/1     Running   0          22s
tf-k8s-deploy-9c7b8d989-j7ngj     1/1     Running   0          10m
tf-k8s-deploy-9c7b8d989-mf7qr     1/1     Running   0          10m
tf-k8s-deploy-9c7b8d989-pkw9x     1/1     Running   0          22s
[cloud_user@ip-10-0-1-124 section2-hol1]$
```

10. View file's replicas attribute tracked by Terraform state, using **terraform state show kubernetes_deployment.tf-k8s-deployment | egrep replicas.** Notice there are four replicas now.

```
[cloud_user@ip-10-0-1-124 section2-hol1]$ terraform state show kubernetes_deployment.tf-k8s-deployment | egrep replicas
       replicas               = "4"
[cloud_user@ip-10-0-1-124 section2-hol1]$
```

11. Takedown the infrastructure you have just built via the **terraform destroy** command. Type yes and hit **Enter** when prompted.

```
Plan: 0 to add, 0 to change, 2 to destroy.

Do you really want to destroy all resources?
  Terraform will destroy all your managed infrastructure, as shown above.
  There is no undo. Only 'yes' will be accepted to confirm.

  Enter a value:
```

12. List the files in the directory using the **ls** command. Terraform creates a backup file called terraform.tfstate.backup if you need to revert to the last Terraform state you deployed.

```
[cloud_user@ip-10-0-1-124 section2-hol1]$ ls
main.tf  README.md  service.tf  terr...        terraform.tfstate.backup
[cloud_user@ip-10-0-1-124 section2-hol1]$
```

Chapter 09: Terraform State

Mind Map

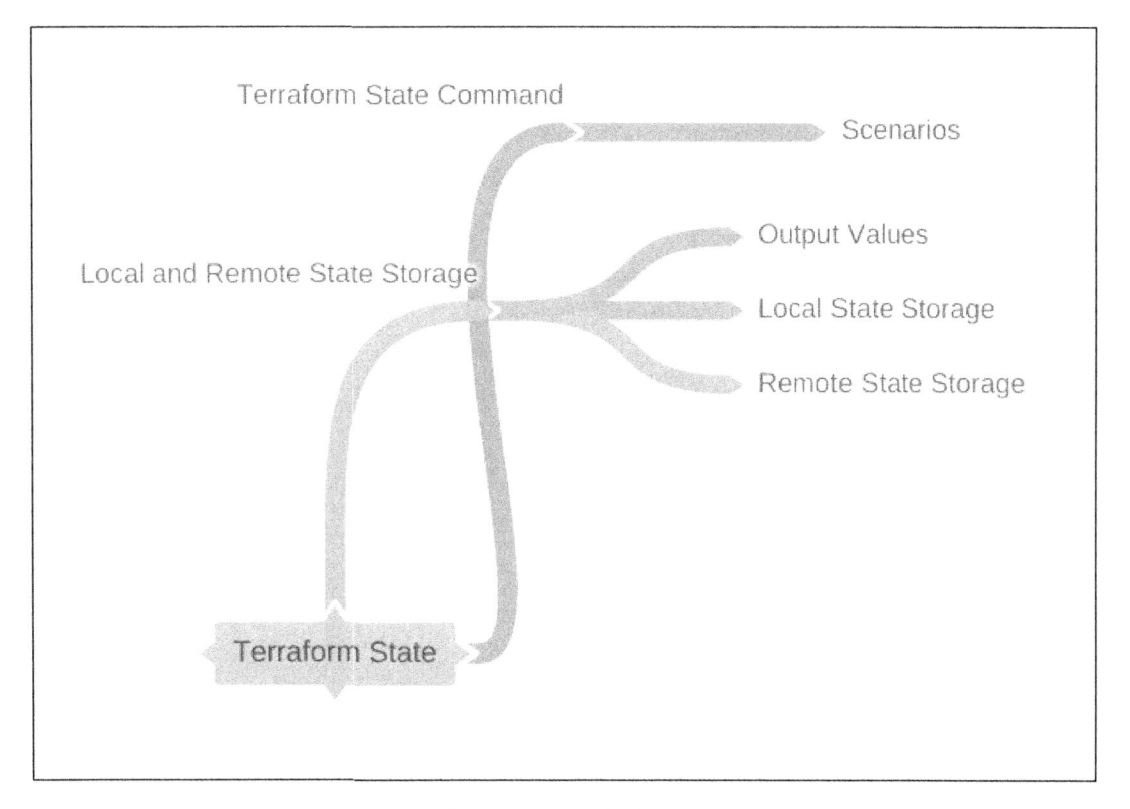

Figure 9-03: Mind Map

Practice Questions

1. Terraform state file is stored only remotely. True or false?

A. True
B. False

2. Terraform state is stored in the file called _____.

A. terraform.tfstate
B. terraform.pystate
C. terraform.jsonstate
D. None of the mentioned

3. Terraform also tracks the _____ resources deployed.

A. Security policies of
B. Health of

C. Dependencies between
D. Both C and D

4. In which of the following scenarios can we tweak the state outside the workflow to remove or change resources tracked by Terraform?

A. For advanced state management
B. To see names of resources managed by Terraform
C. To see details of resources managed by Terraform
D. All of the above

5. What of the following subcommand is used to delete a resource from the Terraform state file?

A. terraform state list
B. terraform state rm
C. terraform state show
D. None of the above

6. By default, Terraform saves state files _____.

A. Locally
B. Remotely
C. Locally and a backup copy on remote services
D. None of the above

7. Local state storage offers greater availability than remote state storage. True or false?

A. True
B. False

8. Remote state storage is more secure because _____.

A. Only the owner of the resource can access it
B. You cannot share it in a different region
C. Due to policies created by cloud vendors
D. All of the above

9. _____ backends do not support State locking.

A. AWS S3 storage
B. GCP Storage
C. Hashicorp's console
D. All the remote state storage

10. _____ values can be used by other Terraform projects or code.

A. Variable
B. Output
C. Input
D. None of the above

11. When deploying or removing resources, how does Terraform handle dependencies in your infrastructure?

A. The Terraform state file is used to handle them
B. The operator (user) must manually code each dependence in
C. For detecting dependencies, Terraform Cloud capabilities like Sentinel are used
D. It does not deal with dependencies

12. What are the advantages of storing Terraform state remotely?

A. It provides no benefit; it is the same as storing a state locally
B. Terraform deployments can now be completed more quickly
C. Granular access, integrity, security, availability, and cooperation are all provided
D. It provides agility, memory optimization, and automated Terraform code patching

13. Which command would you use to see all the resources that the Terraform state file has created and is tracking?

A. terraform state list
B. terraform state to show all
C. terraform state rm <name-of-resource>
D. terraform validate

14. What is the purpose of the terraform state mechanism?

A. It enables the synchronization of configuration files between two Terraform projects
B. It maps real-world resources into Terraform configuration and code
C. It determines whether your Terraform bug updates are up to date
D. It allows Terraform to monitor the status of common cloud vendors' services

15. Where can you set the location of the state file in Terraform code?

A. In the aws_instance.web resource
B. The terraform remote state resource is used
C. You cannot specify or change the location of the state file
D. Using the backend attribute in the terraform block

Chapter 10: Terraform Cloud and Enterprise

Introduction

In this chapter, we will cover some best practices, keeping in view the other features offered by HashiCorp in its Terraform Cloud and Enterprise offerings. We will look at the best practices to secure our Terraform code and deployments using HashiCorp Sentinel and the Terraform Vault Provider. We will compare and contrast the workspace feature offered by Terraform Open Source Software (or OSS) and the Terraform Cloud offering. And we will look further at the benefits of using Terraform cloud and its various features.

Terraform Cloud and Terraform Enterprise

Terraform Cloud is a collaboration tool for teams using Terraform. It allows easy access to shared state and secret data, as well as access controls for approving infrastructure modifications, a private registry for sharing Terraform modules, full policy controls for managing the contents of Terraform configurations, and more.

Terraform Cloud is a hosted service that can be found at https://app.terraform.io. Terraform allows small teams to connect to version control, share variables, run Terraform in a reliable remote environment, and securely save remote state for free. Paid tiers allow you to add more than five users, form teams with different permission levels, enforce policies before building infrastructure, and work more efficiently.

Large businesses can utilize the Business tier to scale to numerous concurrent runs, establish infrastructure in private environments, manage user access using SSO, and automate infrastructure end-user self-service provisioning.

Terraform Enterprise, a self-hosted distribution of Terraform Cloud, is available for enterprises with advanced security and compliance requirements. It provides businesses with a private instance that contains all of Terraform Cloud's advanced features.

Benefits of Sentinel - Embedded Policy as Code Framework

Introduction

HashiCorp Sentinel is a framework that enforces adherence to policies within your Terraform code. In other words, its code that enforces restrictions on your Terraform Code Sentinel has the language in which you write policies. These policies ensure that dangerous or malicious Terraform code is stopped, even before it gets executed or applied via the terraform apply command. It is designed to be approachable by non-programmers, so its code is pretty much human-readable. The Sentinel integration with Terraform runs within Terraform Enterprise after the terraforming plan and before terraform applies. The policies have access to data curated plan, and state the resources and the configuration at the time of the plan.

Benefits

Sandboxing-Guardrails for automation

You can apply Sentinel policies against your Terraform code to sandbox your deployments. For example, stop a dev user from deploying into a prod workspace and guardrail against accidental deployments.

- *Codification – Easier understanding, better collaboration*

    It codifies the process of security enforcement in Terraform code, allowing Sentinel policies to be version controlled and shared across the organization.

- *Testing and Automation:*

    It can help to standardize security testing and automation right into your Terraform deployment pipeline, as it automatically runs before your Terraform deployments.

Use Cases

- *For enforcing CIS standards across AWS accounts*

You can use Sentinel policies to enforce CIS security standards for your AWS accounts.

- *Checking to make sure only t3.micro instance types are used*

You can also use it to ensure that only a certain type of EC2 instance can be spun up by your Terraform code, for example, t3.micro.

- *Ensuring Security Groups do not allow traffic on port 22*

Sentinel policy ensures that no security groups in AWS openly allow traffic from all IP addresses on port 22.

> **Note:** Sentinel policies are written using the Sentinel language.

Sentinel Sample Code for Terraform

Ensure that all EC2 instances have at least 1

In the following code in Figure 10-01, we have Sentinel check that any AWS EC2 instances created through our Terraform deployment have at least one tag applied to them. Otherwise, it will fail and cancel the deployment.

```
import "tfplan"

main = rule {
    all tfplan.resources.aws_instance as _, instances {
        all instances as , r { (length(r.applied. tags) else 0) > 0
        }
    }
}
```

Figure 10-01: Sentinel Sample Code for Terraform

Best Practice: Terraform Vault Provider for Injecting Secrets Securely

HashiCorp Vault

HashiCorp Vault is secret management software. It stores sensitive data securely and provides short-lived, temporary credentials to users in place of actual long-lived credentials, like AWS CLI access keys. Vault handles rotating these temporarily provided credentials in the backend as per an expiration schedule, which is configurable in Vault. It can also generate cryptographic keys to encrypt data at rest and while in transit. You can control access to encrypted data inside Vault via fine-grained ACLs within Vault. More examples of Vault's data can store, encrypt, and work with secrets like usernames and passwords, database credentials, API tokens, and TLS certificates.

Why Do We Need Vault?

Usually, as we build complex secure applications and networks, we experience credentials sprawl, where some of the credentials might be in a plain text file, others inside a database or configuration files, which opens up the attack surface and increases the probability of mismanagement of those secrets. With Vault, you can get all the secrets and centrally manage access to them and integrate with Terraform and other popular cloud vendors.

Vault workflow is used to inject secrets into Terraform during a deployment, on the fly.

- **Scenario:**

You are deploying to AWS and want to use Vault to inject the CLI access keys for the deployment.

Considering the given scenario, the following steps are involved in the workflow:

1. The first step would be for the Vault Admin to provision ACLs and long-lived credentials in Vault. Moreover, using Vault's integration with AWS Identity and Access Management service, you will generate temporary, short-lived credentials with toned down permissions to the users who are invoking those keys.
2. In the next step, you as the user, integrate Vault within your Terraform code using the Vault Provider.
3. Now, the Vault Provider is just like any other Terraform provider that you may have come across. It just helps configure Vault with Terraform so that you can pass back secrets to Terraform securely. With the Vault integration in place and your code ready for deployment, you can issue the **terraform apply** command.
4. Terraform will reach out to the Vault server configured via the Vault Provider and inquire about credentials to go through with the deployment. Vault will check the ACLs and permissions and return temporary, short-lived credentials with appropriate AWS IAM permissions to the user invoking the deployment.
5. Using the credentials given back by Vault, Terraform will proceed with the deployment and execute it. As soon as Vault had returned temporary credentials to Terraform, it had started a configurable expiration timer for the temporary keys, which will expire the keys to render those temporary credentials useless, and a new set of temporary credentials will need to be generated for the next deployment.

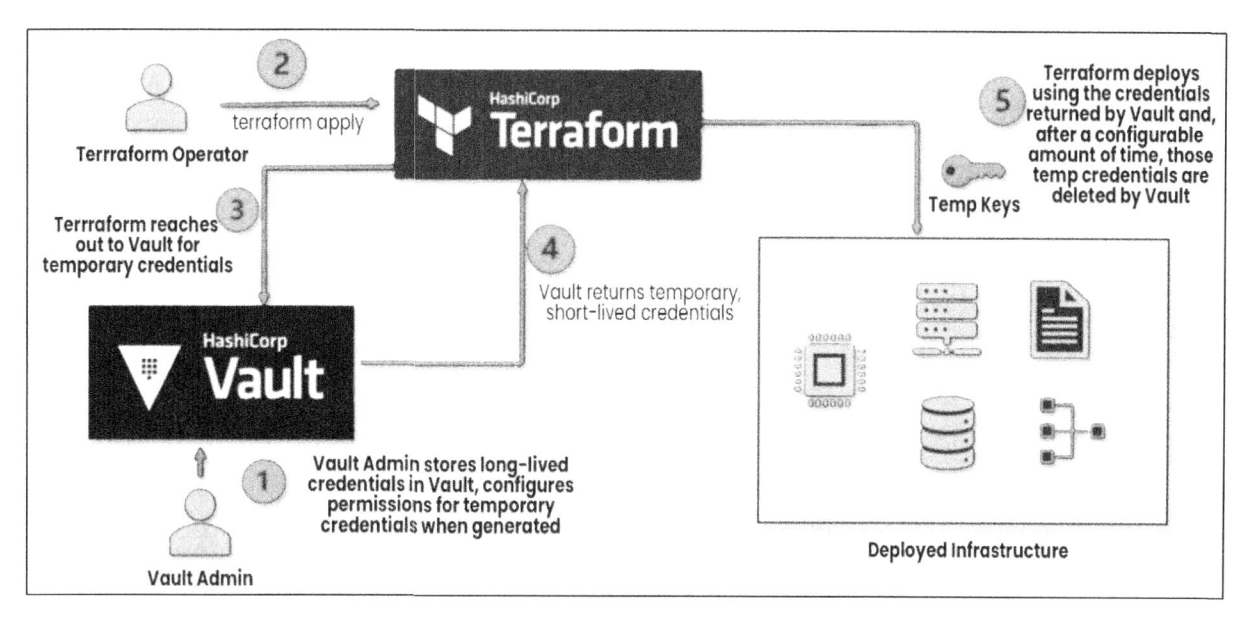

Figure 10-02: Workflow of Vault to Inject Secrets into Terraform during a Deployment

Benefits of Vault Provider to Inject Secrets into Terraform

- *Developers do not need to manage long-lived credentials*

    Developers and end-users do not need long-lived credentials on their machines and hence do not open up larger attack surface areas. Concisely, developers do not have access to real secrets; they only have short-lived credentials, with only their permissions.

- *Inject secrets into your Terraform deployment at runtime*

    The temporary credentials are short-lived and deleted soon. So they are only generated when required and then deleted. And even though your long-lived credentials that are stored in Vault can have less restricted access to resources, you can still configure Vault to hand out more restrictive permissions to temporary keys, which are generated instead of those long-lived keys

- *Fine-grained ACLS for access to temporary credentials*

    Vault is flexible. It offers a user interface, CLI- and API-based access, and an Enterprise offering for large organizations, allowing for distributed Vault deployments and high availability.

> **EXAM TIP:** Vault allows storing your secrets in a centralized way and allows you to provide both temporary credentials for usage in your deployments and encryption of data at rest and in transit.

Terraform Registry

The Registry is a repository of publicly available Terraform providers and modules. It is an integral part of Terraform's adoption by the masses because it is publicly accessible to anyone using Terraform. It has official providers, as well as third-party-provided modules. By default, fetching a provider or module from the Terraform Registry is built into Terraform's workflow. It will look for the provider or module in the Terraform Registry first before searching for that same thing in a private registry or repository. All of this happens when you execute the **terraform init** command.

Benefits of Terraform Registry

- **You can collaborate with other contributors to make changes to providers and modules**

    HashiCorp allows anyone to contribute their modules to the Registry. The Registry also provides useful links to GitHub pages for the code of the hosted providers, modules, and documentation of all the hosted content.

- **You can publish and share your modules**

    With the links provided in the hosted GitHub code to various open-source providers and modules, you can collaborate with HashiCorp and other third-party providers to push for feature requests and even changes to the code.

- **Can be directly referenced in your Terraform code**

    You can declare an AWS provider or some module, and Terraform knows to fetch it from the Registry.

Terraform Cloud Workspaces

The workspace feature in Terraform Cloud does the same thing as the open-source Terraform workspace feature. It is slightly different in the sense that it is all hosted in the cloud instead of your local system. Moreover, you can interact with the Cloud workspace using APIs as well. Think of Cloud workspaces as directories for distinct deployments, hosted in the cloud where you do not need to worry about segregation, storage, and even security of your workspaces. The Terraform Cloud workspaces store all the state files in Terraform's managed cloud and can be shared between organizations. Another feature of the Terraform Cloud workspaces is that Terraform deployment execution and all related activity are recorded via Cloud workspaces, which allows for auditing and investigating deployments more readily and easily. Another advantage with Cloud workspaces is that you do not need to have a local CLI terminal with Terraform installed to kick off deployments with manual 'terraform applications. You can trigger deployments via a workspace's API, or version control system triggers such as GitHub actions, or even the Terraform Cloud User Interface, and HashiCorp will execute your 'plan,' 'apply,' and 'init' commands on their own hosted and managed VMs in the HashiCorp cloud.

Difference between Terraform OSS and Terraform Cloud Workspaces

The workspace feature offered in the freely available Terraform version creates alternate state files against code in the same directory. It does that to issue multiple, distinct deployments against the same code. For example, you could have a workspace for developer deployments and another workspace for production deployments set against the same Terraform code. It creates a separate directory within the leading Terraform directory called the **terraform.tfstate.d**. It houses a folder for each state file tracked by the different workspaces.

Component	Workspace	Cloud Workspace
Terraform Configuration	On-disk	In linked version control repository or periodically uploaded via API/CLI
Variable Values	As .tfvars files, as CLI arguments, or in the shell environment	In workspace (in Terraform Cloud)
On-disk	On-disk or in the remote backend	In workspace (in Terraform Cloud)
Credentials and Secrets	In shell environment or entered at prompts	In workspace (Terraform Cloud), stored as sensitive variables

Table 10-01: Differentiating Between Terraform OSS and Terraform Cloud Workspaces

Features and Benefits of Terraform Cloud

Some of the major features of Terraform Cloud are as follows:

Remote Terraform execution - We have the remote Terraform executions via Terraform Cloud.

Workspace based organization model - Cloud workspace offers an organization-based model where each organization or team can have its workspace. And this enables cross-workspace sharing of data.

Version control integration (Github, Bitbucket, etc.) - Integration with version control systems, such as GitHub and Bitbucket, in addition to VCS-triggered runs, is a nice feature.

Remote State management and CLI integration - You can manage the state remotely via CLI-based integration with the Terraform Cloud. It also offers better resilience and security of state files within the Terraform Cloud itself.

Private Terraform Module registry - If you are concerned about security or have proprietary modules, you can host them in private registries offered by Terraform Cloud. And, of course, Terraform Cloud offers API, UI, and CLI-based access, which gives you great flexibility when working with it.

Cost estimation and Sentinel integration features - You get a cost estimation feature, which can look at your terraform plan output and estimate the cost of deployment. This feature is currently available for AWS, GCP, and Azure. Integrating Sentinel for enforcing policies on your code before it is deployed is also a good feature.

Chapter 10: Terraform Cloud and Enterprise

Mind Map

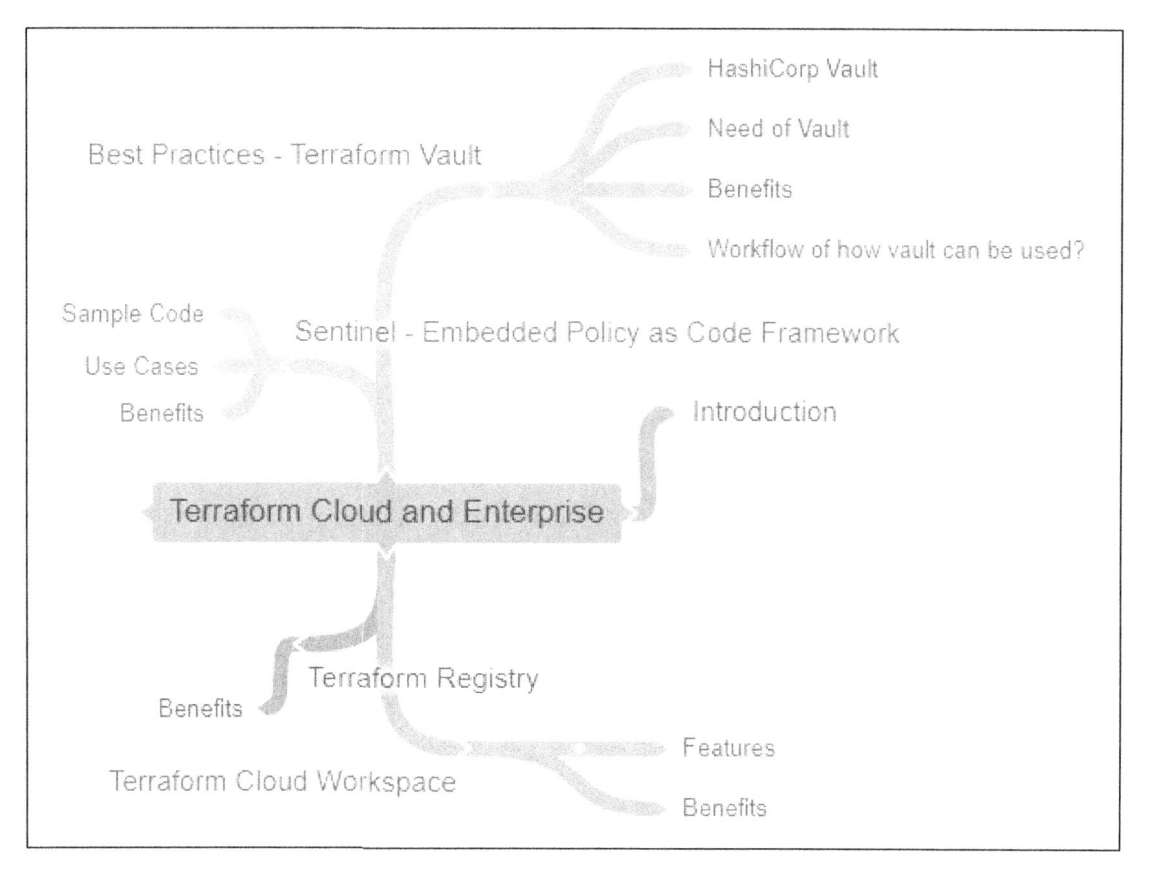

Figure 10-03: Mind Map

Practice Questions

1. What does the Terraform Registry consist of?

A. Publicly available Terraform providers
B. Publicly available modules
C. Images similar to Docker
D. Both A and B

2. What is the purpose of Terraform Cloud?

A. It manages your Terraform configuration in a fluid, ever-changing environment

B. It provides easy access to shared state and secret data
C. It helps teams use Terraform together
D. Both B and C

Chapter 10: Terraform Cloud and Enterprise

3. What are the benefits of using HashiCorp Sentinel with your Terraform deployments?
   A. It can execute multiple terraform apply commands in the backend to speed up deployments
   B. It can optimize your code and format it to make it look better
   C. It can store your deployment information in the cloud to keep it secure
   D. It can help make your deployment more secure and to protect against accidental deployments

4. What is the Terraform public registry?
   A. A repository of publicly available Terraform providers and modules
   B. A Linux package repository that contains Terraform binaries
   C. A paid access repository that has proprietary modules and providers
   D. A public repository of all the Terraform projects that HashiCorp is working

5. Which of the following statements is NOT accurate about the difference between open-source Terraform workspaces and Terraform Cloud workspaces?
   A. Variable values are stored in Terraform local workspaces in .tfvars files or a shell environment
   B. Open-source Terraform workspaces can automatically back up your configuration to Terraform Cloud
   C. A state can be stored on a disk or remote backend for open-source Terraform workspaces
   D. Terraform Cloud workspaces store the Terraform configuration in a linked version control repository

6. How can HashiCorp Vault help secure your Terraform deployments?
   A. It can execute multiple terraform apply commands in the backend to speed up deployments
   B. It can securely store your long-lived credentials and dynamically inject short-lived, temporary keys to Terraform at deployment
   C. It can optimize your code and format it to make it look better
   D. It can store your deployment information in the cloud to keep it secure

7. Which one of the following answers is NOT a key benefit of Terraform Cloud?
   A. Remote Terraform execution
   B. Cloud cost estimation

C. Remote state management
D. A built-in version control similar to GitHub

8. What does the Terraform Vault provider offer to Terraform users?
A. Allows you to store sensitive data securely that can be used for your Terraform configurations
B. A secure place to manage access to the secrets for your Terraform configurations, in addition to integrating with other popular cloud vendors
C. Provides short-lived, temporary credentials for users with only the permissions needed for infrastructure creation
D. All of these

9. Which of the following is a framework that enforces adherence to policies within your Terraform code?
A. Vault
B. HashiCorp Sentinel
C. Terraform OSS
D. None of the above

10. Terraform Code Sentinel has its language in which you write policies. True or false?
A. True
B. False

11. Which of the policy ensures that no security groups in AWS openly allow traffic from all IP addresses on port 22?
A. CIS
B. Vault
C. Sentinel
D. All of the above

12. The following is used to store sensitive data securely and provide short-lived, temporary credentials to users in place of actual long-lived credentials, like AWS CLI access keys. Which one is it?
A. HashiCorp Vault
B. HashiCorp Sentinel
C. Terraform OSS
D. None of the above

13. With HashiCorp Sentinel, you can get all the secrets and centrally manage access to them and integrate with Terraform and other popular cloud vendors. True or false?
A. True
B. False

14. Vault is pretty flexible. True or false?
A. True
B. False

15. Developers and end-users do not need long-lived credentials on their machines and hence do not open up larger attack surface areas. True or false?
A. True
B. False

16. Access to encrypted data inside Vault can be controlled via fine-grained ACLs within Vault. True or false?
A. True
B. False

17. HashiCorp Sentinel is a framework that enforces adherence to policies within your Terraform code. True or false?
A. True
B. False

18. What is meant by Terraform Cloud Workspaces?
A. The workspace feature in Terraform Cloud does the same thing as the open-source
B. The terraform workspace feature is slightly different because it is all hosted in the cloud instead of your local system
C. You can interact with the Cloud workspace using APIs as well
D. All of the above

19. What is meant by Terraform Registry?
A. The Registry is a repository of publicly available Terraform providers and modules
B. It is an integral part of Terraform's adoption by the masses because it is publicly accessible to anyone using Terraform

Chapter 10: Terraform Cloud and Enterprise

C. Both A and B
D. None of the above

20. What is meant by HashiCorp Vault?
A. HashiCorp Vault is secret management software
B. It stores sensitive data securely and provides short-lived, temporary credentials to users in place of actual long-lived credentials, like AWS CLI access keys
C. Both A and B
D. None of the above

21. Which of the following statement is true about codification?
A. It codifies the process of security enforcement in Terraform code
B. It can help standardize security testing and automation right into your Terraform deployment pipeline, as it automatically runs before your Terraform deployments
C. Both A and B
D. None of the above

22. Which of the following statement is true about Testing and Automation?
A. It automatically runs before your Terraform deployments
B. It can help standardize security testing and automation right into your Terraform deployment pipeline
C. Both A and B
D. None of the above

23. Sentinel policy ensures that no security groups in AWS openly allow traffic from all IP addresses on port 22. True or false?
A. True
B. False

24. Which of the following are the benefits of Sentinel?
A. Sandboxing-Guardrails for automation
B. Codification
C. Testing and Automation

D. All of the above

25. You can apply Sentinel policies against your Terraform code to sandbox your deployments. True or false?
A. True
B. False

Appendix A: Answers

Answers

Chapter 01: Introduction

1. **Answer: A** (DevOps)

Explanation: Faster speed and consistency: The purpose of IaC is to make things faster by removing manual processes and slack in the system, which is the backbone of DevOps.

2. **Answer: C** (Version control)

Explanation: The codification of deployment can be tracked in version control such as Git. Now distributed can work on the same chunk of code that can deploy infrastructure and ensure that they agree on immutable and stored in version control before it is deployed. It enables better visibility and collaboration across teams.

3. **Answer: D** (All of the above)

Explanation: AWS Cloud Formation, Red Hat Ansible, Chef, Puppet, Salt Stack, and HashiCorp Terraform are examples of infrastructure-as-code tools. Some tools employ a Domain-Specific Language (DSL), while others use YAML or JSON as a standard template format.

4. **Answer: C** (SDNs)

Explanation: A control layer and an infrastructure layer are common in SDN systems. Terraform may be used to codify software-defined network setup. By interacting with the control layer, terraform may use this configuration to set up and adjust settings automatically.

5. **Answer: B** (False)

Explanation: Terraform is your multi-cloud all-in-one solution! Terraform enables you to create infrastructure across numerous cloud providers dynamically, allowing you to maintain your workflows and processes even while the world around you changes. You can use terraform domains in highly available solutions across two public clouds and achieve high availability beyond what a single vendor can offer.

Appendix A: Answers

6. **Answer: D** (All of the above)

Explanation: If you go inside database providers, you will notice that terraform has providers for interfacing with MySQL, MongoDB, and influx DB.

7. **Answer: D** (All of the above)

Explanation: The most crucial element of the Terraform language is its resources. Each resource block describes one or more infrastructure items, such as virtual networks, computes instances, and higher-level components like DNS records.

8. **Answer: B** (Terraform is free)

Explanation: HashiCorp's Terraform Cloud is a commercial SaaS offering. Many of its capabilities, such as remote state storage, remote runs, and VCS connections, are free for small teams. They offer premium solutions with additional collaboration and governance capabilities for larger teams.

9. **Answer: B** (Orchestration)

Explanation: Terraform, developed by HashiCorp, is an open-source Infrastructure as Code (IaC) infrastructure orchestrator. The necessity to automate the lifespan of environments is addressed by orchestration.

10. **Answer: D** (All of the above)

Explanation: Terraform Cloud provides a team-oriented remote Terraform process that is easy to understand for new Terraform users and comfortable for the established ones. Remote Terraform execution, a workspace-based organizational architecture, version control integration, command-line integration, remote state management with cross-workspace data sharing, and a private Terraform module registry serve as the foundations of this workflow.

Chapter 02: Getting Started With Terraform

1. **Answer: C (Both A and B)**

Appendix A: Answers

Explanation: HashiCorp's Terraform is a simple yet effective open-source infrastructure management tool. It allows you to manage your infrastructure safely and predictably by codifying APIs into declarative configuration files.

Terraform is a fantastic suite of tools for automating infrastructure in both public and private cloud environments.

2. Answer: B (True)

Explanation: Terraform must be installed before it can be used. Terraform is distributed as a binary package by HashiCorp. Terraform can also be installed using major package managers.

3. Answer: D (terraform --version)

Explanation: To verify the installation of the Terraform, you can use the following command.

terraform --version

4. Answer: C (terraform init)

Explanation: The terraform init will check for all plugin requirements and, if necessary, download them; this information will be used to build a deployment strategy.

5. Answer: A (Provide Infrastructure)

Explanation: Terraform is an Infrastructure as Code (IaC) tool that lets you build, edit, and version infrastructure in a secure and efficient manner. This covers both low-level and high-level components, such as compute instances, storage, networking, DNS records, SaaS services, etc.

Chapter 03: Understanding Infrastructure As Code

1. Answer: D (Programmable Infrastructure)

Explanation: IaC is an IT infrastructure provisioning method in which systems are designed, managed, and provisioned automatically using code rather than less flexible

Appendix A: Answers

scripting or a human procedure. That is why IaC is sometimes referred to as programmable infrastructure.

2. Answer: A (Automated)

Explanation: By using automated configurations compared to weeks or months of tedious configuration, deployment of each system can often be shortened to a few seconds by reducing the time required to manually specify communication interfaces, alert limits, and how data is to be saved and presented.

3. Answer: C (IT Staff)

Explanation: IaC makes the information technology processes easier, not just a single process.

4. Answers: D (HCL)

Explanation: The HashiCorp Configuration Language (HCL) is the syntax for Terraform configurations. It aims to achieve a balance between being both human-readable and editable as well as machine-friendly.

5. Answer: C (Provide Infrastructure)

Explanation: Terraform is an Infrastructure as Code (IaC) tool that lets you build, edit, and version infrastructure in a secure and efficient manner. This covers both low-level and high-level components, such as compute instances, storage, networking, DNS records, SaaS services, etc.

6. Answer: C (HashiCorp)

Explanation: HashiCorp invented Terraform, an open-source infrastructure as a code software application. The HashiCorp Configuration Language is a declarative configuration language that allows users to define and deliver datacenter architecture.

7. Answer: D (All of the above)

Appendix A: Answers

Explanation: Terraform supports all the major cloud providers, including Alibaba, Oracle, AWS, GCP, Azure, and smaller ones.

8. Answer: A (True)

Explanation: Terraform is a declarative language that describes an intended objective rather than the processes to get there. Terraform solely evaluates implicit and explicit associations between resources when establishing an order of operations; the ordering of blocks and the files they are arranged into are often unimportant.

9. Answer: D (Both B and C)

Explanation: Both your recovery and deployment operations are automated with IaC. It enhances monitoring and testability, lowers the cost of innovation and experimentation, and streamlines deployments. When you do run into challenges, IaC can help you overcome them faster.

10. Answer: D (None of the above)

Explanation: Terraform is capable of managing infrastructure across a variety of cloud platforms. The human-readable configuration language aids in the rapid development of infrastructure code. Terraform's state feature allows you to keep track of resource changes as they happen throughout your deployments.

11. Answer: C (Both A and B)

Explanation: Despite its benefits, IaC has potential drawbacks. Additional tools, such as a configuration management system, are required. Errors can swiftly spread across systems. As a result, it is critical to keep an eye on version control and do thorough pre-testing.

12. Answer: C (When a technology is not tied to a single cloud and can function similarly across a variety of cloud environments)

Explanation: Cloud agnostic refers to tools, platforms, or applications that are interoperable with any cloud infrastructure and may be moved between them without causing any problems.

Appendix A: Answers

13. Answer: A (Enables better DevOps methods)

Explanation: Infrastructure as Code is a fantastic technique to enable rapid deployments and cross-team cooperation.

14. Answer: D (A way for deploying resources in the Cloud and elsewhere using human-readable code)

Explanation: Instead of managing your infrastructure resources manually through a user interface, IaC is code that delivers them across numerous platforms.

15. Answer: A (True)

Explanation: Kubernetes has been around for a few years and allows you to write your infrastructure as code. This is advantageous in two ways: your infrastructure can now be versioned and committed to a Git repository, and it can be easily "deployed" elsewhere.

Chapter 04: IaC with Terraform

1. Answer: A (Write>Plan>Apply)

Explanation: In the Terraform workflow, first, we write the code, then we review changes the code will make, and then we deploy the code to real infrastructure. We generally start either with a version control system as a best practice or a flat-file working individually in the writing phase. In the planning phase, we see what changes the code will make within our actual environment. Finally, you deploy changes to the actual environment and create real resources in the Cloud.

2. Answer: C (Version control system)

Explanation: Version control is considered best practice so you and your team can collaborate over the issues within your code. We are generally starting either with a version control system as a best practice or a flat-file working individually in the writing phase.

3. Answer: B (False)

Appendix A: Answers

Explanation: After reviewing the code, you can go back and modify your code. Planning and reviewing changes that our code will make is an important step because, at this point, we are not deploying any infrastructure. Still, you can see in detail what changes the code will make within our actual environment.

4. Answers: B (Apply)

Explanation: In the writing phase, we generally start either with a version control system as a best practice or a flat file if you are working individually. Planning and reviewing changes that our code will make is an important step because, at this point, we are not deploying any infrastructure. Finally, we deploy changes to the actual environment and create real resources in the cloud.

5. Answer: D (terraform init)

Explanation: Terraform init is a command written as terraforming in it. It initializes the working directory that contains your Terraform. Plan command reads the code and then creates and shows a "plan" of deployment. Terraform apply is the final command to realize your code into real infrastructure being deployed. The terraform destroy command looks at the recorded, stored state file created during deployment and destroys all the resources created by your code.

6. Answer: A (Downloads supporting components)

Explanation: The first step that Terraforms init does is download the supporting or ancillary components required code to work. Such as providers that provide the libraries and code for your resources to make API calls to the infrastructure you are deploying into.

7. Answer: B (False)

Explanation: The terraform init can either download modules or plugins from Terraform public registry over the internet or from your custom URLs where you have uploaded your custom modules written for Terraform.

**8. Answer: B (any number of)

281

Appendix A: Answers

Explanation: With Terraform plan command, we can do any number of iterations between the write and plan phase of our project. After reviewing the code, you can go back and modify your code. Planning and reviewing changes that our code will make is an important step because, at this point, we are not deploying any infrastructure. Still, you can see in detail what changes the code will make within our actual environment.

9. **Answer: A** (terraform plan)

Explanation: Plan command reads the code and then creates and shows a "plan" of deployment. It allows the user to review the action plan before executing anything. You can look at this plan as a team or individually and decide on the final execution. At this point, Terraform also authenticates with the credentials of the platform that you are trying to deploy into.

10. **Answer: A** (terraform plan)

Explanation: Plan command is a sort of read-only command. It makes API calls in the backend with your preferred platform, but it does not change to your environment.

11. **Answer: B** (terraform apply)

Explanation: Terraform applies the final command to realize your code into real infrastructure being deployed. It also updates the deployment state tracking mechanism known as "state file." Terraform apply creates this state file essential to Terraform working because subsequent commands will come back and look at the state file before making changes to your Terraform infrastructure.

12. **Answer: C** (terraform destroy)

Explanation: The terraform destroy command looks at the recorded, stored state file created during deployment and destroys all the resources created by your code. Use this command with caution as it is a non-reversible command. It is best to take backups and be sure that you want to delete infrastructure before you use this command.

13. **Answer: B** (False)

Appendix A: Answers

> **Explanation:** Terraform fetches data of an already existing resource environment with the data source. The main difference between a data source and a resource block is that a data source block fetches and tracks details of already existing resources.
>
> 14. **Answer: D** (Resource Block)
>
> **Explanation:** Terraform creates and starts tracking resources from scratch with resource blocks. The resource configuration arguments change according to which resources you are creating.
>
> 15. **Answer: A** (.tf)
>
> **Explanation:** The Terraform language uses plain text files to store code with the .tf extension. There is also a JSON-based version of the language with the suffix. tf.

Chapter 05: Terraform Fundamentals

> 1. **Answer: B** (2)
> **Explanation:** There are two methods to install Terraform.
>
> 2. **Answer: B** (False)
> **Explanation:** The syntax for using the sensitive parameter would be a Boolean value to either be true or false. And by default, it is false.
>
> 3. **Answer: C** (3)
> **Explanation:** There are three base variable types for Terraform variables.
>
> 4. **Answer: B** (Output)
> **Explanation:** In the curly braces, you have the description for the output and a value.
>
> 5. **Answer: B** (2)

Appendix A: Answers

Explanation: There are two types of provisioners, which cover two events of your Terraform resource's lifecycle.

6. **Answer: B** (Output)

Explanation: In the Destroy provisioner, you have to output the value one to the same status .txt file upon being deleted or destroyed.

7. **Answer: A** (Independent)

Explanation: Provisioners are not tracked and are independent of the Terraform state file, and there is no mention of the provisioner.

8. **Answer: B** (Linux)

Explanation: You set up the Terraform repository on your system, and it is only available for Linux systems.

9. **Answer: B** (Curly)

Explanation: Between the curly braces, you have the configuration parameters for the variable.

10. **Answer: C** (Both of the above)

Explanation: Providers can be sourced locally or internally and referenced within your Terraform code.

11. **Answer: B** (2)

Explanation: Method 2 is a bit more guided with the help of Linux repositories.

12. **Answer: B** (init)

Explanation: Terraform pulls down the providers when you initialize your different projects, using the terraform init command.

Appendix A: Answers

> **13. Answer: B** (JSON)
>
> **Explanation:** Terraform state is stored into flat files as JSON data.
>
> **14. Answer: A** (State)
>
> **Explanation:** The state file helps Terraform calculate deployment deltas.
>
> **15. Answer: A** (Curly)
>
> **Explanation:** All the config parameters within the curly braces are optional for declaring the variables.

Chapter 06: Terraform CLI

> **1. Answer: A** (fmt)
>
> **Explanation:** The fmt command only modifies the look of the code, but it does not change anything else otherwise.
>
> **2. Answer: B** (taint)
>
> **Explanation:** The taint command marks an existing Terraform resource to be deleted and recreated.
>
> **3. Answer: B** (taint)
>
> **Explanation:** Provisioners only run when a resource is created or destroyed, you can use Terraform taint command to delete and recreate a resource.
>
> **4. Answer: B** (taint)
>
> **Explanation:** You can use the Terraform taint command to replace misbehaving resources forcefully.
>
> **5. Answer: C** (import)
>
> **Explanation:** The import command takes an existing resource that Terraform manages and maps it to a resource within Terraform code using an ID.

Appendix A: Answers

6. Answer: A (Values)

Explanation: The configuration block only allows constant values, and you cannot use named resources or variables within this block.

7. Answer: C (13)

Explanation: Terraform only runs if the Terraform binary version is greater than version 13.

8. Answer: B (Indpendent)

Explanation: Each workspace tracks a separate independent copy of the state file against Terraform code in that directory.

9. Answer: C (Both of the above)

Explanation: The **terraform workspace select** command selects or switches to the workspace of your choice that already exists.

10. Answer: B (Five)

If the terraform dot workspace variable has the value default when the Terraform applies is executed, it will spin up to five instances.

Explanation: Providers can be sourced locally or internally and referenced within your Terraform code.

11. Answer: A (One)

Explanation: If the workspace is not default, then only one instance will be spun up, as evident in this logic.

12. Answer: B (init)

Explanation: Terraform pulls down the providers when you initialize your different projects, using the terraform init command.

Appendix A: Answers

> **13. Answer: B** (JSON)
>
> **Explanation:** Terraform state is stored into flat files as JSON data.
>
> **14. Answer: A** (Destroy)
>
> **Explanation:** You can tear down the infrastructure you just created in the test workspace by using destroy command.
>
> **15. Answer: A** (Curl)
>
> **Explanation:** Use the curl command to view the contents of the webpage.

Chapter 07: Terraform Modules

> **1. Answer: D** (0.14.10)
>
> **Explanation:** Terraform v0.14.10 is a significant new release; thus, there are a few minor changes in behavior to be aware of when upgrading.
>
> **2. Answer: A** (Root Module)
>
> **Explanation:** Each Terraform configuration contains at least one root module, which is made up of the resources defined in the .tf files in the primary working directory. A module can call other modules, allowing you to quickly integrate the resources of a child module in the setup.
>
> **3. Answer: D** (All of the above)
>
> **Explanation:** Modules can be downloaded or referenced from the Terraform Public Registry, which contains a collection of all publicly available modules. Terraform downloads and places them in a directory on a system when referencing modules from Terraform Public Registry. You can also host your modules in a private registry hosted by yourself or an organization and reference them in the same way as Public Registry. You can use it when your concern is security and closed source code. You can also have

Appendix A: Answers

the module code saved in a local folder on your system and reference that folder using its path.

4. Answers: B (False)

Explanation: The Module is a reserved keyword. A keyword cannot be used to identify a variable, function, or another object.

5. Answer: B (Iterating over complex variable)

Explanation: The few parameters allowed inside the module block include count, which allows spawning multiple separate instances of the module's resources; for_each parameter. This permits iterating over a complex variable. Providers parameter allows you to tie down specific providers to your module, while the depends_on module allows you to set dependencies for your module.

6. Answer: C (Arbitrary number of)

Explanation: Modules can take an arbitrary number of inputs and written outputs back into your main code. Once you have invoked a module using the module block in your code, you can use these outputs that it returns and plug them back into your code.

7. Answer: B (Variable)

Explanation: Terraform module inputs are arbitrarily named parameters that you pass inside the module block. These inputs can be used as a variable inside the module code.

8. Answer: B (var.<variable-name>)

Explanation: Terraform module code is just like any other module code that you may come across. You pass the input variable. Once the module consumes this input variable, you will be able to use this variable via the standard variable reference notation interval; var. server-name.

9. Answer: C (Feedback)

Appendix A: Answers

Explanation: The outputs declared inside Terraform module code can be feedback in the root module or your main code. For example, when using an output returned by a module back inside your main code, the output invocation convention is the module.<name-of-module>.<name-of-output>

10. Answer: C (Both A and B)

Explanation: There are various applications for output values:

A parent module can access a portion of a child module's resource properties via outputs. After running the terraform apply command, a root module can use outputs to print specific values in the CLI output. Root module outputs can be accessed by other configurations using a terraform_remote_state data source when using a remote state.

11. Answer: D (To avoid reinventing the wheel by making code reusable elsewhere)

Explanation: Terraform's major method for packaging and reusing resource configurations is through modules. The main purpose of these modules is to reuse the code instead of reinventing the wheel.

12. Answer: C (module.prod-module.returned-variable)

Explanation: The outputs declared inside Terraform module code can be feedback in the root module or your main code. For example, the output invocation convention when using an output returned by a module back inside your main code is the module.<name-of-module>.<name-of-output>

13. Answer: D (In the Terraform module code, **output** block resources are used)

Explanation: The outputs indicated by the output block in Terraform module code can be sent back into the root module or your main code.

14. Answer: C (version)

Explanation: The inclusion of the usual variable reference notation, var, indicates that an input variable is being given.

Appendix A: Answers

15. Answer: D (.tf)

Explanation: The Terraform language uses plain text files with the .tf extension to store code. A JSON-based form of the language with the .tf.json file extension is also available. Terraform configuration files are files that contain Terraform code.

Chapter 08: Built-in Functions and Dynamic Blocks

1. **Answer: A** (All the built-in functions)

Explanation: By default, Terraform comes bundled with all the built-in functions. You do not need to use any additional providers or modules to use these functions.

2. **Answer: B** (False)

Explanation: In Terraform, you cannot create your user-defined functions like in a programming language because the Terraform language does not support user-defined functions; only the built-in functions are available for use.

3. **Answer: B** (Parenthesized comma-separated arguments)

Explanation: The general syntax of the function is just like how you would invoke functions anywhere else in a programming language. You pass the function some arguments and get values in return.

The general syntax for function calls is a function name followed by parenthesized comma-separated arguments.

4. **Answer: A** (file function)

Explanation: The **file** function returns the contents of a file at the specified path as a string. Since strings in Terraform are Unicode character sequences, the file function will interpret the file contents as UTF-8 encoded text and return the resulting Unicode characters. If the file contains invalid UTF-8 sequences, this function will fail.

5. **Answer: C** (flatten function)

Appendix A: Answers

Explanation: The **flatten** function takes a list and replaces any list elements with a flattened sequence of the list's contents.

6. **Answer: B** (max function)

Explanation: The **max** function will return us the greatest value from the list of values entered.

7. **Answer: A** (Expressions)

Explanation: The Terraform console command displays an interactive console where expressions can be evaluated. If the current state of your deployment is empty or has not yet been created, the console can be used to experiment with expression syntax and built-in functions.

8. **Answer: B** (Two)

Explanation: Type constraints control the type of variable values that you can pass to your Terraform code. There are two types of constraints: primitive and complex types.

9. **Answer: A** (Primitive)

Explanation: Primitive Constraints allow for a single type of value to be assigned to a variable, such as a number type, string type, or boolean (or bool) type.

10. **Answer: B** (Complex types)

Explanation: Complex types constraints include multiple value types in a single variable; such value types can be constructed using list, tuple, map, or object data structures.

11. **Answer: B** (Two)

Explanation: Complex types include multiple value types in a single variable. Such value types can be constructed using list, tuple, map, or object data structures. The complex types can be broken into two further types.

- Collection type

Appendix A: Answers

- Structural type

12. Answer: B (False)

Explanation: Complex type is divided into two further types, which are collection and structural type. Primitive does not divide into any further types.

13. Answer: A (collection type)

Explanation: Collection types allow multiple values of a single or one primitive type to be grouped against a variable. For example, you can have a list of type strings, or you can have a map of type numbers, or you can have a set of type strings, but you cannot mix more than one type against a single variable.

14. Answer: B (Structural Type)

Explanation: Structural types allow multiple values of different primitive types to be grouped. So, as opposed to the type of the collection, which only allows a single type of value within a variable, the structural type allows more than one type of values assigned within a variable.

15. Answer: C (dynamic Blocks)

Explanation: Dynamic blocks help construct repeatable nested configuration blocks inside Terraform resources. They can be used inside resources, such as resource blocks, data blocks, provider blocks, and provisional blocks inside a Terraform resource.

Chapter 09: Terraform State

1. Answer: B (False)

Explanation: By default, Terraform state is stored locally in a file called terraform.tfstate, but it can be stored remotely in services such as AWS S3. Before any modification operation, Terraform refreshes the state file.

2. Answer: A (terraform. tfstate)

Appendix A: Answers

Explanation: Terraform uses this state to map real-world resources to your configuration, keep track of information, and optimize large-scale infrastructure performance. This state is kept in the "terraform. tfstate" file, but it can also be saved remotely, which is more useful in a collaborative environment.

3. Answer: C (Dependencies between)

Explanation: Terraform tracks the dependency between the resources deployed. For example, Terraform must know that it needs to configure a subnet before deploying a virtual machine in AWS. State file also helps boost deployment performance by acting as a cache for resource attributes.

4. Answers: D (All of the above)

Explanation: Normally, we do not need to mess with the Terraform state file outside the core workflow of Terraform. There are some scenarios in which you might want to tweak the state outside the workflow to remove or change resources tracked by Terraform. It can be used for advanced state management. We can remove resource so that it is not tracked by Terraform. You can use The terraform state commands list subcommand to drag the details of resources and names of resources that are being managed by Terraform.

5. Answer: B (terraform state rm)

Explanation: terraform state list is used to list out all resources tracked by the Terraform state file. Terraform state rm is used to delete a resource from the Terraform state file. The terraform state show is used to show details of a resource tracked in the Terraform state file.

6. Answer: A (locally)

Explanation: By default, Terraform saves state files locally on the same system that generates these commands. This method is usually used for individual projects or testing purposes.

7. Answer: B (False)

293

Appendix A: Answers

Explanation: The advantages of storing files remotely are reading files across the distributed teams and better security and availability in the Cloud, which ensure solid backups.

8. Answer: C (Due to policies created by cloud vendors)

Explanation: Different cloud vendors offer different security policies for access to files; you can get granular in who can read and write to the files. This is how a remote state enables collaboration between distributed teams securely.

9. Answer: D (All the remote state storage)

Explanation: State locking locks the state file, so another operator who has access to your system or code repository does not end up executing a parallel run of Terraform deployment by mistake. State locking is not supported by all remote state storage backends. Some of the backends that support state locking include AWS S3, GCP storage, and Hashicorp's console.

10. Answer: B (Output)

Explanation: State files also contain the output values in your Terraform code, which means these output values can be used by other Terraform projects or code. If a state file is stored remotely is extremely useful for distributed teams working on data by plans, which requires successful execution, and output from previous Terraform deployment. Suppose you have a Terraform code that deploys a database. You execute it and deploy infrastructure to the Cloud and configure Terraform to save state remotely. Another team that perhaps deploy the application can reference your state file remotely and access output values.

11. Answer: A (The Terraform state file is used to handle them)

Explanation: A map of all resources and their dependencies may be seen in the Terraform state file. Terraform's correct operation requires it. Prior to any modification operation, Terraform refreshes the state file. It also tracks the dependency between the resources deployed. For example, Terraform must know that it needs to configure a subnet before deploying a virtual machine in AWS.

Appendix A: Answers

12. Answer: C (Granular access, integrity, security, availability, and cooperation are all provided)

Explanation: Unlike local state storage, which does not offer flexibility in collaboration and availability, Terraform offers remote state storage. There are several platforms on which you can set Terraform to store state remotely, including AWS S3 storage and GCP Storage. The advantages of storing files remotely are reading files across the distributed teams and better security and availability in the Cloud, which ensure solid backups.

13. Answer: A (terraform state list)

Explanation: When you use the list with the terraform state command, all of the resources in the Terraform state will be listed.

14. Answer: B (It maps real-world resources into Terraform configuration and code)

Explanation: It is essentially mapping real-world resource IDs and configurations to Terraform logical resources.

15. Answer: D (Using the backend attribute in the terraform block)

Explanation: Terraform state files are files that contain Terraform code. Terraform can be configured to save state remotely on various platforms, including AWS S3 storage and Google Cloud storage.

Appendix A: Answers

Chapter 10: Terraform Cloud and Enterprise

1. **Answer: D** (Both A and B)

   Explanation: Publicly available Terraform providers and publicly available modules both the Registries consist of both publicly available Terraform providers and modules. Images similar to the Docker registry consist of available providers like AWS, Azure, GCP, and modules that allow easy integration in your Terraform configuration.

2. **Answer: D** (Both B and C)

   Explanation: Terraform Cloud was created to allow easy access to shared state and secret data that a team can use and modify easily. It includes easy access to shared state and secret data, access controls for approving changes to infrastructure, detailed policy controls for governing the contents of Terraform configurations, and more.

3. **Answer: D** (It can help make your deployment more secure and act as protection against accidental deployments)

   Explanation: The policies inherent to the Sentinel framework ensure that dangerous or malicious Terraform code is stopped, even before it gets executed or applied via the terraform apply command.

4. **Answer: A** (A repository of publicly available Terraform providers and modules)

   Explanation: The Terraform public registry links end-users with the providers that power all of Terraform's resource types or helps them find modules for quickly deploying common infrastructure configurations.

5. **Answer: A** (Variable values are stored in Terraform local workspaces in .tfvars files or a shell environment)

   Explanation: Terraform does not automatically back up your configuration to Terraform Cloud. If you are running Terraform locally, it stores the configuration in the designated directory on your machine.

Appendix A: Answers

6. **Answer: B** (It can securely store your long-lived credentials and dynamically inject short-lived, temporary keys to Terraform at deployment)

Explanation: HashiCorp Vault is a centralized and secret management software.

7. **Answer: D** (A built-in version control similar to GitHub)

Explanation: Though Terraform Cloud integrates and can use repositories like GitHub and BitBucket, it does not have built-in version control.

8. **Answer: D** (All of these)

Explanation: Vault allows you to store any sensitive data securely and can be used with all your configurations. It helps, especially once your infrastructure configurations get large and complicated. Vault allows you to store any sensitive data securely and can be used with all your configurations. It also integrates with cloud vendors like AWS, Azure, and GCP to allow for easy configuration across all your cloud vendors. Vault allows you to provide short-lived, temporary credentials that allow users to have only the permissions they need to deploy the infrastructure. The credentials will rotate according to the rotation schedule you define. It allows you not to worry about keeping up with long-lived credentials.

A built-in version control similar to GitHub Vault allows you to store any sensitive data securely and can be used with all your configurations. This helps, especially once your infrastructure configurations get large and complicated.

9. **Answer: B** (HashiCorp Sentinel)

Explanation: HashiCorp Sentinel is a framework that enforces adherence to policies within your Terraform code. In other words, its code that enforces restrictions on your Terraform Code Sentinel has its language in which you write policies.

10. **Answer: A** (True)

Explanation: HashiCorp Sentinel is a framework that enforces adherence to policies within your Terraform code. In other words, its code that enforces restrictions on your Terraform Code Sentinel has its language, in which you write policies.

Appendix A: Answers

11. **Answer: C** (Sentinel)

Explanation: Sentinel policy ensures that no security groups in AWS openly allow traffic from all IP addresses on port 22.

12. **Answer: A** (HashiCorp Vault)

Explanation: HashiCorp Vault stores sensitive data securely and provides short-lived, temporary credentials to users in place of actual long-lived credentials, like AWS CLI access keys. In the backend, Vault handles rotating these temporarily provided credentials as per an expiration schedule, which is configurable in Vault.

13. **Answer: B** (False)

Explanation: With Vault, you can get all the secrets and centrally manage access to them and integrate with Terraform and other popular cloud vendors.

14. **Answer: A** (True)

Explanation: Vault is pretty flexible. It offers a user interface, CLI- and API-based access, and an Enterprise offering for large organizations, allowing for distributed Vault deployments and high availability.

15. **Answer: A** (True)

Explanation: Developers and end-users do not need long-lived credentials on their machines and hence do not open up larger attack surface areas. Developers do not have access to actual secrets, only short-lived credentials, with only the permissions.

16. **Answer: A** (True)

Explanation: HashiCorp Vault is secret management software. It stores sensitive data securely and provides short-lived, temporary credentials to users in place of actual long-lived credentials, like AWS CLI access keys. Vault handles rotating these temporarily provided credentials in the backend as per an expiration schedule, which is configurable in Vault. It can also generate cryptographic keys to encrypt data at rest and while in transit. Access to encrypted data inside Vault can be controlled via fine-grained ACLs within Vault.

Appendix A: Answers

17. Answer: A (True)

Explanation: HashiCorp Sentinel is a framework that enforces adherence to policies within your Terraform code. In other words, its code that enforces restrictions on your Terraform Code Sentinel has the language in which you write policies.

18. Answer: D (All of the above)

Explanation: The workspace feature in Terraform Cloud does the same thing as the open-source Terraform workspace feature; it is slightly different because it is all hosted in the cloud instead of your local system. And you can interact with the Cloud workspace using APIs as well. Think of Cloud workspaces as directories for distinct deployments, hosted in the cloud where you do not need to worry about segregation, storage, and even security of your workspaces.

19. Answer: C (Both A and B)

Explanation: The Registry is a repository of publicly available Terraform providers and modules. It is an integral part of Terraform's adoption by the masses because it is publicly accessible to anyone using Terraform.

20. Answer: C (Both A and B)

Explanation: HashiCorp Vault is secret management software. It is used to store sensitive data securely and provide short-lived, temporary credentials to users in place of actual long-lived credentials, like AWS CLI access keys

21. Answer: A (It codifies the process of security enforcement in Terraform code)

Explanation: It codifies the process of security enforcement in Terraform code, which allows for Sentinel policies to be version controlled and shared across the organization.

22. Answer: C (Both A and B)

Appendix A: Answers

Explanation: It can help standardize security testing and automation right into your Terraform deployment pipeline, as it automatically runs before your Terraform deployments.

23. Answer: A (True)

Explanation: Sentinel policy ensures that no security groups in AWS openly allow traffic from all IP addresses on port 22.

24. Answer: D (All of the above)

Explanation: Sandboxing, Codification, Testing, and Automation are the benefits of Sentinel

25. Answer: A (True)

Explanation: You can apply Sentinel policies against your Terraform code to sandbox your deployments. For example, stop a dev user from deploying into a prod workspace and act as a guardrail against accidental deployments.

Appendix B: Acronyms

Acronyms

AMI	Amazon Machine ID
API	Application Program Interface
AWS	Amazon Web Services
CDK	Cloud Development Kit
CI	Continuous Integration
CLI	Command Line Interface
CPU	Central Processing Unit
DB	Database
DBA	Database Administrator
DC/OS	Distributed Cloud Operating System
Dev	Development
DevOps	Development and Operations
DNS	Domain Name System
EC2	Elastic Compute Cloud
GCP	Google Cloud Platform
IaaS	Infrastructure as a Service
IaC	Infrastructure as a Code
IAM	Identity and Access Management
ID	Identity
IP	Internet Protocol
JSON	JavaScript Object Notation
OS	Operating System
PaaS	Platform as a Service
SDNs	Software Defined Networks
SQL	Structured Query Language

Appendix B: Acronyms

SSH	Secure Shell
SSL	Secure Socket Layer
TCP	Transmission Control Protocol
URL	Uniform Resource Locator
UTC	Coordinated Universal Time
VM	Virtual Machine
VPN	Virtual Private Network

Appendix C: References

References

https://learn.hashicorp.com/tutorials/terraform/infrastructure-as-code

https://www.devopsschool.com/blog/terraform-taint-and-untaint-explained-with-example-programs-and-tutorials/

https://www.terraform.io/language/providers

https://www.terraform.io/language/state

https://docs.microsoft.com/en-us/azure/developer/terraform/overview

https://learn.acloud.guru/course/hashicorp-certified-terraform-associate-1/learn/012df419-ecf6-441b-8e6a-f9eeb827b53e/012b0b8d-7aa2-4c84-aa1e-4c86bb8a8588/watch

https://www.opensourceforu.com/2022/04/terraform-the-cloud-agnostic-solution-for-infrastructure-as-code/

https://www.terraform.io/language/modules/develop

https://www.terraform.io/language/modules/syntax

https://www.terraform.io/cloud-docs/overview

https://learn.acloud.guru/course/hashicorp-certified-terraform-associate-1/learn/012df419-ecf6-441b-8e6a-f9eeb827b53e/5fa535c1-d01b-426a-92ac-c561272d95fd/watch

https://learn.acloud.guru/course/hashicorp-certified-terraform-associate-1/learn/012df419-ecf6-441b-8e6a-f9eeb827b53e/96f1013e-cfdb-449b-9794-034fe1eb942e/watch

https://learn.acloud.guru/course/hashicorp-certified-terraform-associate-1/learn/012df419-ecf6-441b-8e6a-f9eeb827b53e/b53b7a55-deaa-40cb-9582-cfc2d7923449/watch

https://learn.acloud.guru/course/hashicorp-certified-terraform-associate-1/learn/012df419-ecf6-441b-8e6a-f9eeb827b53e/0b41c90e-0648-45b0-9159-0e946fb562c5/watch

http://man.hubwiz.com/docset/Terraform.docset/Contents/Resources/Documents/docs/commands/taint.html

https://www.terraform.io/cli/commands/taint#:~:text=The%20terraform%20taint%20command%20informs,the%20next%20plan%20you%20create.

Appendix C: References

https://www.terraform.io/language/settings

https://learn.acloud.guru/course/hashicorp-certified-terraform-associate-1/dashboard

https://learn.acloud.guru/course/hashicorp-certified-terraform-associate-1/learn/8082ae1e-6a81-4819-a607-e466765c0f54/05cd7c68-965d-4904-a98f-8834024152f3/watch

https://learn.acloud.guru/course/hashicorp-certified-terraform-associate-1/learn/8082ae1e-6a81-4819-a607-e466765c0f54/34b3df4d-9975-48cc-9254-aefff7ba5440/watch

https://learn.acloud.guru/course/hashicorp-certified-terraform-associate-1/learn/8082ae1e-6a81-4819-a607-e466765c0f54/d1fb38c4-befb-401e-bc49-3323aec7d1e9/watch

https://learn.acloud.guru/course/hashicorp-certified-terraform-associate-1/learn/38e2e518-92e0-40ec-9a0f-c251f70ded38/0597b82c-744b-47b4-b47b-cef938b732af/watch

https://www.terraform.io/language/functions

https://learn.acloud.guru/course/hashicorp-certified-terraform-associate-1/learn/38e2e518-92e0-40ec-9a0f-c251f70ded38/840e1bb1-698b-4ff4-9e49-c6436df46c17/watch

https://learn.acloud.guru/course/hashicorp-certified-terraform-associate-1/learn/38e2e518-92e0-40ec-9a0f-c251f70ded38/b11d3db8-aac6-4970-8257-ee318d3bb7c9/watch

https://docs.microsoft.com/en-us/devops/deliver/what-is-infrastructure-as-code

https://www.terraform.io/registry/providers/publishing

https://registry.terraform.io/browse/providers?category=database

https://www.terraform.io/language/values/variables

https://www.terraform.io/language/modules/syntax

https://www.terraform.io/language/values/outputs

https://www.terraform.io/language/values

https://docs.microsoft.com/en-us/devops/what-is-devops

https://learn.acloud.guru/course/hashicorp-certified-terraform-associate-1/overview

https://www.terraform.io/language/state

Appendix C: References

https://www.terraform.io/language/state/remote

https://www.terraform.io/language/state/backends

https://www.terraform.io/language/state/locking

https://www.terraform.io/language/state/sensitive-data

https://www.terraform.io/language/values

https://www.terraform.io/language/resources/provisioners/syntax

https://learn.acloud.guru/course/hashicorp-certified-terraform-associate-1/dashboard

https://learn.acloud.guru/course/hashicorp-certified-terraform-associate-1/learn/9c2e6d25-bd6c-46b2-80b1-1b7da7c2c4a7/166835c7-f9f4-4ff1-9c19-14a1328de54e/watch

https://learn.acloud.guru/course/hashicorp-certified-terraform-associate-1/learn/9c2e6d25-bd6c-46b2-80b1-1b7da7c2c4a7/1ed9bec9-ee35-436a-a696-f96843ebe2e5/watch

https://learn.acloud.guru/course/hashicorp-certified-terraform-associate-1/learn/9c2e6d25-bd6c-46b2-80b1-1b7da7c2c4a7/c4aa724f-68d2-4eb1-9461-5ee5e2cfc5aa/watch

https://learn.acloud.guru/course/hashicorp-certified-terraform-associate-1/learn/9c2e6d25-bd6c-46b2-80b1-1b7da7c2c4a7/1d1aa68f-ed03-4296-85ea-b19cb0f69780/watch

https://www.terraform.io/registry/providers/publishing

https://registry.terraform.io/browse/providers?category=database

https://www.cloudbolt.io/blog/3-advantages-and-challenges-of-infrastructure-as-code-iac/

https://www.xenonstack.com/insights/terraform

https://en.wikipedia.org/wiki/Infrastructure_as_code\

https://www.terraform.io/

https://www.terraform.io/docs/configuration/providers.html

https://registry.terraform.io/browse/providers?category=database%2Cpublic-cloud

https://searchitoperations.techtarget.com/definition/DevOps

https://www.baeldung.com/ops/terraform-intro

Appendix C: References

https://www.youtube.com/watch?v=POPP2WTJ8es

https://www.youtube.com/watch?v=0yWAtQ6wYNM

https://learn.acloud.guru/course/hashicorp-certified-terraform-associate-1/dashboard

https://learn.acloud.guru/course/hashicorp-certified-terraform-associate-1/learn/72caad05-a776-4803-b0e6-226ea8163168/bf4b03be-9a38-4693-9648-4f8a15e0c2d4/watch

https://learn.acloud.guru/course/hashicorp-certified-terraform-associate-1/learn/72caad05-a776-4803-b0e6-226ea8163168/1601ad79-2e4a-4d8c-8bfa-9465ad33f9fb/watch

About Our Products

Other products from IPSpecialist LTD regarding CSP technology are:

AWS Certified Cloud Practitioner Study guide

AWS Certified SysOps Admin - Associate Study guide

AWS Certified Solution Architect - Associate Study guide

AWS Certified Developer Associate Study guide

AWS Certified Advanced Networking – Specialty Study guide

AWS Certified Security – Specialty Study guide

AWS Certified Big Data – Specialty Study guide

AWS Certified Machine Learning – Specialty Study guide

Microsoft Certified: Azure Fundamentals

About Our Products

- Microsoft Certified: Azure Administrator

- Microsoft Certified: Azure Solution Architect

- Microsoft Certified: Azure DevOps Engineer

- Microsoft Certified: Azure Developer Associate

- Microsoft Certified: Azure Security Engineer

- Microsoft Certified: Azure Data Fundamentals

- Microsoft Certified: Azure AI Fundamentals

- Microsoft Certified: Azure Database Administrator Associate

About Our Products

- Google Certified: Associate Cloud Engineer

- Google Certified: Professional Cloud Developer

- Microsoft Certified: Azure Data Engineer Associate

- Microsoft Certified: Azure Data Scientist

- Ansible Certified: Advanced Automation

- Oracle Certified: OCI Foundations Associate

- Oracle Certified: OCI Developer Associate

- Oracle Certified: OCI Architect Associate

About Our Products

Kubernetes Certified: Application Developer

Other Network & Security related products from IPSpecialist LTD are:

- CCNA Routing & Switching Study Guide
- CCNA Security Second Edition Study Guide
- CCNA Service Provider Study Guide
- CCDA Study Guide
- CCDP Study Guide
- CCNP Route Study Guide
- CCNP Switch Study Guide
- CCNP Troubleshoot Study Guide
- CCNP Security SENSS Study Guide
- CCNP Security SIMOS Study Guide
- CCNP Security SITCS Study Guide
- CCNP Security SISAS Study Guide
- CompTIA Network+ Study Guide
- Certified Blockchain Expert (CBEv2) Study Guide
- EC-Council CEH v10 Second Edition Study Guide
- Certified Blockchain Expert v2 Study Guide

Printed in Great Britain
by Amazon